THE NEW WORLD ORDER

DATE DUE

The New World Order
*Corporate Agenda
and Parallel Reality*

EDITED BY
GORDANA YOVANOVICH

McGill-Queen's University Press
Montreal & Kingston · London · Ithaca

© McGill-Queen's University Press 2003
ISBN 0-7735-2555-6 (cloth)
ISBN 0-7735-2613-7 (paper)

Legal deposit fourth quarter 2003
Bibliothèque nationale du Québec

Printed in Canada on acid-free paper that is 100% ancient forest
free (100% post-consumer recycled), processed chlorine free.

This book has been published with the help of a grant from the
University of Guelph.

McGill-Queen's University Press acknowledges the support of the
Canada Council for the Arts for our publishing program. We also
acknowledge the financial support of the Government of Canada
through the Book Publishing Industry Development Program (BPIDP)
for our publishing activities.

National Library of Canada Cataloguing in Publication

The new world order: corporate agenda and parallel reality/edited by
Gordana Yovanovich.

Includes bibliographical references
ISBN 0-7735-2555-6 (bnd)
ISBN 0-7735-2613-7 (pbk)

1. Globalization – Social aspects. 2. Globalization – Political aspects.
I. Yovanovich, Gordana, 1956–

HD2755.5.N49 2003   306   C2003-900691-3

Typeset in Sabon 10/12
by Caractéra inc., Quebec City

Contents

Acknowledgments

I would like to thank the School of Languages and Literatures and the College of Arts of the University of Guelph for their financial support. The publication of this book has also been made possible thanks to a grant provided by the Social Sciences and Humanities Research Council of Canada at the University of Guelph.

This multidisciplinary manuscript was written in collaboration with the internationally acclaimed authors with whom I was honoured to work, and prepared with the assistance of Jeanne Stegeman, secretary of the School of Languages and Literatures, and my two research/editorial assistants. I am particularly grateful to Sabrina Ramzi, my research assistant, for her excellent work on this project. I would also like to thank Shahina Jamal for her help with proofreading.

THE NEW WORLD ORDER

Introduction

GORDANA YOVANOVICH

The New World Order that emerged after the fall of the Berlin Wall (President Bush Sr proclaimed a "new world order" at the time of the Gulf War in 1991) has not declared itself to be ideologically different from the international order that grew out of World War II. However, it is different; in fact, the two are almost antithetical. The post-World War II era was symbolically marked by the global role of the United Nations as an agent for the promotion of peace; the New World Order compels a destructive and value-negative agenda on states and on the poor population within states around the world. Nonetheless, the main centres of power conceal change. The New World Order has developed under an ambiguity and secrecy that threaten civil society, undermine democracy, and work to invalidate national sovereignty. The unnamed and non-elected sources of power in the New World Order hide behind the ideology of universal human rights. As leaders pretend to promote human rights, they weaken the state and undermine national civil codes – as if the modern urban individual human being can survive without the support of the state and civil society.

The "humanitarian" NATO bombing of Yugoslavia was, according to Noam Chomsky, "a defining moment in world affairs."[1] It not only vexed the Russians and the Chinese but began to worry Europe. Contrary to CNN stories, the United States and NATO are no longer motivated by the same humane concerns they had at the end of the Second World War when the United Nations was formed as a means to promote peace.[2] Fifty years later, as the European Union develops its potential for economic, intellectual, and military independence, the

U.S. has shown itself to be unwilling to abide such autonomy. Had there not been the Yugoslavian crisis, Gwynne Dyer writes, "the North Atlantic Treaty Organization would be bidding farewell to the last U.S. troops as they finally went home from Europe."[3] The U.S. found reasons for its troops not to leave. It was argued that Europe could not solve the Balkan problem on its own. But, as James Bissett explains in the third essay of this collection, Europe was not able to solve the Yugoslavian problem precisely because the U.S. orchestrated and supported the conflict. Having seen enough pictures on TV of suffering in the former Yugoslavia, the general public of the West was not only ready to allow a foreign military institution to enter an independent state without a declaration of war but demanded that NATO interfere in the affairs of a sovereign state in order to protect the human rights of minorities. Help, however, came mainly in the form of bombing, in arming and training minorities, and in empty economic promises for future recovery. After the Kosovo conflict and four years of civil war in Bosnia, the human rights of minorities and majorities of former Yugoslavia are not guaranteed as people find themselves in an extremely dire economic and social situation. However, two NATO military bases are firmly established and well equipped in the Balkans. U.S. soldiers from former military bases in Germany are now stationed in Tuzla (Bosnia) and in Kosovo. As Gwynne Dyer has observed, the U.S. will not go home from Europe. They will stay to enforce the New World Order where it is not accepted willingly.

The secretive decision-making practices of the New World Order and the subsequent manipulation of public opinion through CNN and other media require a particular method of inquiry. A strictly academic approach is restrictive because it is no longer possible to take "evidence" at face value. A diplomat's testimony, such as James Bissett's or a lawyer's documented case against the main establishment, such as that by Michael Mandel, may be closer to the truth than scholarly articles that support their arguments with newspaper "evidence." Given that CNN and other official sources of information are driven by corporate interests, it is necessary to hear other voices. Scholars writing in this volume are not guided by scepticism. Their purpose is not to criticize but to study the present globalization through deeper logical deduction and enlightened interpretation. As feminist studies have exhaustively shown, the discourse of the patriarchy must be analysed carefully; as Mihai Spariosu observes, "rulers have always found it convenient to rule in the name of an abstract idea (i.e. Family, the People, God, Communism, Universal Justice, Universal Human Rights)."[4] In the name of humanitarian protection, NATO, the most powerful executive organization of the New World Order and corporate interests, has become an offensive military organization that does not respect international law.

According to the official interpretation of events, NATO is a neutral guardian of international stability. NATO was presented in the Yugoslavian conflict as having the military muscle and strategic determination to end conflicts the UN was unable to solve. Is it not logical, therefore, to replace the inefficient UN with the effective NATO? But what political system, what ethical position, and what authority guide the present change in the developing New World Order? James Bisset and Michael Mandel address these questions specifically. John McMurtry examines goals and values of the New Order from the point of view of ethics.

This collection of articles begins with the suggestion that the gradual change in our modern value system is reaching the point of culmination. In "The New World Order: The Hidden War of Values," social philosopher John McMurtry shows that the New World Order is marked by a negative change of values, and that it is a a global *coup d'etat* in the wake of the collapse of the Soviet bloc. With the disappearance of the balance of powers, capitalism is no longer a national economic system. The new capitalism is determined by interests of international corporations. Consequently, NAFTA and other multinational agreements impose their rules over the laws of a state. Arguing from "a life-value standpoint," McMurtry indicates that the very meaning of capital has also undergone major change. Wealth is no longer production *for* life but appropriation *from* life. The most dangerous or, in McMurtry's terms, lethal aspect of this unseen inversion of our value system is that it has not been recognized, much less understood.

Most people believe that capitalism is still in its original phase, where commodities serve life. In the past, gold-based money, for example, was invested in buying factors of production such as labour, instruments of labour, and natural resources, which were then organized to produce the means of life, such as clothing, food, and homes. McMurtry argues that most people still use money in this way: not for money gain but for life gain. However, the New World Order has inverted the pattern so that life and society itself are made to serve stockholder profit. He warns that "the rapidly emerging dominance of the 'speculative economy' over the 'real economy' resembles a carcinogenic circuit. International corporations of the New World Order are systemically appropriating society's life nutrients in order to multiply. However, they perform no committed function to the host body."

McMurtry's view can be read as excessively mistrustful, almost cynical. However, employees who have been laid off so that their companies could declare a year-end profit understand his reasoning. The pensions and entire life savings of Enron employees were lost due to that corporation's misjudgments and speculations in the stock market. McMurtry's article is a synopsis of two of his books, *Unequal Freedoms: The Global Market as an Ethical System* (1998) and *The Cancer Stage of Capitalism* (1999), both of which are thoroughly documented and internationally recognized. McMurtry's views are supported not only by his scholarship but also by current events. In recent years, thousands of informed protestors and political activists in Quebec City, Seattle, Washington, Edmonton, Halifax, Genoa, and other cities have shown that his thinking is, in fact, based on economic and ethical realities. McMurtry's writing is not a bleak portrayal of an ethical bankruptcy but a diagnosis of a moral ill and a call for an appropriate consciousness of it and response to it. McMurtry's conclusion, that "civil society [must] defend the life code of value against life-blind circuits, or human and planetary life will be increasingly stripped," states the position of all the authors in this collection. With understanding and effort, the world must embrace life-giving forces and defend civil society.

In the second essay, "Intelligence Agenda and the Need for Constructive Intellectual Intervention in the New World Order," I argue that political intelligence and the *intelligentsia* of the primary institutions of society, including the majority of intellectuals, are not guided by life-giving values. However, ordinary people, particularly in oppressed countries, hold on to spirituality and a desire for continuity as they endure the hardships of the new order. The intellectual agenda of the New World Order is imperialistic and insensitive to the needs of ordinary citizens, and the *intelligentsia* which has traditionally voiced humanistic concerns, is now marked by intellectual nonchalance, modern emphasis on individualism, and a general unwillingness to deconstruct contemporary illusions. In short, it has played a passive role in the creation of the New World Order. On the other hand, the wisdom of the people and the popular ability to endure are creating a parallel reality. They give hope that all is not "rotten in the kingdom of Denmark," as Shakespeare would say.

The United States employs the most educated people from all over the world to protect the economic and political interests of one country. The American Academy's Commission on the Year 2000 is a testimony that rich countries have the resources to pay capable and informed citizens of the world to help shape the New World Order. The commission is also an example of intellectual servitude, bureaucratization, and human alienation. Its agenda works towards, as McMurtry would say, "a global *coup d'etat*." Intellectuals in the former Eastern bloc, people like Alexander Solzhenitsyn and Andrei Sakharov, collaborated with their colleagues in the West and helped bring the system down in the Soviet Union. However, one imperfect system has been replaced with another. It is quite evident that Eastern European intellectuals have offered little help to those who are living in the post-Soviet chaos, where the state is in the hands of the Mafia and once famous musicians of classical music play in subways.

Eastern European artists and academics clearly did not understand the tricks of purported globalization. This, however, has not been the case with Latin American thinkers. Two poems by Nicaraguan modernist poet Rubén Darío from the early 1900s explain why the idea of Pan-Americanism failed at the beginning of the twentieth century. These poems also explain the problems of the contemporary attempt to globalize: Darío shows that a fair union is impossible because the United States exploits smaller countries. He believed that the hegemony can be resisted by cultures with a profound spiritual base that adhere to the natural chain of being, which ensures continuation. Darío and other Latin American writers, such as the Cuban modernist poet José Martí, had a holistic vision of the world. Unfortunately, they did not make an impact on the general intellectual development of the twentieth century because economic inequality demonstrates itself in intellectual reality as well. Had there been a greater dialogue between writers of the Third World and the developed world, modernism might have been a positive intellectual foundation for the contemporary world. In the Renaissance and in the eighteenth century intellectuals and writers were more involved in the creation of social and political order. These were progressive moments in human history because, unlike today, the spiritual and intellectual visions of life were integrated with economic progress.

At the present moment, it is difficult to resist globalization. Small countries like Cuba or Yugoslavia, for example, cannot directly challenge the power of corporate globalization. However, they can, as Keith Ellis indicates, live by their ingenuity and celebratory attitude towards life. To understand the second general theme of this collection of essays – the theme of spiritual strength and survival through ingenuity – we may recall Mikhail Bakhtin's study of medieval celebratory or "grotesque" laughter. With no hint of a Marxist slant or glorification of the working people, Mikhail Bakhtin demonstrated in *Rabelais and His World* that medieval peasants were able to resist the seriousness of the official order; they did not oppose their kings, but they turned the gravity of the official story into their own grotesque laughter.

Neither Bakhtin nor Rabelais romanticized the general population. For them, ordinary people are not revolutionaries, peasants are not "noble savages," and the power of the establishment, be it the G7, IMF, NATO, or medieval king, is undeniable. Yet people as a human collective have an ability to survive even the most difficult social and political orders, and they are able to create a reality that is different from the one designed by the established order. Bakhtin showed that official culture is marked by hierarchy and rational order and that popular culture is characterized by a continuous chain of being. He explained the natural chain through ornaments found in the fifteenth-century excavation of Titus's baths. The bath ornaments, or "grottesca," are made up of a number of figures that are interwoven as if giving birth to each other. The boundaries of these figures are visible, but they are also boldly infringed as the inner movement of being itself and its ever-incomplete character are expressed in the violent passing of one form into the other. In Rabelais's work, which portrays the life of the medieval peasant, it is emphasized that hardship is unavoidable. However, in the natural world, violence is not superfluously destructive.

The violence, crudeness, and open-ended movement forward in Bakhtinian grotesque laughter bring to mind Joseph Meeker's explanation of the ecological whole, and its relation to comedy – the genre of the lower classes. Meeker argued that comedy demonstrates that humankind is "durable" even though specific people may find themselves in a weak and undignified position: "Comedy is careless of morality, goodness, truth, beauty, heroism, and all such *abstract* values men say they live by. Its only concern is to affirm man's capacity for survival and to celebrate the continuity of life itself, despite all morality. Comedy is a celebration, a ritual renewal of biological welfare as it persists *in spite of any reason* there may be for feeling metaphysical despair."[5] As María Figueredo argues in her essay, Latin American music was a voice of resistance that was unsuccessful in preventing the political events of the harsh 1970s and 1980s. Yet music that stems from people's souls and folk tradition, like medieval grotesque laughter, was and still is a means of *healing* that recreates life from created situations, and is not a form of sedation or escape. It is a means of maintaining positive, life-giving values. Just as grotesque laughter sought not to subvert the official order but to laugh at the seriousness of the establishment, today people in small countries – especially poor women – treat the establishment with a certain degree of disrespect. Women in particular have the strength to "fight for fertility," as Turner and Brownhill show in their study of women in Kenya.

John McMurtry, James Bisset, Michael Mandel, Jorge Nef, Jennifer Sumner, and Meenakshi Bharat analyse the present global situation

from the point of view of the defence of civil society, national sovereignty, and international protection through the UN. Keith Ellis, María
Figueredo, Terisa E. Turner, Leigh S. Brownhill, and Edward Vargo
illustrate positive challenges to corporate globalization. They present
hope that people's enduring spirit and celebratory attitude towards life
might be able to withstand the New World Order. They show that
countries with a history of difficult survival, a strong folk culture, and
deep spirituality are again faced with challenges, but that these countries are not giving in to the contemporary, sophisticated form of
colonization. From harsh reality they are able to create a parallel,
spiritually rich reality that is driven by positive natural life forces.

Michael Mandel and James Bissett argue that NATO's lack of respect
for international law, national sovereignty, and the rules of the United
Nations lead to the destruction of civil society and cultural diversity
and annihilates the essence of Western civilization. To prevent abusive
human practices, humanity has created law and order to protect the
weak. Bissett reminds us that the United Nations and NATO were
created to deal with the aggression and violence of the Second World
War, when "might was right," as Mandel says. The New World Order
still pretends to protect the weak through NATO and tribunals such as
the one in The Hague. However, the new court and the new NATO are
in reality a threat to national sovereignty and international peace.

In "Humanitarian Intervention and the Sovereignty of a State in the
New World Order: Undermined Authority and Undefined Rules of
Engagement," James Bissett, a former supporter of NATO, objects to the
aggressive direction the military organization has taken. As Canadian
ambassador to Yugoslavia from 1990 to 1992, Bissett writes as a
witness to the failures of Western diplomacy. He does not disagree that
the rules of engagement need to change as the world evolves, but he
explains that the Kosovo bombing broke the groundrules for NATO
engagement. He insists that in the Kosovo conflict diplomatic negotiations were not exhausted before military intervention took place. This
signals a fundamental change in the nature and purpose of the organization.

If NATO's rules of engagement are being changed and precedents are
being set for the future, then it is only logical to ask: under what
authority does the most powerful war machine on earth operate?
Bissett is aware of the importance of the human rights argument and of
people's willingness to support it. However, he warns well-intentioned
citizens that this argument may be manipulated and that Western
intervention may exacerbate rather than help solve problems in countries with a complex history.

Writing from an insider's perspective, Bissett explains how the break-
down of Yugoslavia came about. He exposes and documents the lies

fabricated by NATO. But Bisset is more concerned for a world in which any sovereign state can be destroyed under similar circumstances. He wonders about the state of democracy in Canada if Canadian armed forces can be engaged in an offensive military action authorized by neither the United Nations, the Canadian Parliament, nor the Canadian people. Bissett points out: "If it is essential that countries give up some of their sovereignty as the price they pay for membership in global institutions such as NATO, it is mandatory, then, that such institutions follow their own rules, respect the rule of the law, and operate within the generally accepted framework of the United Nations charter." He also expresses concern about the ease with which the mainstream media in the West accepted and even supported NATO military action.

In "The Legal Institutions of the New World Order: 'Might Makes Right' and the International Criminal Tribunal for the Former Yugoslavia," Michael Mandel provides a legal apology for basing international relations and civil society on law and order. Mandel, a professor and practicing lawyer, argues that in the New World Order, "courts have proven themselves to be essentially an antidote to democracy, a way in which elites fight the democratic tendencies of representative institutions (like the United Nations)." Mandel, like McMurtry, exposes a malady, in his case a legal ill, that seriously harms the body and the spirit of civil society. His article stems from his disapproval of the creation of pseudo-legal institutions such as the International Criminal Tribunal for the Former Yugoslavia in The Hague. This court was created not to serve justice but as a cover for politically and economically motivated wars. In May 1999, Mandel led an international team of lawyers who brought formal complaints of war crimes against sixty-eight NATO leaders. In his legal dealings with Canadian judge Louise Arbour and Swiss judge Carla Del Ponte, Mandel became convinced that quickly assembled, blatantly political tribunals of the emerging world order have the potential to turn law-based societies into Hobbesian jungle-like kingdoms.

Mandel explains that the tribunal in The Hague was sponsored by only one country, and that the UN Security Council Resolution establishing the tribunal was written by a U.S. State Department lawyer on Madeleine Albright's instructions. In May 1999, Albright publicly announced that the U.S. was the major provider of funds for the tribunal and that America had pledged even more money to the tribunal, despite the outstanding U.S. debt to the UN. Given that most ordinary citizens believe in law and order and that politicians need public support in the West, the presence of judges appears to lend legitimacy to wars that are in fact illegal according to international

law. In his article, Mandel asks us to recall that at the beginning of
the bombing in Yugoslavia, Judge Arbour made successive television
appearances with British foreign secretary Robin Cook and American
secretary of state Madeleine Albright. Mandel and a number of other
international experts are convinced that the politicians needed the
judge to legitimize the war.

The lawyers' request to Judge Arbour that no one be above the law
is a justifiable request on behalf of ordinary citizens. A true legal system
must be defended because it is the backbone of any civil society. The
case Mandel took on was not to defend Yugoslavia but to defend
international law and justice. International law is still far from guar-
anteeing success, but it is one of the few existing attempts to insure
the peaceful coexistence of nations. Unfortunately, he and the group
of lawyers were not given the opportunity to present their case in court.
Not being able to seek justice in court, the lawyers are increasingly
forced to present their case in the court of public opinion.

The indictment of Slobodan Milosevic and the legal process regarding Augusto Pinochet that were happening around the same time have
confirmed that in the New World Order "might is right." Pinochet,
who has served the New World Order, is a free man because he has
been defended by people like former British prime minister Margaret
Thatcher. She and other proponents of the New World Order make
the message clear: leaders like Pinochet who comply with the neo-
liberal economic model are protected, while disobedient leaders like
Milosevic are punished. Guided by the American institutional intelligentsia (and the CIA), the Pinochet regime in Chile in the 1970s and
1980s was an experiment in which the New World Order was tested.
The dirty work of this brutal dictator has even been hailed as a positive
step because it brought order and stability to the Latin American
country. However, it is not clear that the Chilean example was truly
successful.

In "Neo-Liberalism and the Chilean Model: A Forerunner of the
New World Order," Jorge Nef explains that the New World Order,
presented by the U.S. as a victory over socialism, has been growing in
strength since 1989. Yet in 1973 in Chile the balance was tipped in
favour of capitalism with massive U.S. assistance. At the time, most
saw the Chilean military coup as simply a typical Latin American
violent change of government. However, the coup marks the time when
liberal capitalism, through the Chilean "experiment," started to prevail
and transform itself into neo-liberalism.

The neo-liberal economic model was conceptualized by ideologues
such as Friedrich von Hayek, Ludwig von Mises, Milton Friedman,
Karl Popper, Louis Baudin, and Ayn Rand. Their six major policy

recommendations have been adopted by the corporate world as the basic economic model of the New World Order: 1) reestablishment of the rule of the market, 2) tax reduction, 3) reduction in public expenditure, 4) deregulation of the private sector, 5) privatization of the public sector, and 6) elimination of the collectivist concept of the "public good" and promulgation of "individual responsibility." In the 1994 Human Development Report to the United Nations it is shown that in 1991 the global neo-liberal elite controlled 80 per cent of world trade, 95 per cent of all loans, 80 per cent of all domestic savings, and 80.5 per cent of world investments.

In his analysis of the Chilean model, Jorge Nef agrees with Italian thinker Antonio Gramsci that the old is dying and the new cannot be born. International socialism has been killed, yet there is no new system in place to protect ordinary citizens. For over a decade, mainstream politicians, intellectuals, and the media have praised Chile as a model for Latin America, the Third World, and beyond. Unfortunately, in the New World Order money creates little else but itself. Nef indicates that the 1973 coup in Chile and the subsequent experiment in the economy have served only the big corporations.

In an earlier time setting, U.S. General Smedley D. Butler explained the role of the U.S. military in Latin America in a manner that foretold future events: "I spent thirty-five years and four months in the service as a member of our country's most agile military force – the Marine Corps …. And during that period I spent most of my time being a high-class muscle man for Big Business, Wall Street, and for the bankers. In short, I helped make Honduras *right* for American fruit companies in 1903."[6]

William Walker performed a similar job in El Salvador in the 1980s. He later became leader of the war-crimes verification team in Kosovo. His team set wheels in motion, as Chomsky says, for the indictment of Milosevic and for the American occupation of part of Yugoslavia and Europe. The work of people such as Walker and Butler is never presented in terms of economic domination. The intervention is portrayed as a struggle for efficiency, order, stability, and predictability. Given that order and stability are of supreme importance for most people, this rhetoric enables aggression towards apparently unstable sovereign states. There is no doubt that today Chile enjoys relative stability. The Pinochet regime destroyed dissidence and imposed order. However, Nef explains that Chile remains, on the whole, "a structurally vulnerable and underdeveloped country, which bears the scars of a brutal military regime and lives still under its shadow." He shows why success is largely a triumphalist narrative, that hides the reality of a fragile normalization.

Jennifer Sumner's article, "The New World Order and the Destruction of Public Education: The Case of Canada," argues against the privatization of public education. Sumner reminds us that the vast majority of our public institutions were once the property of the private sector. They were made public precisely because it was determined through past experience that this was the only effective way to insure that the institutions would serve the needs of all citizens, regardless of their individual wealth.

What drives the privatization of education today is the fact that, worldwide, it is worth $2 trillion annually, and $60 billion in Canada. The New World Order hails the economy in which the neo-liberal notion of "individual responsibility" is promoted, as if most individuals could become successful if only high taxes did not stand in their way. We are told that responsible citizens should take care of their own affairs, including their education. Promoting the image of the clever young computer wizard, the new establishment suggests that all capable people could become millionaires. It is also implied that those who are unsuccessful are not responsible enough. This "blame-the-victim" attitude is generally accepted because it exploits the Calvinist principle of responsibility and hard work, which is at the basis of Canadian society. What most people do not realize is that in the new global corporate economy, the Calvinist moral principles of charity and community are replaced by market principles measured strictly in dollars.

Within this privatization context, Sumner examines the impact of corporate globalization on primary and secondary education, higher education, and lifelong learning (distance, adult, and extension education) in Canada. In her discussion of primary and secondary education, she cautions against the recent trend of charter schools and questions the spread of YNN, the Youth News Network, into the school system. This private commercial network provides Canadian schools with televisions, audio-visual equipment, and computers in exchange for airing its 12.5-minute "newscast." Sumner poses the question whether we know what values are being passed on to school children.

If the New World Order is negative for rich countries such as Canada, it is even more damaging to poorer countries. Yugoslavia was chosen for this collection as a country where military enforcement of the New World Order was obvious and brutal. Chile is often used by the power establishment as an example of supposed economic, political, and social success. However, this country, which had a strong public sector and the strongest democratic tradition in Latin America, lives today under "authoritarian capitalism," where its non-unionized workers are forced to support the low-wage economy. For the ordinary citizen, there is no improvement in this Latin American economic model. In Canada wages are still respectable and the standard of living is high, but even so, it is witnessing negative effects of the world order where privatization destroys the achievements of years of civilization. India is the largest Asian country, and has an ancient culture and a history of difficult survival. In "Women and the New World Order: The *New* Face of the Indian Woman?" Meenakshi Bharat, a professor of English Literature and Women's Studies in New Delhi, examines the effects of the "free market" on India where 80 per cent of the population is rural and where a feminization of agriculture has taken place. Bharat takes a closer look at the changing position of women in her country, and is shocked that the thinking women of India have barely considered and much less debated the impact of the New World Order. According to Bharat, the pleasant image of creating a global village has allowed "the sweeping winds of the new order the run of the world." In that one world are two groups: a smaller prosperous elite/ head and a much larger impoverished and suffering body of people.

Changes created for the woman in the boardroom or in the entertainment industry are markedly different, Bharat indicates, from the changes imposed on the woman working in agriculture, or living in the poor parts of the city where prostitution and hunger are prevalent. In the upper strata of society, globalization has brought women more power and therefore more gender parity. Indian women executives fly all over the world working for multinational firms, while Indian women film directors such as Deepa Mehta, actresses such as Shabana Azmi, and writers such as Arundhati Roy are making waves around the globe. Bharat concludes that "this has done wonders for our sense of self-worth and has fostered a confidence to stand up to global challenges." The pitfalls of globalization are more conspicuous, however, for women from less privileged sections of society. Liberalization, privatization, and globalization have opened doors to a variety of products and have caused a surge of unprecedented consumerism within India. The desire to buy has been stoked, but more often than not it cannot be satisfied. The inability to buy has harsh reverberations for all, but especially for women. Bharat explains how this adds to the stress of mothers. They have to tell their children that they cannot have what is aggressively advertised to them. In some cases this leads women to prostitution.

In Africa, as in India and Asia, the New World Order enacts a new and subtle form of colonialism. Terisa Turner and Leigh Brownhill argue in "Kenyan Women's Fight for Fertility: Globalization from Above and Reappropriation from Below" that what is driving the impetus for change in Africa is not so much politics as the need to

survive. They define "the fight for fertility" as "the capacity to reproduce and sustain life in all its forms." Given that women have always
borne and nourished human life, their struggle with the corporate
world and globalization is part of the instinctive effort to survive. This
effort may become a challenge to the New World Order, particularly
if resistance becomes what is called a "globalization from below,"
because the sophisticated masculine world of air planes, cellular
phones, and the Internet is incompatible with the feminine instinctive
drive for life. Although Turner and Brownhill do not refer to this, the
infamous incident with the American-born UN soldier in Somalia is
an example of the clash between the two worlds. Most of us remember
the televised image of the women of Somalia dragging the naked
American soldier through the streets and dancing on the downed U.S.
plane. Their motivation was a feeling that foreign soldiers were there
not to bring peace but to harm Africa, as foreigners have been doing
for centuries. The women's protests and dances succeeded in removing
foreign soldiers from Somalia – perhaps like ants that force a lion to
move from the place the ants had as their space.

Turner and Brownhill point out that conflicts in Kenya and many
other African countries are not ethnic clashes, as they are often portrayed by the media, but a "fight for fertility" against transnational
capital and the neo-liberal privatizing state. They examine three
moments in this fight in post-colonial Kenya: the Maragua women
coffee farmers' flight from coffee growing from the 1980s to the mid
1990s; the 1992 hunger strike at Nairobi's "Freedom Corner," carried
out by mothers of political prisoners – the fruits of their own fertility;
and the large-scale reappropriation of land by landless people across
Kenya (and Zimbabwe). The two authors briefly describe the historical
antecedents to the fight for fertility and explain how and why Maragua
peasant women replaced export crops (mainly coffee) with local food
crops (mainly bananas). According to the World Bank, real international prices for Africa's coffee exports fell by 70 per cent during the
eighties. Increasing numbers of women coffee cultivators received nothing from the coffee payments, and at the same time had no land on
which to cultivate food for their children. This situation forced women
to uproot coffee trees illegally and replace them with beans and other
crops. The Maragua women thus started a parallel, grotesque reality,
as they extracted themselves from state-mediated relationships with
foreign suppliers of agrochemical inputs and from a global coffee
market that enriched commercial traders at the expense of producers.

In their struggle against the state, which is in the service of the global
marketplace, women use the only weapons they possess: their bodies
and folkloric superstitions. A seventy-year-old woman remembers a

1992 women's protest to free their sons who were held political prisoners. She told Turner that they were teargassed and beaten with clubs, and the whole area was sealed off by policemen. The old woman then stripped her clothes and remained stark naked. When women, especially old women or groups of women, expose their genitals to people who have offended or threatened them, they are in effect declaring that "this is where your life has come from. I hereby revoke your life." Those so cursed believe that they will lose their virility, that their land will lose its fertility, and that they as individuals will be outcasts from society. To the Western mind the curse is a foolish act, but most minds are not Western minds.

The struggle that is taking place in many African countries today for the reappropriation of land and of a way of life is rooted in the tradition of living in tune with the rhythms of the local ecosystem. However, the Internet and telephone may become useful tools, Turner and Brownhill observe, to connect the African women with their Indian sisters and their Zapatista brothers in Mexico. The hungry and dispossessed of all countries may inadvertently be united through the efficient tools of the New World Order.

The unofficial culture, or the reality that is developing parallel to the New World Order, is not based only on folkloric spiritual strength and survival instinct. Cuba has survived years of colonialism and economic blockade thanks to its strong national feeling and a sophisticated intellectual struggle that seeks to work with the potential of the natural world. The main Cuban scientific discoveries are in the area of traditional herbal medicine, acupuncture, and homeopathy. The combination of the highest per capita number of doctors and other medical personnel in the world, an excellent distribution of these practitioners throughout the island, and the type of medical research have kept this small country in good health, despite its economic difficulties. Infant mortality in Cuba (6.2 per 1,000 live births in 2001) is lower than infant mortality in the U.S. The island's high life expectancy of seventy-five years is also an important achievement. In "Cuba's Encounter with the Changing Faces of Imperialism," Keith Ellis lists the major difficulties Cuban people have encountered under colonial pressures from both Spain and the United States. He argues, however, that Cuba has demonstrated that "national sovereignty is the necessary condition for the development of people." Ellis also indicates that the hallmark of Cuba at the present stage of its development is a "humanitarian concern that has at its service *the cultured intelligence of the people.*" As John McMurtry demonstrates, the quality of "cultured intelligence of the people" does not carry much weight in the present dominant value system. However, for the Cuban national poet, José

Martí, the way to be free is to be cultured: *"Ser culto es el único modo de ser."*

Ellis's essay draws from the present Cuban reality and from the writings of Cuban journalist, poet, and soldier José Martí (1853–95), who fought for Cuban independence from Spain and who emphasized to his last day the peril of looming U.S. imperialism. He used a tiger metaphor to show that danger is not always obvious. A tiger approaches its prey with "velvet-covered claws. When the prey awakens, the tiger is already upon it." If we are to learn from history, Cuba can be a valuable lesson to those who naïvely believe that the United States is a benevolent rich uncle.[7] More importantly, Cuba shows that national dignity can triumph over national humiliation and protect its people from degradation.

Enduring the hardships imposed by U.S. exploitation and, since the revolution, hostility, Cuba not only has virtually eliminated basic illiteracy but has been able to provide its scientists and artists with the infrastructure necessary for them to achieve the highest levels of accomplishment. In North American terminology, Cuba has built its human resources. Educated people are not money-makers but enriched human beings who enhance the general situation of their country. For Jennifer Sumner they would be model public servants, and for Edward Vargo, who also discusses education in the New World Order, they would be good "servant-leaders." Ellis points out that 56 per cent of Cuban scientists are women, and that medical research is not controlled by profit-oriented pharmaceutical companies. The goal of the medical culture and of education in Cuba is a healthy community instead of a profit margin.

In "The Latin American Song as An Alternative Voice in the New World Order" María Figueredo agrees with Keith Ellis that culture frees and invigorates peoples and nations. There is a difference between the "knowledge based society" envisioned by the corporate world and the "cultured society" promoted by José Martí, Rubén Darío, and other humanist thinkers. Culture and music in Latin American and Third World countries, like the music derived from North American slaves, is a cultural expression in which knowledge comes from profound human experience. There is a marked difference between the music of Louis Armstrong, for example, and Michael Jackson or between Mahalia Jackson and Madonna. The music of North American jazz singers is similar in its emotional intensity and empirical wisdom to that of Chilean singer Violeta Parra and other musicians María Figueredo studies. This music is a force that aids the survival of the human spirit and the human world. This music is characterized by faith that the corporate world does not hold or understand.

In moments of violence, music keeps the idea of justice alive, it nurtures the spirit against despair, and elucidates a meaning of life. Given its power of simultaneity, music can mobilize large numbers of people, and lead us to receive its message(s) in ways we may not be fully analytically aware. It is also a means of reaching out to the rest of the world. Figueredo explains that Latin American music and song are born from the integration of European, Native, and African influences. Modern Latin American song is clearly connected to traditional heritage and is an expression of the collective spirit. She examines Latin American music of the period when the New World Order was being tested in Latin America, beginning with the post-World War II period, when the United States assumed a more defining role in international relations and became a determining factor in Latin America's search to define its own voice in the world.

As a universal art form, music and song are an alternate voice, a communal fountain that preserves and nurtures life. Argentinian singer Horacio Guaraní sings, "If the singer falls silent, so does life" ("Si se calla el cantor, calla la vida"). Even so, Figueredo does not idealize music. As she shows, it is excruciatingly difficult to be an alternate voice to the New World Order, but the artistic spirit is constructive, or celebratory and grotesque, as Bakhtin would say, and for this reason able to withstand the ruling pragmatic materialism or, as McMurtry calls it, the "economics of death."

Discussing the educational importance of Latin American music, Figueredo quotes a Brazilian scholar who explains that the university in her country is beginning to consider the type of music Figueredo studies as "the new matrices of [academic] knowledge." The New World Order could evolve in a positive direction if arts and music were to influence the world of politics and economics. As traditional music has evolved into a "new song" without abandoning the essential humanistic spirit and feeling for community, the whole world could at least try to move in this direction.

In his article "Higher Education and the New World Order" Edward Vargo argues that a spiritual presence in education could also enrich the world. He reasons that the implementation of the business model in higher education will work only if education and business are led by life-giving "servant-leaders" (using Robert Greenleaf's term) that "trust the human ability to bring surprises, and have faith in human potential." Professor Vargo, an American professor of English literature and a former dean of Arts in Taiwan and Thailand, indicates that one of the greatest lessons of the Asian economic crisis has been that we live in an interdependent but non-convergent world. "Like it or not," he says, "it is futile to resist globalization despite the fact that the International

Monetary Fund is controlled by Western macroeconomists who do not understand the social and cultural factors active in different countries." Stating the present "contextual imperative," Vargo disagrees, however, that the university curriculum must be in line with market forces and funding needs. Vargo does not believe that universities in developing countries must forge new links with business and industry. Taking a humanistic point of view, Vargo would like to believe that the American system, out of which the New World Order has emerged, not only pushes free enterprise, market forces, and new technologies, but also has a concern for human rights, democracy, and social justice. He knows that to trust this agenda to the free market or to the foreign policies of corporations driven by self-interest is foolish, and for that reason suggests that "[w]e cannot allow the market economy to proceed on its own without a concern for the public good."

As he looks for alternatives to the New World Order's agenda for higher education, Vargo refers to Robert Zemsky from the University of Pennsylvania, who suggests that universities must be mission-centred, and that they must have a soul, "even as they chase after every business out there." Vargo then argues that a drive for change in universities be entrusted to a special breed of leaders who are "gifted with strategic vision," who are "well versed in financial management and resource allocation," and who are "capable of leading a team in addition to performing traditional functions, such as curriculum planning and research development." He argues that a blind belief in the marketplace needs to be replaced by a human perspective. He advocates, therefore, the business model developed by Greenleaf's servant-leadership concept, used in both for-profit and non-profit organizations. This institutional model is based on teamwork and community. The model seeks to involve others in decision-making, it is strongly based in ethical and caring behaviour, and it attempts to enhance the personal growth of students and workers. "Servant-leadership holds that the primary purpose of a business should be to create a positive impact on its employees and community. Profit is not its sole motive." In "The Servant as Leader" (1970), Greenleaf concludes that the most effective leaders are those motivated not by power and greed but by a desire to serve.

The desire to serve almost always comes from deep transcendent spiritual impulses. The key test of servant-leadership is the effect it has on its followers. In the existing "scientific management model," leaders control and discipline employees. In the proposed "human relations management model," leaders aim at full development of workers and of students who will be future workers. If higher education wants to prepare students for the age of globalization, Vargo argues, it must be concerned not only with their tuition fees but with their mental and physical health, with their intellect and knowledge, and with their morality and integrity.

As McMurtry's article elucidates, the "economics of death" is a serious social malady that threatens the health of the capitalist system. With excruciating effort, it is true, the immune system can begin to intercept the economics of death by the necessary economics of life as peasants in Latin America, Africa, and Asia in grassroots protests all over the world reappropriate their land and right to fertility. The world will endure the present ethical value crisis; history demonstrates that positive forces become stronger as situations worsen. The simulation of tanks and other creative tactics of the weaker party in the Kosovo conflict clearly showed that creative spirits can at least frustrate if not combat or challenge the powerful machine of the New World Order. The Kosovo conflict was, as the American president said, a war for credibility. NATO bombing did, in fact, start a complex debate, but the general public is less and less credulous.

The public is beginning to realize that the New World Order does not mark a period of progressive development in world history. As they are forced to think about modern manifestations of evil, some journalists agree that the Western world is too rational, perhaps too manipulative. In a *Toronto Star* article, "There is no Modern Therapy for Evil," Richard Gwyn writes that liberalism is too secular. He quotes columnist Robert Fulford, who wrote in *National Post* that liberalism "does not speak to the heart. It cannot evoke awe before the mystery of existence. It has no cure for self-obsession that is the major infirmity of our age. It offers only reason."[8] In *Democracy in Europe*, Edward Skidelsky argues that if modern liberalism is going to refind itself it can only do this by refinding its roots in Christian faith. Given that the New World Order is the new order for the entire world, it must not concentrate on one religion. If the world's immune system is to be revitalized, we do not need to return to institutionalized religions. Instead, the New World Order needs to listen to individuals and cultures that are still in touch with nature and with living, creative spirits. Societies must be ruled by law and order. Therefore, reason has a place in the modern world, and reason must be distinguished from calculated manipulation. As the German poet Rainer Maria Rilke has written, we must go beyond "mere skill and petty gains":

> As long as you catch what you yourself threw into the air
> all is mere skill and petty gains;
> only when you become the catcher of the ball
> that the Goddess, your eternal playmate,

threw toward you ...
only then is being able to catch the ball an ability
to be cherished –
not yours, but the world's.

Richard Gwyn is right that "we may be on the cusp of one of those radical transformations in human affairs – certainly the most radical in more than a century – in which this time modernity tries to come to terms with religion." The modern world has to have faith that the New World Order will be challenged by spiritual and humanistic concerns that keep the Third World alive. As Uruguayan writer Eduardo Galeano says: "We are being obliged to accept a world without soul as the only one possible. In this system, there are no *pueblos* (peoples), only markets; no citizens, only consumers; no nations, only companies; no cities, only conglomerations; no human relations, only economic competitions! ... We will have to invent something as an alternative to the present system."[9]

NOTES

1 Noam Chomsky, *The New Military Humanism: Lessons from Kosovo*, Monroe: Common Courage Press, 1999, 14.

2 America's apparent generosity, i.e. acts of protecting and feeding the displaced, wounded, and hungry in the forties and fifties, fueled a dream of peace and Western unity, and made it difficult to suspect that the U.S. was anything but a good and trustworthy moral leader through the Marshall plan. This was a part of the struggle against communism, which resulted in a strong and united Europe, and this success offered the hope of unity and prosperity, as well as generating guarantees of cultural tolerance.

3 Gwynne Dyer, "Human Rights Take Centre Stage as West Rewrites World Order." *The Globe and Mail*, 12 June 1999, 17.

4 Mihai Spariosu, *Literature, Mimesis and Play*, Tubingen: NARR, 1982, 17.

5 Joseph W. Meeker, *The Comedy of Survival*, New York: Charles Scribner's Sons, 1976, 24.

6 Don Cockburn, ed., *An Anti-Intervention Handbook*, Toronto: Latin American Working Group, 1985, 3.

7 When the Cuban war of independence ended, Cuba was given no voice by the Americans in negotiating the terms of the Treaty of Paris. This injustice was repeated in the signing of the 1995 Dayton Agreement, for example, that ended the war in Bosnia and Herzegovina. The

United States dictated the terms of agreement without giving voice to Bosnian Serbs.

8 Richard Gwyn, "There is no Modern Therapy for Evil." *Toronto Star.* 23 January 2002, A25.

9 *Presencia.* 20 October 1995. Quoted in Murray Luft, "Latin American Protest Music – What Happened to 'The New Songs'?," *Bulletin de musique folklorique canadienne* 30, no. 3 (1996), 17.

The New World Order: The Hidden War of Values

JOHN McMURTRY

The techniques which induce a paradigm change may well be described as therapeutic, if only because, when they succeed, one learns one had been sick before. – Thomas Kuhn[1]

Since the fall of the Soviet Union in 1991, transnational market forces have moved rapidly across the world's national and cultural boundaries in a sweeping restructuring of local and regional economies. The new system is called "the New World Order."

The "globalizing" system being instituted, however, is not at all what it seems. It is not, as it is represented in the mass media and political ideology, an "international free market." In fact, most of its trade is between the firms of interlocked oligopolist corporations that have the power to affect supply, create demand, and dominate governments making rules for economic agents.[2] The tidal wave of change to achieve this "New World Order" is not "globalization" either. Only the rights of transnational capitalist corporations have been "globalized" in any trade and investment treaty since 1988. Workers' rights, national environmental regulations, and post-1945 norms of wealth redistribution have all been *de*-globalized and driven back into pockets of local resistance under ever-increasing pressure to "adapt to global competition." "There is," the authorities of the New World Order sinisterly proclaim, "no alternative."

THE NEW WORLD ORDER AS GLOBAL COUP D'ÉTAT?

The sudden reversal of half a century of the welfare state and the post-war social contract between labour and capital has been described by its most trenchant critics as a global coup d'état. Swiftly exploiting the collapse of the Soviet bloc and the yawning absence of an opposing military and economic order, world rule by transnational corporations has become a reality imposed with the strategic speed of a long-planned operation. In view of the general fact that transnational trade and investment regulations fashioned by corporate trade lawyers now override national economic sovereignty across continents, the analysis of a global coup d'étatcoup d'état has much to substantiate it. In the real world underneath saturating slogans of "free trade" and induced presupposition of the dominant market paradigm as a law of nature, a worldwide economic revolution has occurred by the force of transnational trade and investment decrees with no accountability to any electorate or law beyond itself.[3]

Transnational trade and investment agreements, over 20,000 pages of regulatory specifications and still growing in the case of the World Trade Organization, have in effect rewritten the laws of nations – striking down their regulatory control over national and regional markets; the right to preferential domestic ownership of natural resources; the powers of governments to receive concessions in return for foreign access to their societies' markets, materials, and infrastructures; and the established rights of states to regulate, subsidize, or nationalize ownership of strategic resources or industries in favour of national firms and citizens.[4] More specifically, these new investment and trade decrees prescribe unlimited foreign access to domestic markets without employment or other "performance requirements" permitted; guarantee unqualified license of foreign corporations to exploit natural resources with the same rights of "national treatment" as local citizens; open up public and social sectors, including multi-billion health and education budgets, to foreign corporate bidding and appropriation; and enable the one-way suing of sovereign governments by private foreign corporations for any public policy that is deemed by secretly operating trade panels to have offended against these new transnational regulations.[5]

In a real sense, responsible government is being usurped step by step via a transnational economic apparatus prescribing exclusively corporate rights to override any domestic legislative policy or law that is inconsistent with them. Yet the sweeping terms and regulations of this "New World Order" have been read by few elected officials. At the same time, the very transnational corporate beneficiaries of the new regime have provided the main sources of election finance, policy advice, and media support to the political parties that have sponsored the foreign takeover of their own economies under the name of global freedom and prosperity.[6]

While party governments have in this way been fully complicit in the appropriation of their societies' economic bases, the global occupation of domestic economies has met widespread unofficial opposition. Growing hosts of ordinary citizens, sustenance farmers, environmentalists, intellectuals, students, and workers from across continents have risen up to oppose this transnational regime as an enemy of democracy, the planet's faltering ecosystems, and the human rights of workers and citizens.[7] But what, the question is asked to this growing opposition, could be *wrong* with competitive principles of maximally efficient production and distribution regulating the world's markets?

THE REPRESSED ISSUE OF VALUES

The opposition answers by arguing that the global corporate system is not a "free market" but a transnational oligopoly; not truly "efficient" but selective of the lowest-common-denominator standards of environmental and labour protection; and not an engine of universal prosperity but a multiplier of human inequalities to levels never before seen.[8]

In short, a global war of values has emerged. Instead of a Cold War of opposing military superpowers confronting each other across geographically divided camps, this conflict has grown up *within* the societies of the world – from the American hemisphere across Europe and Africa to East Asia. While the corporate media dismiss the rising worldwide opposition to the corporate global system as "confused," "uninformed," "afraid to compete," "protectionist," and the like, a deeper current of reality erupts in the streets of Paris, Seattle, and Prague, the cities of India and Malaysia, the urban cores of Latin America, and in the pages of electronic and scholarly analyses from across the planet. The reality of the emerging world resistance has become too widespread to be ignored.

Academic research might seem a natural terrain for this argument or "war of values" to be clarified and resolved. Academic discourse itself, however, has become increasingly dependent on corporate funding in the new "knowledge economy," in which scholars' search for private and strategic funding determines academic survival. As a result, the deep-structural issues dividing the advocates and opponents of corporate globalization have been screened out of view in learned analysis as well as popular discourse. The underlying principles of the value war raging beneath the surface images and slogans have for this reason remained concealed, and hardly understood by the leading agents of the conflict themselves.

We know that the conventional outlook upon which the new global order depends for its legitimacy is that the free market organization of production and distribution promotes the well-being of citizens better than any alternative system. More problematically, it is also supposed as an unexamined causal law that corporate globalization promotes and universalizes the freedom of peoples and individuals. The analysis below will demonstrate that, in truth, this is a legitimating narrative that is opposed by the actually regulating principles of the global corporate system. More careful analysis of the real system-deciders of the world economy discloses, on the contrary, underlying value sequences whose determination of economies has neither been exposed nor understood.

On the other hand, active participants in the growing opposition to the new global corporate system seem to be an incoherent mélange of species protectors, human rights activists, Third World farmers, industrial workers, feminists, civic nationalists, and festive malcontents. Their common cause seems to be beyond the capacity of the mind to integrate into unified meaning. For this reason the "anti-globalization" protest has been repudiated as an uprising that is ultimately incoherent in its bearings. The striking mix of oppositional interests has led to outright derision from the corporate camp. Its media and government representatives declare the protestors represent nobody beyond themselves and have no idea of what they're standing for or protesting against.

The explanation below lays bare the regulating value principles of the warring sides, and it does so from what we may call "the life-value standpoint," the ethical ground of human and planetary life itself from which we can best understand and judge the rival positions. Once the global war of values is cast in the light of this underlying normative ground, the concealed life-and-death stakes of the conflict emerge clearly.

THE LIFE SEQUENCE OF VALUE

Life is not a given but is always a conditional process. That is, it is a process that requires a complex set of highly specific conditions to continue as life. Buddha recognized this ultimate principle of our existence as *pratityasamutpada*, which means that everything depends on everything else at once and in unison. We need to understand this principle of planetary interdependency well, because the essential problem of the global market system is that its economic paradigm is blind to the conditionality of all life, conceiving of "the real world" as decoupled transactions among self-maximizing buyers and sellers who look only to commodity prices and money returns for themselves.

Reality is more complex. Life is always a conditional sequence in which the beginning and ending terms of any extent of it are mediated by the countless means of life it requires to continue and reproduce as life. Here we refer not only to priced means of life, which can be bought in the market if one possesses the money-demand to pay. We refer also and more basically to the *unpriced* means of life – nature, such as clean air and sunlight, and one's community, such as language, personal affection, and education.

The unfolding of the life process at all the levels of its possibility is what we can call *the life sequence of value*. This life sequence of value is infinitely complex in its variations and complexities, but can be formulated in simple axiom as the sequence:

Life → Means of Life → More Life (L → MofL → L^1)

In this formula, *life* refers specifically to sentient life. Sentient life, in turn, is life that can move, feel, and – in the case of humans – think in concepts. These three planes of being – organic movement, sensation, and thought – are all processes that can only continue into the next moment if they are sustained by means of life of various kinds, not only immediate requirements like an exactly composed air to breathe, but remote conditions like a stratospheric layer of ozone to mediate the ultraviolet rays of the sun. At the same time, depending on the species, these three planes of life admit in accordance with the means of life available to their host widely different *ranges of vital function*. In the case of humans, for example, these ranges of life-capability can be drastically curtailed by economic conditions (as with the vital capabilities of a malnourished child), or increased (as with the opening horizons of movement, felt being, and cognition of the same child with access to nutritious food).[9]

Means of life refer to *whatever enables life to be preserved, or to extend its vital range on these planes of being alive*. Clean air, food, water, shelter, affective interaction, environmental space, and accessible learning conditions are the basic means of human life. But they are complemented in their necessity by countless other conditions of life, which are typically presupposed or ruled out of attention by the confinement of the dominant market paradigm to money values. In consequence, these non-monetary values can be degraded or despoiled by massive pollutions, extractions, and exploitations without any deficits whatever registering in the monetized accounts of states or corporations.

In short, means of life must be somehow sustained and available to humans for their life sequences to reproduce and grow rather than decline or die. To *reproduce* life is not simply for a body or bodies to go on living. It is to maintain life's *achieved ranges of capability* – of thinking, of acting, of feeling in all the very rich and complex parameters of each of these fields of life. For example, it is false to think that a generation is being reproduced in its organic capabilities when fewer children are being educated to literacy, as in sub-Sahara Africa over the heyday of "restructuring for globalization," or when the

saturation of the world's richest market with junk food leads to a
doubling of obesity rates in less than a decade, as in the "booming
U.S. economy" between 1991–98.[10] Here life-value is being reduced,
whatever global market figures of "vastly increased exports" or "spec-
tacular growth" may tell us.

In general, to reduce life value is to diminish or to extinguish *any*
domain of vital life capability, whether it be cognitive, emotional, or
physical capability. This is "the bottom line" of the life-value metric, and
it can be identified by social as well as individual indicators. Market
figures do not register either. For this reason, the paradigm is life-blind
in principle. To increase global corporate trade, for example, dictates
the reduction of public health and education financing as well as environmental protection systems across the globe. If we examine the many
fronts of opposition to the corporate market system, we will find that
underlying their diversity of standpoint is a single unifying principle of
concern – that life's reproduction and growth matters more than the
reproduction and growth of monetized trade and profit, and the belief
that global trade and life systems are not mutually re-enforcing but are
increasingly in deadly conflict.

THE QUESTION OF DEVELOPMENT:
WHY THE NEW WORLD ORDER
IS A FAILED EXPERIMENT

To increase life-value is to widen or deepen organic capabilities to a
more comprehensive range – as in education, whose root meaning is
"to cause to grow." What indicators of this growth of life-value do
we find anywhere since the restructuring of economies began in the
1990s? On both human and environmental levels, the pattern on
almost all life indicators has been, in fact, downwards – in particular on
the environmental level where species extinctions are now 1,000 times
greater than since the last ice age, and forest, fish, and water habitats
and stocks have precipitously fallen or collapsed.[11]

Greater or lesser ranges of humanity and of the world "being alive"
are the defining parameters of all value, on whatever scale of judgment
we care to analyse. They are the real bearers of growth or decline of
societies and economies. But no country or international trade region
has yet constructed a life value index of what is going on at the level
of the life economy itself. Worse, what indicators we have of human
and environmental life-fare point to a global decline on aggregate
biodiversity, health, educational and social security indices.

This deteriorating global life profile is not paid much attention in
economic circles because life value is confused with other kinds of

value, like consumers spending more in the market, or monetized trade increasing between countries. But life registers its gains and losses on its bearers independently of increases in consumer demand or global trade. Having money may certainly be a condition of having access to means of life in a current market society. But even possessed in sufficient quantities, even for the decreasing minority who have enough money to spend, monetary possession does not ensure life reproduction or growth. The global market may be, and increasingly in fact is, dominated by ever more unnourishing food, polluted air, saturating noise levels, alienated civil relations, mindless entertainment, iatrogenic pharmaceuticals, a demolished life-environment, and so on. A "booming economy" may boom despite all of these life-insulting conditions. But since there is no life-value GNP, or any adequate set of life standards by which economies judge themselves, the global corporate market could unravel the life-webs of the planet with no markers to recognize the problem in its metrics of "growth" and "development."

We may summarize these oppositions of value in a single general principle and its converse. An economy succeeds in reality rather than in claim *to the extent that life's ranges of vital being are maintained and/or increased for its members*. It fails to the extent that the opposite occurs, and the life of its members declines on these planes of life capability and enjoyment. It becomes a death economy to the extent that life is rapidly reduced and destroyed in its forms at the levels of species, cultures, and individual life capabilities.

Although the parameters of the life code of value are not computed in the global market paradigm, their lines of quality and quantity reveal to what extent an economy serves, or violates, life. These parameters are not mysterious or opaque. Even very small reductions of the vital range of breath, feeling, organ, or limb are normally experienced by us as "something wrong," whether or not they register in the priced transactions of an economic metric. The measure of life value is also exactly calibratable in its gains and losses. The entire corpus of scientific medicine, for example, can be understood as the development of ways and means of assessing and responding to deficits of normal life ranges – mainly, by diagnosing disease and prescribing treatment for the deficits of life range that it brings about. Similarly, every principle and practice of formal education can be decoded as the process of judging and enabling more comprehensive levels of thinking across defined breadths and depths of cognition. Yet again, environmental protection can be understood as the body of practices that effectively defend the evolved scopes of life of the species and ecosystems around us.

From the standpoint of the life ground of value, the more life's breadths and depths are reproduced and extended, the better is our objective condition.[12] Conversely, the more these life domains are reduced or lost, the worse is our real condition. Our global predicament is that public health, educational, and environmental expenditures to realize this life sequence of value have been increasingly "cut back" and "axed" across the world in accordance with the demands of the corporate market paradigm of value. Its standards of value judge these expenditures on health, education, and ecological security to be "unaffordable." The inner logic of this value system is we call "the money sequence of value." All of the recent evidence of its demand-effect sequence indicates that its system by nature increasingly imperils the conditions of human community and planetary life.[13]

THE MONEY SEQUENCE OF VALUE: ITS ORIGINS AND DEFORMATIONS

The money sequence of value has been traditionally confused in its outcomes with the *maximization of utility*. Although the money sequence of value can certainly have this serendipitous effect, its regulating objective is to maximize money returns over money inputs by whatever means is perceived to best achieve this outcome. Its original structure of "profitable investment" is represented by the formula:

$$\$ \to Means\ of\ Life \to More\ \$\ (\$ \to MofL \to \$^1)$$

In its initial historical form, money is only a medium of exchange. The baker or the shoemaker exchanges shoes or bread for money, in order to buy other life-goods with the money received. Here the money received and spent stands in as equivalent to means of life, because its reproduction is solely to exchange means of life. Most people normally use money in this way – not for money gain, but for life gain. We could therefore add an intermediate formula here to represent this value sequence:

$$Life \to Money \to Means\ of\ Life \to More\ Life\ (L \to \$ \to MofL \to L^1)$$

In this form, the sequence is *not* the money sequence of value, but the life sequence of value. It is not invested as money to have more money, but to have more life.

The money sequence of value, in contrast, begins with money and ends with money in its reproductive cycle. Means of life are what money, in the person of its agent, uses as a middle term to become more money. More money, not more life, is the regulating objective of thought and action throughout this value cycle, a cycle that is normally reiterated in compounding sequences to ever greater accumulations of money value. Value judgment here does not calculate whether life gains or loses by this reiterating money sequence. The objective is to net more money for money investors. Indeed, it is famously held that any other objective is a betrayal of fiduciary trust to stockholders. It follows from this value calculus that wars, ongoing car crashes, or endemic diseases can be occasions of momentous "value adding" and "economic prosperity," so long as they promote increased profits or priced transactions in the aggregate. This "money sequence of value" regulates every decision and every sector of the global market system.

Since those programmed by the money sequence of value always assume that more real money demand expresses more value, they conclude more real money demand is always better for the individual or for society. This value metric has become socially institutionalized in such standard measures of social well-being as the GNP (the total money value of the goods and services sold in and by a national economy, which registers no life debits in people killed by it or environments degraded by its activities).

Such a value system suppresses the distinction between life and death itself. In failing to distinguish between life-wealth and money demand *on* life-wealth, it systemizes a fateful confusion. Money demand on the wealth of life keeps increasing, and the wealth of life keeps decreasing by its demands, but the market or money calculus cannot recognize the problem. According to its metric, all is well and prosperity and development are being won. This can lead, if its logic is not exposed, to the stripping of the life-world until the life fabric can no longer hold.[14]

THE DEATH SEQUENCE OF VALUE

But the problem here is not fully fathomed. The money value program also undergoes fundamental mutations in its sequence over time. In its classical capitalist form, it invests in buying factors of production (labour, instruments of labour, and natural resources), and organizes them to produce means of life (e.g., clothes, foods, homes). Then, to complete the investment sequence, these commodities are converted back into money again, with the "value added" of profit by sale to buyers in the market. This is the capitalist sequence analysed so trenchantly by Karl Marx. But the money-into-more-money sequence mutates insofar as its middle term is no longer means of life but *means of life destruction*. This mutation in is not registered in market theory or practice. By not being recognized, it is more lethal. The need to inhibit its growth does not register to the value system's feedback loop.

The primary form of this money sequence is to invest in producing and selling means of destruction, or military armaments, which are produced so as to maximize their capacity to maim or kill life.[15] Armaments are researched, designed, and produced so as to achieve this capability with the maximal efficiency that physical, biological, and engineering sciences can program. Most public research money in the world's richest nation is assigned to this research, which is then applied to producing arms for profit. The weapons commodity, which began its truly modern history with the study of falling objects and projected missiles by Galileo, consists in ever more lethal instruments to obliterate people and settlements. In the life-blind calculi of the money sequence, however, these systematic negations of life – by resource diversion as well as by destruction – are not factored into value designations or judgments. The debits of life and its resources may be immense, but since only monetary returns count as values, no economic problem can be perceived. The armaments commodity has become the single most profitable manufacture of global trade, but the problem can no more be discerned at a high level of life loss than at a low level by this value paradigm. *What kills and deprives human life is the same in value in its monetized calculus as what serves and enhances life.* This deadly confusion follows unnoticed from the paradigm's regulating metric of worth.

The global market paradigm's indifference to the distinction between life and death is systematic, and reaches far beyond military means of life destruction. Other forms of this commodity are also manufactured and sold as the middle term of the money sequence as well, even though their content is known to cause disease to and kill human beings in predictable millions. A cigarette, for example, bears an estimated 4,000 to 5,000 chemicals into its consumer, a number known to be highly toxic and deadly. Unlike weapons, however, its life-assaultive properties have traditionally been denied rather than asserted by manufacturers. The feeling its consumption produces of enhanced being is, in fact, the response of the body's immune system to deadly toxins entering the life-system.[16] But here as well, even though the commodity between money input and money output destroys life by its design, this consequence to life is not a problem that registers to the money sequence of value. We may represent this, directly deadly form of the money sequence, then, as follows:

Money → Means of Destruction → More Money ($ → MofD → $¹)

Means of life destruction as a whole have become, without the current economic paradigm recognizing the pattern of the sea-shift, a more dynamic middle term of the money sequence than means of life. But there are two species of this quintessential New World Order commodity that require distinction – commodities that are produced and sold for the assault and destruction of life, and commodities that are produced and sold to *represent* the assault and destruction of life. The latter is still more pervasive. The global production and marketing of images, films, games, and other portrayals of terrorizing, wounding, and murdering people increases in both sites and vehicles every year. As the leading edge of the entertainment industry, the representation of bodily harm and death has ever more branches of manufacture and sale. Although its portrayals and images often have as their referents real injury or killing (as in mass-market "sports" and television "news"), this commodity form is representational, not real in its assaults on living structures. With the screens of the media watched up to five hours a day across the world, thousands of killings, shootings, acts of terror, fatal disasters, tortures, and, in general, irreversibly violent insults and deaths to human bodies in single or mass numbers are portrayed or re-enacted on a daily basis to "attract viewers." The regulating principle of their manufacture is that they advance money-sequence gains, and all are contrived, selected, and marketed in accordance with this final criterion of worth.

In sum, whether real or representational, the $\$ \rightarrow MofD \rightarrow \$^1$ sequence always has as its middle term the destruction of life as its logic of money gain. We might properly call this second form of the global market money sequence, therefore, *the death sequence of value*.

Means of destruction of life are also at work in other monetary sequences of value in the New World Order – principally, in the use of *non*-human life as raw materials for this or that commodity in the ceaseless transformation of money-demand inputs into increased money-demand outputs. The levelling of forest ecosystems to raise domestic animals for killing for meat, for example, also erodes and depletes topsoils, water supplies, and natural ecosystems. This commodity production alone, it is estimated, slaughters 6,000,000 animals a year in the U.S., has resulted in the destruction of 260,000,000 acres of its forests, appropriates half of all the country's water supplies, and, by deforestation, extinguishes an estimated 1,000 species a year across the world.[17] But none of these life costs enters the ledgers of the market calculus as losses. One might say that the mechanized conversion of the organic into the inorganic to maximize the returns of the money sequence is the meta-value theme of our era. Its systems of expression include, more generally, the worldwide industrial extraction of natural resources that leave behind them extinguished ecosystems above and below the earth and the water, and which pervasively contaminate the life-systems remaining with the poisonous effluents of their processes of production and sale.[18] Strictly speaking, however, the death sequence of value is confined to investment circuits in which means of life-destruction are the *commodity* that is manufactured and sold.

The death commodity is especially prominent in the New World Order's manufacture of ever more efficient machineries to tear natural life-fabrics apart – for example, rainforests, ocean bottoms, and earth strata – in order to extract their marketable elements. Large-scale factories of slaughter on land and sea to transform myriads of domestic and aquatic animals into meat is another form. These highly articulated machines to dismantle and to slaughter life-systems and animals develop scientifically alongside armament commodities for killing human beings. Similarly efficient in their technical capacities, they rip up soil communities, demolish forest worlds, and strip aquatic ecosystems in minutes so as to ensure the maximum velocity and volume of competitive money-sequence gains. They cage, kill, and process animals at the rate of millions an hour with the biological sciences as their servant. But, again, none of these advancing forms of the death sequence of value is recognized as constituting a deepening global market pattern. Here as well the received economic paradigm as it is constructed not to distinguish between life and death in its value judgments.

THE DECOUPLED MONEY SEQUENCE OF VALUE

A third kind of money sequence of value has become even more dominant since the New World Order's emergence at the end of the Cold War. Like the second, it remains unrecognized and is, by its nature, in conflict with the sequence of life. As I have written elsewhere, the money sequence of value *mutates* in another way when it bypasses the production of *any commodity at all*.[19] In this form of the money sequence, the investment circuit transforms money into more money in a self-multiplying circuit that is decoupled from the middle term of commodity production altogether. This exponentially escalating money sequence now commands a conservatively estimated forty times more money value daily than all expenditures on goods and services put together. We can represent this pattern of money begetting money in the formula:

Money $\rightarrow$ More Money $\rightarrow$ More money or $\$ \rightarrow \$^1 \rightarrow \$^2 \rightarrow \$^3 \rightarrow \$^n$

This money-into-more-money cycle is reproduced and expanded in many forms – currency and derivatives speculation, arbitrages, leveraged buyouts to strip assets for sale, and, most well known, compound interest demands. All of these variations on the pure money sequence multiply money outputs with no input of production. Because they appropriate revenues from the production and distribution of means of life in society – for example, from budgets for social infrastructures to pay rising compound interest payments to banks and bondholders – they also attack the life sequence of value, but by deprivation rather than by direct assault.[20] The money sequence of value like the death sequence, is a basic ordering pattern of the New World Order that most lethally attacks the integrity of macro life organization. By appropriating revenues devoted to producing public goods to increase the returns of private financial circuits that produce nothing but more demand for further returns, the pure money sequence deprives social life-organization of its life means – for example, by rerouting former expenditures on public health, education, social welfare, pensions, civil arts, and communications to payments to expanding $\$ \to \$^1 \to \$^2 \to \$^3 \to \$^N$ rounds.

The rapidly emerging dominance of the "speculative economy" over the "real economy" resembles in this way a carcinogenic circuit, in its systemic appropriation of society's life nutriments to multiply itself with no committed function to the host body.[21] The inner logic of this money sequence, however, is not recognized, even by Marxian economics.[22] Rather, all three money sequences, the destructive and the parasitic as well as the productive, are conflated under the masking general concept of "capitalism," although the meaning of "capital" as wealth that is used to produce more wealth has shifted from production for life to appropriation *from* life as the ruling pattern.

THE MORAL DILEMMA CONFRONTING CITIZENS OF THE NEW WORLD ORDER

In all three expanding sequences of the money value program, global market prescriptions come into ever sharper and more destructive contradiction with the life sequence and its internal requirements for maintenance and growth. As the mutant sequences grow, the life sequence on both social and environmental levels is systemically depleted and degraded. In the end, an emergent crisis poses a life-and-death choice to human society: either its people defend civil and environmental life organization against these life-blind global market demands, or civil and planetary life will be increasingly stripped by the cumulative money-to-more-money circuits as "free world" imperatives and "value adding."[23]

As with other lethal value programs in other places and other times, the pathological pattern is not seen because its normative structure is presupposed as the ground of the real and the good, and its harshest consequences as the "necessary" workings of its inviolable laws. The New World Order's language of an "invisible hand," "necessary sacrifices," and "no alternative" disclose its fundamentalist nature. As planetary climate patterns destabilize, extinction spasms increase, the ozone layer disappears, and human inequality multiplies to unheard of extremes, those living within this New World Order are confronted with an ever starker and more urgent choice between its fanatic value program for the world, and civil and planetary life itself.

NOTES

1 Thomas Kuhn, "Incommensurability and Paradigms," in Harold Morick, ed., *Challenges to Empiricism*, Belmont, Ca.: Wadsworth, 1965, 206.

2 These points are developed in more detail in my *Unequal Freedoms: The Global Market as an Ethical System*, Toronto and Westport, CT: Garamond and Kumarian Press, 1998, 13–15, 132–42, and *The Cancer Stage of Capitalism*, London: Pluto Press, 1999, 37–59.

3 For an extended analysis of the value system underlying this "New World Order," see *Value Wars: The Global Market versus the Life Economy*, London: Pluto Press, 2002.

4 For an anatomy of these regulating principles of the emerging global corporate system, see my "World Order By Trade and Investment Decree: The Global Corporate System," in Walter Dorn, ed., *World Order for A New Millennium*, New York: St Martin's Press, 1999, 45–57.

5 For a shorter, accessible report of this still expanding regulatory regime, see Stephen Shrybman, *The World Trade Organization: A Citizen's Guide*, Toronto and Ottawa: Lorimer Press and the Canadian Centre for Policy Alternatives, 2000.

6 See, for example, David Korten, *When Corporations Rule the World*, Westport, CT and San Francisco: Kumarian and Berrett-Kohler Press, 1996.

7 For a systematic analysis and detailed documentation of these patterns, see my *Unequal Freedoms* and *The Cancer Stage of Capitalism*, and monthly articles from June 1998 in *Economic Reform*, the journal of the Toronto-based policy research group the Committeee on Monetary and Economic Reform (er@comer.org).

8 The United Nations Human Development Report 2000, for example, reports that the world's 200 richest people have doubled their wealth within just the last four years, with the result that the assets of just three corporate owners now exceed the GNP of all of the least developed societies of 600 million people ("Overview," *Human Development Report 2000*, Cary, NC: Oxford University Press, 2000, 3).

9 These facts may seem self-evident, but they are ignored even by the richest countries of the world, where one in six children, 47 million in all, "remain poor despite a doubling and redoubling of national incomes" (*United Nations Report on Child Poverty in Rich Nations*, 2000, Torstar News Service, 13 June 2000).

10 "Hog Nation: U.S. Wallows in Obesity," *Earth Island Journal* (Spring 2000), 23.

11 Digby J. McLaren, "Reply to Colin Rowat," *Delta Newsletter of the Global Climate Change Program* (Royal Society of Canada) 7, no. 3 (1996), 3. Such figures are typically suppressed, however. The foregoing journal ceased publication after these disclosures, perhaps coincidentally. There was no coincidence, however, in the case of the European Union and the World Wide Fund For Nature, which suppressed, demanded rewrites, and then pulped their own commissioned expert report on the state of the world's tropical rainforests after World Bank and IMF programs restructured African, Caribbean, and Papuan economies to sell their forests for cash to pay back debts to foreign banks (Paul Brown, "Report on Forests Suppressed," *Guardian Weekly*, 1–7 June 2000, 3).

12 It is worth noting here that the life-world refered to in this paper is not the "lifeworld" that Jurgen Habermas refers to in his theory of communicative action. Habermas, typically of contemporary philosophers whose analysis is confined to the linguistic plane of existence, means by the term only the symbolic realm of life. See, for example, Jurgen Habermas (trans. Thomas McCarthy), *The Theory of Communicative Action*, Boston: Beacon Press, 1984, 1:xxxiv.

13 I argue this systemic diagnosis in *The Cancer Stage of Capitalism*.

14 A graphic example of the block against recognizing the extent of life-destructive "externalities" by money sequences of growth is provided by Lawrence Summers, former chief economist of the World Bank and now president of Harvard University. He proclaims, with no relevant expertise in the life sciences, that there are "no natural limits to [monetized economic] growth" and "no limits to the carrying capacity of the earth." The claim that there are, he states, "is a profound error" (cited by Susan George, associate director of the Transnational Institute, in the *Globe Report on Business*, 29 May 1992, B15).

15 A more developed account of the political economy of the armaments commodity may be found in my monograph *Understanding War*, Toronto: Science for Peace, 1989. Lest it be thought that armaments are means of life in the sense of means of defending civilian populations from aggressors, we need to bear in mind that over three of four people killed by the armaments commodity in war are non-combatant civilians, and most of them are killed by their own governments (Ruth Leger Sivard et al., *World Military and Social Expenditures 1996*, Washington DC, 1996).

16 International epidemiologist Richard Peto of Oxford University estimates that smoking is responsible for 3,000,000 deaths per year worldwide, which will likely reach 10,000,000 in three decades. In China alone,

Peto estimates that 50,000,000 people will eventually die from smoking-induced diseases. Former U.S. surgeon-general C. Everett Koop observes: "I think one of the most shameful things my country ever did was to export disease disability and death by selling our cigarettes to the world." Clayton Yeutter, the U.S. trade representative, however, exults on the increased trade figures and exports of the U.S. in the global market: "I just saw the figures on tobacco exports a few days ago and, my, have they turned out to be a marvellous success story." Here we see in clear expression what we will call the global market's "death sequence of value" affirmed as an optimum good. Figures and quotations are cited in Glenn Frankel, "U.S. Aided Tobacco Firms in Asia Conquest," from *The Washington Post* in the *Guardian Weekly,* 1 December 1996, 15.

17 M.I.T. Vegetarian Support Group, "How our Food Choices Affect Life On Earth," *World-Wide-Web,* 22 November 1996, 1.

18 Together these economic operations of extraction and pollution "lead to the extinction of plants and animals at about 1000 times the normal rate" (Digby J. McLaren, "Reply," *Delta Newsletter of the Global Climate Change Program* 7, no. 3 (1996), 3), with "about $500 billion a year subsidizing the destruction of the oceans, atmospheres and land" (John Vidal, "World Turning Blind Eye To Catastrophe," Reports of U.N. Environment Agency, British Panel on Sustainable Development, and World-Watch Institute, *Guardian Weekly,* 7 February, 1). According to the Rio Plus Five Forum Earth Summit meeting in March 1997, these processes of life destruction and deterioration had not abated since 178 nations had pledged to "clean up the world" five years previously but had increased. At the same time, the money sequence of value had multiplied the world's billionaires by more than ten times since 1987 (Associated Press, 14 July 1997).

19 See my "The Social Immune System and the Cancer Stage of Capitalism," *Social Justice* (Winter 1995, 1–25. The nature of the pure money sequence of value and its rapid overwhelming of the life economy is analysed in detail in this account, with the relevant documentation not repeated here.

20 The precise ways in which compound interest charges on national debts strip societies' capacities to protect and enable the lives of their citizens is tracked in depth in the analysis cited in note 7, which reports, for example, that Zambia's expenditure on interest payments to foreign banks is five times its total expenditures on public health.

21 Interest demands on public debt in Canada, for example, escalated nearly eightfold in real terms in Canada between 1962–81 and 1981–95, requiring a corresponding dismantling of health, education,

and social security budgets to pay the compound interest demands. In the U.S., it is estimated that at the 1967–87 rate of the interest-demand share of the U.S. national income, *all* of the national income would be required to pay off compound interest payments to money lenders by 2020 (William F. Hixson, *A Matter of Interest: Re-Examining Debt, Interest and Real Economic Growth*, New York: Praeger, 1991, 177, 176).

22 Marxist theory would seem to have the methodological resources to pick out this decoupled circuit of capital, which secures accumulating money gains without the production of any use-value, but in fact Marx himself rules out this possibility when he argues in *Capital* that "movements of money capital are therefore once more merely movements of an individualized *part of industrial capital engaged* in the reproduction process" (*Capital*, Vol. 3, ch. 29).

23 Again, the gross outcome patterns disclose the growth and development of life and money sequences in inverse relation, as opposed to the correlation that the current paradigm assumes. Thus, for example, while almost 100 species are made extinct every day from the impact of "economic activities" (U.N. Environment Program, *Canadian Press*, 20 April 1996) and while the number of all of the world's children who are malnourished increases past one in three (World Health Organization, *Guardian Weekly*, 21 May, 1995), the money value of shares in the broad U.S. market skyrockets to six times total value (*Globe and Mail Report on Business*, 25 July 1977), and bank assets in money value delinks from legal-tender reserves to a ratio of almost 400 to 1 (William Krehm, *Economic Reform*, September 2002, 4). The assumed correlation between aggregate real dollar value increases in the world economy and increases in the world's well-being is in such ways increasingly the reverse of the facts.

Intelligence Agenda and the Need for Constructive Intellectual Intervention in the New World Order

GORDANA YOVANOVICH

The New World Order has been created by politicians and by political intelligence. It is an artificial order that has been imposed from above. The New World Order is global in nature, yet it does not encompass the universal spirit that has nurtured ordinary lives throughout history. At the time of the imposition of the New World Order, intellectuals were not ready to cope in a profound and holistic way with new developments; some of the intellectuals who were not living in their academic towers were employed to work for narrow political agendas, and some were naïve in their belief that the struggle against communism was a struggle for true freedom and democracy. Others were in their avant-garde world, unaware of social and political changes. If we compare the present situation to the time of the French Revolution and the Renaissance, we see how little modern philosophers, writers, and artists are engineers of the contemporary worldview. Perhaps that is the reason why the New World Order lacks a humanistic vision: the life-respecting spirit is absent in the order created by intelligence services of the main establishment. However, it can be found in countries and peoples with a tradition of difficult endurance. This spirit was celebrated by Rubén Darío, for example, at the beginning of the twentieth century. Intellectuals today, who should assume a more engaged and constructive role in society, can learn from the Nicaraguan poet.

The challenge of harmonizing material and immaterial, social and individual aspects in life and culture is eternal. However, the delicate balancing act has taken a sinister turn in recent times. The material world or the world of business and money is seizing leadership. A holistic approach to life and the traditional wisdom that "money is the root of all evil" have been replaced with the new view that "money makes the world go around." The art world is now ruled by art industry, while academics are guided by research and publishing grants. With the exception of Nelson Mandela, no visionary figures comparable to Galileo, Erasmus, Cervantes, Mozart, Gandhi, Whitman, Martin Luther King, Cezanne, or Picasso can be found on stage in the new millennium theatre, yet major developments have been led throughout history by bold intellectual and cultural dialogue. At the time of the fall of the Berlin Wall, intellectuals on both sides of the now tumbled Iron Curtain had nothing significant to say, yet the event marked a major change in the alignment of power. In the last few years, writers and academics in Eastern Europe are beginning to discover their naïvete in their attitude towards the American agenda, but their comments are no longer broadcast on American television. Intellectuals in the West, on the other hand, do not seem to be concerned with the new developments in the world because they are not ready, it seems, to deconstruct the present. More importantly, if we exclude well-educated politicians, there are few intellectuals in the West who are able to make an impact on the making of society. Writers and academics are no longer enlightened leaders whose job is to articulate a humanist voice with a philosophical conception and an artistic vision for the future.

In the New World Order cultural intelligence in the traditional sense of the word plays a much less important role than political intelligence. We are given a revealing insight in a 1964 U.S. House Report of the thinking of the Committee on Foreign Affairs. In Report No. 2 it is explained that "certain foreign policy objectives can be pursued by dealing directly with the people of foreign countries, rather than with their governments. Through the use of modern instruments and techniques of communication it is possible today to reach large or influential segments of national populations – to inform them, to influence their attitudes, and at times perhaps even to motivate them to a particular course of action. These groups, in turn, are capable of exerting noticeable, even decisive, pressures on their governments."[1] Commenting on this mobilization of people of other countries to work for American interests, Herbert I. Schiller comments that "if Free Trade is the mechanism by which a powerful economy penetrates and dominates a weaker one, the 'free flow of information,' the designated objective incidentally of UNESCO, is the channel through which lifestyles and value systems can be imposed on poor and vulnerable societies."[2] But, Eastern European *intelligentsia* and former dissidents are only beginning to understand that "American interests" are not synonymous with true "personal freedom and democracy." A book that is particularly revealing is Valdas Anelauskas' *Discovering America as It Is* (Atlanta: Clarity Press, 1999). Other former dissidents have been using the Internet to warn against accepting help from the Soros Foundation, which financially supported their struggle against communism. Blagovesta Doncheva, a Bulgarian intellectual, is only one of many emerging anti-communists who are beginning to recognize their mistakes. In an article posted on her website "Emperor's Clothes," for example, as she warns Serbs who support the "democratic opposition," she writes that "whatever terrible suffering they have gone through, these are nothing compared to what will befall them if the IMF and the Soros foundation get hold of them."[3]

When in the eighteenth century the industrialized world emerged in Europe out of a combination of changes in the economic structure and enrichment of the middle class, it was in response to equally important philosophical and political dreams of liberty, fraternity, and equality. The philosophical exchange lead by Voltaire and Rousseau was both sincere and profound enough to find support among the masses and it helped move the world in a new direction. As Joachim Ritter says, the modern bourgeois society emerged from the French Revolution as the "locus of emancipation." Secularization, reason, democracy, and law and order have played an important role in human history. However, reason and created order must work together with other aspects of life. Most importantly, they must be accompanied by good will. The French Revolution was imperfect in practice, but it was based on positive and profound philosophical thinking.

The contemporary attempt to guide culture and societies through meetings and conferences of groups such as the G7+1, WTO, IMF, NATO, and so on is, however, the eighteenth-century faith in logic and reason taken to the ridiculous. It is a deviation of philosophy because the New World Order is not created through philosophical reasoning but rather through manipulative agendas and bureaucratic procedure. The American Academy's "Commission on the Year 2000" is an example of bureaucratization, human alienation, intellectual servitude, and academic arrogance. Lawrence K. Frank, in proposing the creation of the commission in 1964, argued that the modern situation was "somewhat similar to that of the eighteenth century, when such inquiring thinkers as John Locke, Adam Smith and the French philosophers formulated the premises that underlie the democratic polity and market economy of the past two hundred years."[4] The creation of the commission was to be taken as "the first step toward meeting this urgent need for a new social philosophy." The task of implementing the proposal fell to Paul Freund of Harvard Law School, as president of the Academy, and John Voss, as the new executive officer. The first commission meeting was held in October of 1965. With Daniel Bell as chairman, twenty-seven academics were involved in "Working Session One: Baselines for the Future." Daniel Bell's *Toward the Year 2000* transcribes the work of this group and lists all its participants.[5] The book reproduces the agenda for the meeting and the group and testifies that rich countries have the resources to pay its most intelligent and most educated citizens to help shape the world. But can lasting worlds and cultures be created without the inspiration of the cosmic and human spirit? Is the predominance of a mindset ordered by premeditated plans and conference agendas not dangerous when it is not accompanied by good will, when dreams and positive emotions are not the warp and weft of society?

One of the leading participants/discussants of the Commission 2000, Zbigniew Brzezinski, showed extreme formal erudition and computer-like intelligence on public television as he helped advance NATO's "humanitarian" involvement in the bombing of Yugoslavia. Brzezinski's[6] academic colleagues such as the former American secretaries of state Madeleine Albright and Henry Kissinger have shown similarly remarkable academic knowledge. In their struggle against communism in Latin America and Europe, they have made an impact on the world that is comparable, at least in magnitude, to the impact the French philosophers made in the eighteenth century. But are power and erudition impressive if they, as in the case of the Second World War, destroy and spoil millions of human lives? The French Revolution did not happen without loss of life and suffering, but it did give a direction for the future. What is the vision of modern world makers?

In 1968 Daniel Bell wrote that "[t]echnology is not simply a 'machine,' but a systemic, disciplined approach to objectives, using a calculus of precision and measurement and a concept of system that are quite at variance with traditional and customary religious, aesthetic, and intuitive modes."[7] In the NATO display of power in Yugoslavia, it was quite clear that the machine is only a component of a larger, intellectually elaborated system. As in Hitler's Germany, the war machine is a product of the educated elite that not only works on the advancement of technology but also perfects its ways of controlling the ordinary citizen's mode of thinking. In his defence of German nationalism, Thomas Mann wrote that "[t]here are not two Germanies, an evil and good, but only one, which, through devil's cunning, transformed its best into evil."[8] Open attacks by the United States on countries such as Vietnam, Panama, Iraq, and Yugoslavia under the guise of a moral purpose and concern for human rights combine military might and unmerciful propaganda in precise coordination. Viewers marvel at the modern technological inventions because their precision and performance support the postmodernist claim that humans, not God, are the makers of the world. Given that, as the

German-born NATO general briefed, "six hundred und forty-five sorties in good weather" were sent a day in the bombing of Yugoslavia, the small number of accidents was impressive. Even those who watched the destruction of their work places, heating centres, children's schools, and so on were impressed that a missile launched in Italy could target a particular building in downtown Belgrade and that only one particular building would be destroyed while leaving the adjacent ones intact. In earlier centuries, such exactitude would have been thought to be a true miracle. However, we must remember that there are good miracles and there are bad miracles.

If the strength of the technologically oriented culture of today were to work together with the wisdom of traditional, religious, and intuitive cultures, the two could wonderfully complement each other to create a holistic society where neither body nor soul, figuratively speaking, would suffer in isolation. Unfortunately, Western European and North American culture harbours the mentality of colonizer and hunter, as Nicaraguan diplomat and poet Rubén Darío observed at the beginning of this century, when U.S. imperialism was still in its embryonic form. When, in 1904, Darío wrote "To Roosevelt," the president and his country are portrayed as synonymous:

You are a strong, proud model of your race;
you are cultured and able; you oppose Tolstoy.
You are an Alexander-Nebuchadnezzar,
breaking horses and murdering tigers.
(You are a Professor of Energy,
as the current lunatics say).

You think that life is fire,
that progress is an irruption,
that the future is wherever
your bullet strikes.

Eres soberbio y fuerte ejemplar de tu raza
Eres culto, eres hábil; te opones a Tolstoy.
Y domando caballos, o asesinando tigres,
eres el Alejando-Nabucondonosor.
(Eres un profesor de Energía
como dicen los locos de hoy.)
Crees que la vida es incendio
que el progreso es erupción,
que en donde pones la bala
el porvenir pones.

Rubén Darío could be writing this today. Northern rationality has created an unparalleled military and economic power. The United States not only thinks that it is powerful; it is an empire. Its military force and ruthless deception rule the world, yet they are disguised as guardians and promoters of universal human rights.

Studying the idea of Pan-Americanism, which is comparable to today's idea of globalization, in 1906 Rubén Darío wrote a poem called "Salutación al águila,"[9] in which he celebrated what we today call "free trade," "globalization," and "NAFTA." In this poem he sees the American eagle flying together with the Southern condor. The poet begins with Fontoura Xavier's wish, "May this grand Union have no end!," then calls forth the Latin proverb: "E pluribus unum!" The desire for unity is also accompanied by a desire for economic development. The poet clearly invites the Northern power to open "the great and rich belly of the earth," "el gran vientre fecundo a la tierra," so that "man can have bread with which to circulate his blood," "y tenga el hombre el pan con que mueve su sangre." He even goes so far as to label Latin American youth as mere "rhetoricians" or "los retores latinos," and he earnestly orders them to learn "from Yankees about firmness, vigor and strength of character" "de los yanquis la constancia, el vigor, el carácter." Today, as then, North American practicality, organization, and hard work are respected as a recipe for success all over the world.

Rubén Darío changed his mind about the grand union however because he, like many contemporary thinkers, suspected that the envisioned brotherhood with the U.S. was not to be a union between equal or loving peers. In a letter to Mrs Lugones, Darío writes that he had tried to argue for the great union with a great deal of fear and little faith, "Yo pan-americanicé/ con un vago temor y con muy poca fe." In his diplomatic work on Pan Americanism, he found a nucleus of honest people with souls full of love, dreams and ideals, "encontré también un gran núcleo cordial/de almas llenas de amor, de ensueño, de ideal."[10] But the official politics of the northern brother is to be feared rather than loved and trusted. Hence, Darío addresses Roosevelt as a hunter, "Cazador," referring literally to his passion for hunting and symbolically to his politics of aggressive expansionism:

The United States are grand and powerful.
Whenever it trembles, a profound shudder
runs down the enormous backbone of the Andes.
If it shouts, the sound is like the roar of a lion.
And Hugo said to Grant: "The stars are yours."
(The dawning sun of the Argentine barely shines;

the star of Chile is rising ...) A wealthy country,
joining the cult of Mammon to the cult of Hercules;
while Liberty, lighting the path
to easy conquest, raises her torch in New York.

Los Estados Unidos son potentes y grandes.
Cuando ellos se estremecen hay un hondo temblor
que pasa por las vértebras enormes de los Andes.
Si clamáis, se oye como el rugir del león.
Ya Hugo a Grant lo dijo: Las estrellas son vuestras.
... Sois ricos.
Juntáis el culto de Hércules con el culto de Mammón
y alumbrando el camino de la fácil conquista,
la Libertad levanta su antorcha en Nueva-York.

Referring to Hugo's reproach of General Grant, Darío declares that
American imperialism is threatening the young republics of the South.
Today, this charge could be expanded to say that it is threatening the
world. Might ("the cult of Hercules"), greed ("the cult of Mammon"),
and cynical propaganda ("lighting the road of an easy victory, / the
statue of liberty raises its torch in New York") combine as an unholy
triad. The United States is not simply "grand and powerful," as Rubén
Darío recognized at the beginning of the century. It exercises its power
with chilling precision: "Whenever it trembles, a profound shudder
runs down" not only through "the enormous backbone of the Andes"
but also down the Vietnamese Annamese chain of mountains, the
Balkans, and the barren desert of the Middle East.

The Latin American poet defiantly told the Americans: "And though
you have everything, you are lacking one thing: God!" "Y, pues contáis
con todo, falta una cosa: Dios!" "God" for a Catholic such as Darío,
as for the Orthodox Serbs, for Jews, for Muslim Iraqis, Kurds, and for
Buddhists, is not synonymous with "religious conscience," an abstract
imperative that North American New Conservatives are attempting to
revive as a remedy for modern internal ills. Northern cultures often
understand God as a "religious conscience" and a controlling force in
morality, but in Latin America and many other countries with deeply
rooted spiritual traditions, God is understood in terms of dreams, love,
suffering, endurance, and liberation or redemption. In Darío's poem,
God is to be found in the double heritage of the indigenous and the
Spanish, of Christian and sensual love, of Indian endurance, of the
poet's intoxication and the philosopher's ideals:

But our own America, which has had poets
since the ancient times of Netzahualcoyotl;

which preserved the footprints of great Baccus,
and learned the Panic alphabet once,
and consulted the stars; which also knew Atlantis
(Whose name comes ringing down to us in Plato)
and has lived, since the earliest moments of its life,
in light, in fire, in fragrance, and in love–
the America of Moctezuma and Atahualpa,
the aromatic America of Columbus,
Catholic America, Spanish America,
the America where noble Cuauhtémoc said:
"I am not on a bed of roses" – our America,[11]
trembling with hurricanes, trembling with Love.

Mas la América nuestra, que tenía poetas
desde los viejos tiempos de Netzahualcoyotl,
que ha guardado las huellas de los pies del gran Baco,
que el alfabeto pánico en un tiempo aprendió;
que consultó los astros, que conoció la Atlántida
cuyo nombre nos llega resonando en Platón,
que desde los remotos momentos de su vida
vive de luz, de fuego, de perfume, de amor,
la América del grande Moctezuma, del Inca,
la América fragante de Cristóbal Colón,
la América católica, la América española,
la América en que dijo el noble Guatemoc:
"Yo no estoy en un lecho de rosas;" esa América
que tiembla de huracanes y que vive de amor.

The traditional idealism of the Spanish American people stated in these verses may sound ridiculous to the pragmatic rational mind. They can appear to be simplistic consolations for a poor and naïve people. But there are times when circular reasoning – that something endures because it has survival instincts and has survival instincts because it endures – makes sense because it reflects reality. By gathering for concerts on potential military targets and singing to the thunder of planes and bombs, Serbian artists and historically suffering people stated that their courage and invincible spirit, not NATO bombing, are acts of God. In *Man's Search for Meaning*,[12] Victor Frankl explains how Jewish people survived German concentration camps through spiritual strength; amidst unspeakable horror and great suffering, they overcame despair by creating and performing theatrical skits. Concentration camp theatre, Serbian concerts, poetry composed by Dr Zhivago during the horror of the Russian revolution, and Rabelaisian grotesque laughter are positive energy, or an expression of God, that nurtures life.

It is difficult for a rational mind to understand how small cultures and peoples survive within the official order. To say that they endure because they have survival instincts is analogous to saying to a blind man that green is the colour of the caterpillar: it is obvious, but not apprehensible. Yet it is true. As Rubén Darío believed, there is an *anima mundi* that can still stand up to the mighty and the powerful. In his article "The Trap of Rationality," published in *Newsweek* on 26 July 1971, George Bell observed that "[w]hat misled a group of able and dedicated [U.S.] men [in Vietnam] was that, in depersonalizing the war and treating it too much as an exercise in the deployment of resources, we ignored the one supreme advantage possessed by the other side: a rebuke of the spirit to the logic of number." A similar "rebuke of the spirit" has been seen in half a century of Cuban endurance. More generally, Latin America as a whole has survived despite the fact that the New World Order tested its methods in 1970s and 1980s by means of the Latin American military. While it is true that thousands of young men and women disappeared because they dreamed of creating a different world, their mothers and relatives have not stopped coming every Thursday to the Plaza de Mayo in Buenos Aires, where they keep the memory of their children and their cause alive. CNN cameras and the world's eyes no longer focus on the Southern hemisphere, but this does not mean that the "Latin American problem" has been solved or that the defiant Latin spirit has been tamed. As Maria Figueredo shows in this collection, the spirit lives through music, for example, which is more than merely a form of subversion. Latin musicians sing of brotherhood and love, and thus nurture, give hope, and vitalize individuals and societies.

In North America, the strength of spirit evident in the struggle of pioneers faced with an unfriendly frontier, in the survival of African slaves, and in the Civil Rights movement seems diminished. In recent years, the ready availability of material possessions has incubated a form of modern urban alienation. An abundance of food and an emphasis on the self has isolated and corroded the human spirit, reduced individual vigour, and eroded communal ties. Antonio Benítez-Rojo compares the attitude of the poor in North America to that of their Southern brothers in the following way: "In Chicago a beaten soul says 'I can't take it any more,' and gives himself up to drugs or to the most desperate violence. In Havana, he would say: 'The thing to do is not die,' or perhaps: 'Here I am, fucked but happy.'"[13] South American fortitude is not created by "religious conscience." As the following poem by contemporary Serbian poet Lubomir Simovich testifies, people with a history of being colonized and invaded have developed a resistance that the gentlemen in the American Academy, operating entirely with rational categories, cannot understand. As in the past, the spirit will continue to resist the menace of the soulless, profit-seeking, technologically oriented world order that seeks to set the current agenda. In the case of the destruction of former Yugoslavia, people met terrible torture with humour. Simovich wrote at the time of the war:

Ballad of Family O'Stand

The torturer whips us, God does he ever hit,
our skin breaks, pieces of flesh scatter around;
he whips us one hour, keeps hitting two hours, he whips us for three hours,
where does he find so many sticks and rage?
He hits us unsparingly, hits us wholeheartedly,
his face already twitching from the strain,
loses his breath, stops a while, takes breath, exhausted,
falls down dead tired,
                    and we are still alive.

They line us up tied against the wall,
they shoot at us – our skulls crack,
our shins splitting, our forearms, all bones,
our flesh turns heavy with all that lead in our bodies.
The evening comes. The gunmen become tired.
They untie us. Curse God and our mother.
From the firing squad we return home
                    as from work,
and while the supper is cooking
our wives darn holes in our clothes.

After supper I check my home:
patch up the roof, mend the fence,
gather rain water in barrels and tub.
Then it's time for bed. Before I fall asleep
I tell my wife: they will hang us at five,
try to wake me up a bit earlier.

In the morning, the gallows are brand new, secure,
ropes strong, hangmen dressed up,
– frankly speaking, nothing to object to.
They hang us quickly, they hang us with ease.
We remain hanged until dark,
it's time for supper, they take us down – still alive,
they all kick us and swear; but it does not matter.

Tomorrow morning at dawn they gather wood and branches
stack up the stake, tie us naked to it,
bring matches, and light up,
and it burns, burns one week,
the whole town turns gray with ashes.
When it all burns down, we walk out from under the smoke,
the queen faints, the king
rubs his eyes and looks at us astonished:
God damn you, you are still alive!

They tie us up to horses' tails, they stretch us on a wheel,
they cut off our heads, legs and arms – horror!
They hang us dead, asphyxiate decapitated,
but we don't know why, and it does not matter.

The judges have had enough of this!
They set up new marksmen, let soldiers go,
hang their hangmen – as if it's their fault.
And again at us: with mace, with cannons,
then they hang us, hack us, decapitate us!
                                        We are still alive.

Something is wrong, people are starting to whisper,
someone is trying to save the judges from sinning!
We also started becoming afraid before falling asleep:
we are also mortal, this won't last long,
we are finished
we will end too
we won't endure,
                        we will die
                        of laughter.
                                    (My translation)

In his well-known primitive masks in "Les Demoiselles d'Avignon,"
Pablo Picasso invoked the primordial spirit and crude energies Rubén
Darío and Lubomir Simovich portray as a profound source of empowerment. Unfortunately, the modern world in general did not manage
to re-connect with universal, primitive, or primordial forces. James
Joyce and Virginia Woolf, two other founding members of modernism,
searched for the same life-giving energy in the subconscious mind and
in the "flickering of that innermost flame which flashes its message
through the brain," as Virginia Woolf wrote.[14] Yet, their exploration
of the subconscious became a search that was too sophisticated for the

general reader. Modernism was marked, as Ihab Hassan argues, by "purpose, design, determinacy, transcendence, and origins."[15] Yet, in its effort to discourage emulation of bourgeois morality, modernism became a movement that seemed to reject the past altogether. Daniel Bell argues from a neo-conservative perspective in *The Cultural Contradictions of Capitalism* that modernist culture, as a force, was a negative phenomenon because it contributed to the destruction of the moral bases of rationalized society. In *The New Conservatism*, Jurgen Habermas explains that modernism led to "Bohemian lifestyles with their hedonistic, unrestrainedly subjective value orientations." He laments that it undermined "the discipline of bourgeois everyday life," and he suggests that "only the renewal of a religious conscience, the overcoming of a culture that has become profane, can restore the ethical bases of a secularized society."[16] Habermas is probably right in commenting that modernism made a negative impact on society because the intended liberation led to "Bohemian lifestyles" and "hedonistic unrestrained subjectivity." However, we must also remember that modernism was an avant-garde movement where writers did not write for the general public. Modernist ideas were warped by Hollywood because sex and nudity appeal to masses and make money.

At the beginning of the twentieth century, modernist Irish poet W.B. Yeats foresaw that the end of the twentieth century will not celebrate a birth of Christ but will witness a birth of the Anti-Christ. In "The Second Coming," published in 1921, Yeats wrote:

> Turning and turning in the widening gyre
> The falcon cannot hear the falconer;
> Things fall apart; the center cannot hold;
> Mere anarchy is loosed upon the world,
> The blood-dimmed tide is loosened, and everywhere
> The ceremony of innocence is drowned;
> The best lack all conviction, while the worst
> Are full of passionate intensity.
> ....
>
> The darkness drops again; but now I know
> That twenty centuries of stone sleep
> Were vexed to nightmare by a rocking cradle,
> And what rough beast, its hour come round at last,
> Slouches towards Bethlehem to be born?

Like García Márquez in *One Hundred Years of Solitude*, the Irish poet suggested that the modern world is in the process of creating "a baby with a pig's tail." He saw not Christ but "a rough beast" moving towards Bethlehem because the fragmentation of the world in which "the falcon cannot hear the falconer" had destroyed the poetic and spiritual visions that nurtured life and held it together. Modern destruction of dreams and emphasis on market values and materialism has worsened the human condition and has deepened human solitude. In *One Hundred Years of Solitude*, García Márquez portrays a difficult world from the conception of Macondo. However, exploitation is significantly increased with the arrival of international corporations such as the United Fruit company, and the take-over by corporate lawyers. Their impersonalized manipulation driven by profit created the situation in which "the best lack all conviction, while the worst are full of passionate intensity."

There is no doubt that the modernist struggle for personal liberation was perverted by Hollywood films and television. It was also deviated by postmodernism, which is marked by "play, chance, indeterminacy, immanence, and trace."[17] In its attempt to exclude illusion from its approach to the world,[18] postmodernism left the world without dreams or cohesive forces that keep society together. At the same time it created a new myth that individuals are in control of their lives. In its attempt to deconstruct the past, feminism, for example, has shown that marriage is not a place where girls "live happily ever after" but a social institution where women are exploited. To know that what binds the "I" and "the other" is a set of human constructs, that notions such as love, friendship, and family are not God-given but are created over time for social purposes, is a positive knowledge and a crucial step in liberation. However, postmodernism does not take into consideration that it takes time and serious thinking to create a new and truly profound vision of life. Marriage, as an institution, needed to be reformed. Family has also been redefined. Yet, it is not clear that the "new individual" is happier or more protected.

The twentieth-century deconstruction of illusions was correct, but illusions and dreams have a place in society; they are cohesive forces that keep society together. When dreams are removed, societies are fragmented and left without a direction. Ordinary people are thus placed in isolation and therefore further disempowered. Where would Martin Luther King and his followers be without a dream, and where is the world going with the corporate agenda that stands in a place of a positive, all-encompassing dream? For example, in their struggle against communism, Eastern European *intelligentsia* rightfully deconstructed the socialist myth, but they were also duped by the new myth of individual freedom. They did not realize that they were bought by various anti-communist, capitalist foundations to dream about the West rather than to conceptualize a better world and a better collective future that would be born out of their own circumstances. As they joined forces with Radio Free Europe, with the Soros Foundation, and as they created their own media supported by the West, the intellectuals in Eastern Europe brought down their governments, but they did not understand that destruction was not automatically to be followed by a just reconstruction. The destruction of Eastern Germany did not mean that there would be one large Western Germany. Yet, people were duped into believing in this postmodernist, American-made illusion. William Gass, who is generally credited with coining the term "postmodernism," argues that "the novelist no longer pretends that his business is to render the world; he knows, more often now, that his business is to make one, and to make one from the medium of which he is a master."[19] In this sense, Bill Gates is a postmodern man because he has made a new world out of his technological medium. But how many people have a chance to become Bill Gates? Even less fortunate individuals own a computer and a cellular telephone today, but there is little they can do with modern technology.

The secularized consumer society indeed needs a spiritual revival. But the new "religious conscience" will have to place more emphasis on "spiritual awareness" than on "religious mind-setting." If the Church were to become again an institution that organizes and leads society, it would have to re-connect with the innate aspects of life. Since the French Revolution and the rise of Protestantism, societies have repeatedly rebelled against priests and the union between money, army and popes. Modernism tried to liberate the individual from "religious conscience" because it oppresses and deforms individuals. Spanish modernist writer and theologian/philosopher Miguel de Unamuno wrote "that there is nothing more stagnant than the philosophy of the philosophers and the theology of the theologians."[20] To this, one might add the culture of bureaucrats and cultural theorists. Life and progress come from "the barbarians," Unamuno says, because only they and their artists are brave or foolish enough to be possessed by the kind of resilient, creative cosmic energy on which life itself feeds.

When trying to diagnose what is wrong with the New World Order of the bureaucrats who set the agenda and emphasize economic gains or losses, it is useful to glance briefly at another moment in history in which a powerful worldview married economic prosperity with spiritual enrichment: the European Renaissance. Emerging in Florence and other economically vibrant Mediterranean cities, the Renaissance was a profound humanistic/artistic/religious rebirth in which it was difficult to separate the arts, sciences, and business. Had Leonardo da Vinci's scientific thinking and new understanding of the world not been lent material support, his genius would not have culminated in the discoveries of Galileo and Newton in the seventeenth century. In this case, as in the case of the Medici family's economic support of Michelangelo, one has to recognize that power and money play an indispensable role in artistic and spiritual development. However, power and money are not the *source* of creativity and growth. Even the political prescriptions of Machiavelli, which are often interpreted as turning entirely on power and money, do not emphasize mere skill and wealth. Human values take centre stage. Machiavelli borrows the classical idea that Fortuna is a goddess who could be attracted by the *virtu*, i.e., the qualities that enable a man to withstand the blows of Fortuna. She likes to reward courage, but first she must test a man to see if he possesses it. Hence, shrewd courage is the key to success in *The Prince*. The Prince does not oppress and exploit the weak, as a superficial reading might suggest. He builds their intelligence and courage to respond to the harsh blows that Fortune has already dealt them.

Courageous military ventures and ingenious taxation schemes for the aristocracy were key to the success of Machiavelli's model, Ferdinand of Aragón. The success of Ferdinand and Isabella was achieved by brute force and exploitation. This alone should prevent us from glorifying the past. Still, in order to build the first strong modern state in Europe, and attract the most advanced Italian Renaissance humanists and artists, the Catholic kings established the infamous Inquisition to combat the aristocracy and false converts, censor intellectual opposition, and thus solidify monarchal power. And while "men of God" successfully and brutally led various European inquisitions, the Spanish Inquisition being only the most notorious, it is difficult to glorify spiritual creativity and goodness of this period. The merging of power, money, and culture in the fifteenth and sixteenth centuries was not at all innocent. However, leading Renaissance painters and other intellectuals were not merely servants of the establishment; they dreamed and suffered for the new epoch. Despite the looming danger of the Inquisition, Miguel de Cervantes made a profound impact on Spanish society with *Don Quixote*, a novel he wrote in prison. Through his humorous hero, beaten and trampled in the name of his humanistic ideals, Cervantes promoted higher ideals such as love, justice, and courage without naively declaring that "all you need is love." To combat the economically powerful and politically dangerous establishment, Cervantes, as St John of the Cross, the Spanish mystical poet had done before him, found strength and spirituality not in the official culture but in a human experience of the larger universe. Life develops in the link between the human body and the mystery of the cosmos, and it is expressed through human creativity and imagination. Unamuno comments that "[w]hat was the mysticism of St John of the Cross but a knight errantry of the divine sense? And the philosophy of Don Quixote cannot, strictly speaking, be called idealism: he did not fight for ideas. It was of a spiritual order: he fought for the spirit."[21] The spirit of Cervantes, St John of the Cross, Michelangelo, and even Machiavelli did not come from their religious consciousness but from their erudition, their human experiences, and, most importantly, their connection with the rest of the universe.

We know from personal experience and from the achievements of the eighteenth century that reason plays a positive role in life. We also know that technology is constructive if it is used for a good purpose. Yet, American academics and intelligence are wrong to assume that societies and cultures develop according to theoretically devised agendas. They are even more in error if they think that complex societies can be changed with a flick of the wrist. The Commission on the Year 2000 also failed to see that intelligence that lacks positive emotions and good will is dangerous. There is no doubt that the New World Order lacks the spiritual dimension of the Renaissance, and that it lacks the good will and the intellectual depth of the eighteenth-century Age of Reason. Perhaps it is not too late for humanity to save itself. If intellectuals awaken in time, they could play a constructive role in the New World Order. Modernism in its conception was a positive movement, but the struggle for modernist liberation was either misunderstood or purposely exploited. Given that oppressive moralizing rules of the bourgeois world have been broken, intellectuals could now focus on the constructive aspect of liberation. It would be difficult to rebel directly against the New World Order, but a parallel culture could make an impact. The nonchalant play of postmodernism is exhausting its creativity on its own. More importantly, the world is realizing that in the New World Order there is no true multiculturalism. Some writers from marginalized countries are entering the main canon, but a significant dialogue has not yet been created. We hear of Third World writers predominantly when they are translated into English, and we know about them through the powerful publishing business driven by book agents and reviews in particular journals in New York. Yet, the Third World may be playing a role that will prove to be more important than the artistic developments advertised in New York: the people and artists of the less fortunate parts of the world are still holding on to the life spirit and humanistic emotions that the New World Order lacks.

NOTES

1 88th Congress, House Report No. 1352, 27 April 1964, 7.

2 Herbert I. Schiller, *Mass Communications and American Empire*, New York: Augustus M. Kelley, 1970, 9.

3 http://www.emperors-clothes.com/articles/doncheva/donch3.htm

4 Daniel Bell, "The Year 2000 – The Trajectory of an Idea," in *Toward the Year 2000: Work in Progress*, Boston: Houghton Mifflin, 1968, 9.

5 Bell, "The Year 2000," 20.

6 The uprooted Eastern European elite of fifty years ago, people such as the American Secretary of State Madeleine Albright, have not only been regaining positions of power in the U.S., but they have been reacting passionately and strategically towards the dismantling of communism in Europe. Similarly, Cuban expatriats in Miami who are a significant political voice in the Land of Freedom rightfully and understandably remember that their personal and financial loss during the rise of communism was substantival. It definitely must not be undermined. But, as was obvious in the case of little Elian González, those who were victims of communism not only struggle in the U.S. to regain their wealth and initial superior position in society but they act with a strong dose of revenge and willingness to demonize the other side, as if communism were the only severe international force. And here lies the danger for history to repeat itself. If at the moment of triumph over communism no one takes into consideration that educated and intellectually astute communists came to power not only because they had a wicked plot but because the rich and the powerful did not think of the sorrows of the ordinary folks, the New World Order will merely reintroduce an era of disproportionate inequality. The situation created both by the widening gap between those who have and those who have not and by acts of revenge will, undoubtedly, set in motion a new wave of hatred and violence.

7 Bell, "The Year 2000," 5.

8 Thomas Mann, *Germany and the Germans,* Washington: Library of Congress, 1945.

9 Darío was appointed secretary of Nicaragua's delegation to the third Pan-American conference held in Rio de Janeiro in 1906, where this poem was written.

10 Rubén Darío, *Poesías completas*, Madrid: Aguilar, 1967, 747.

11 In this case the Spaniards abused Moctezuma's hospitality. Similar abuses of hospitality were practiced in the colonization of Africa.

12 Victor Frankl, *Man's Search for Meaning* Boston: Beacon Press, 1963.

13 Antonio Benítez-Rojo, *The Repeating Island*, Durham: Duke University Press, 1992, 10.

14 Virgina Woolf, "Modern Fiction," in David Lodge, ed., *Twentieth-Century Literary Criticism,* London: Longman, 1972, 87.

15 Ihab Hassan, "Postface," in *The Dismemberment of Orpheus: Toward a Postmodern Literature,* Madison: University of Wisconsin Press, 1982.

16 Jurgen Habermas, *The New Conservatism: Cultural Criticism and the Historian's Debate,* Cambridge: MIT Press, 1989, 29.

17 Hassan, "Postface."

18 Philip Stevick, "Scheherazade Runs out of Plots, Goes on Talking; the King, Puzzled, Listens: An Essay on New Fiction," *TriQuarterly* 26 (Winter 1973), 332–62.

19 William H. Gass, *Fiction and the Figures of Life,* New York: Vintage, 1971, 24.

20 Miguel de Unamuno, "Don Quijote and the Contemporary Tragedy," in *The Selected Works of Unamuno,* Princeton: Princeton University Press, 1972, 328.

21 Ibid., 334.

Humanitarian Intervention and the Sovereignty of a State in the New World Order: Undermined Authority and Undefined Rules of Engagement

JAMES BISSETT

As Canadian ambassador to Yugoslavia from 1990 to1992, I was a witness to the tragic breakup of that country. There were a number of reasons why Yugoslavia was torn apart, but one of the primary causes of the tragedy was the failure of Western diplomacy. This is not to say that the Yugoslavs themselves were blameless – not at all. Nevertheless, Western intervention exacerbated the problem and precipitated much of the ensuing bloodshed. It is said that history never repeats itself, but Western interference in the Balkans has repeatedly proven disastrous. Lacking adequate knowledge of the region and ignoring the history and aspirations of the people living there, Western governments have historically tried to resolve Balkan problems by pursuing their own narrow foreign policy objectives, which have little or no relevance to the issues on the ground. This was true in the past and remains true today.

The debate about whether concern for human rights should override sovereignty is topical and ongoing. We will be hearing much about this issue in the months and years ahead because globalization and the New World Order attempt to impose Western norms globally, threatening the national sovereignty and cultural uniqueness of certain countries. The horror of mass killings in Rwanda has given impetus to those who believe the civilized world cannot simply stand by when genocide is taking place. While there is room for intervention in the internal affairs of a sovereign state, no intervention can be undertaken lightly and armed intervention must be undertaken with extreme care. The rules of intervention must clearly be defined and obeyed. Some argue that the rules must change and be adapted to changing conditions, but who has the authority to change them and what the new rules will be must be determined. Until Kosovo the ground rules for such intervention called for UN Security Council authority before intervention could be taken. NATO, however, took upon itself the powers of the Security Council.[1] Until the rules change, we must continue to obey those that still have legitimacy. In the new, anarchic scenario, it is not only dubious what role the UN can have, but also whether Article 1 of the NATO treaty still stands: does NATO still undertake to settle any international disputes in which it may become involved by *peaceful means*? Do the NATO countries still undertake to refrain in their international relations from the threat or use of force in any manner inconsistent with the purposes of the United Nations?

If the rules are being changed and precedents set for the future, it is important to guard against the danger that the human rights argument is used to justify intervention for other quite cynical motives. We recall that Hitler's justification for invading Czechoslovakia was that the Czechs were violating the human rights of the Sudeten Germans. The long and frequently sad history of Western intervention in the Balkans should also serve as a warning about the dangers of taking sides in internal disputes. The NATO military misadventure in Kosovo that has destabilized the Balkans and shaken the framework of international security is another more recent example that calls into question the validity of so-called humanitarian intervention.

NATO's military intervention in Yugoslavia in March 1999 was said to be justified on the grounds that the human rights of ethnic Albanians were being violated by the Yugoslav military authorities. There is no doubt that the human rights violations did take place. We know that approximately 2,000 Albanians and Serbians were killed prior to the NATO bombing. As deplorable as this may be, it is not an alarming figure given that a civil war had been raging in Kosovo for a number of yearsf.

We were told, however, that much bigger atrocities were being carried out in Kosovo. Some NATO leaders charged that genocide was taking place in that Serbian province. U.S. Secretary of Defence William Cohen suggested that more than 100,000 Albanian Kosovars may have been murdered. We were also told that massive ethnic cleansing was under way and that the Serbian government had long- range plans to remove the entire Albanian population from Kosovo. We were confronted daily with atrocity stories in the media of massacres taking place, of young Albanian men being rounded up and taken away, of rape and pillage of a massive and systematic scale.

The alleged massacre of forty-five Albanian Kosovars in the village of Racak in January 1999 was described by U.S. Secretary of State Madeline Albright as the "galvanizing event" for NATO military action. The New York Times wrote in an article dated 18 April of that year that the Racak massacre was a "turning point" in NATO's road to war. The so-called Racak massacre had been challenged from the outset by French journalists who were on the ground when the alleged incident took place. More recently German investigative reporters for the Berlin *Zeitung* charged on 24 March 2000 that the autopsy reports, to which they gained access, showed no evidence of an execution scenario. It appeared the victims might have been killed in combat and later placed in a ditch to simulate an execution. There is a strong suspicion that U.S. General William Walker, in collaboration with the Kosovo Liberation Army (KLA), may have to played a part in staging this incident.

Later, as the NATO bombing campaign was stepped up and thousands of Albanians were being driven out of Kosovo by Serbian security forces, it became evident that the bombing had not stopped ethnic cleansing but on the contrary had intensified it, NATO spokespeople began to talk about Serbia's "Operation Horseshoe": a secret, long-range plan of ethnic cleansing by Serbian forces to rid Kosovo of its Albanian population. We now know as a result of the disclosure of German General Heinz Loquai that "Operation Horseshoe" was a complete falsehood engineered by the German defence minister to swing public opinion in favour of the bombing. There is absolutely no evidence that the Serbs were planning to drive out the Albanian population from Kosovo prior to the NATO bombing campaign. The *Sunday Times* of London exposed this scandal on 2 April 2000. It is interesting that despite this being a major story in Germany and a matter of debate in the German parliament there has been no coverage of the story in the Canadian media.

All of this indicates that the New World Order not only challenges the very concept of national sovereignty but it undermines democracy and sadly manipulates the notion of the freedom of the press. It may well be that Canada and some of the other smaller NATO members were misled and misinformed at the beginning of the war. However, the Canadian ministers of foreign affairs and national defence who stoutly defended the NATO action have not yet made apology for sending the Canadian armed forces to war against a sovereign state and former ally in two world wars. Nor have they as yet expressed any misgivings that, for the first time since the founding of the United Nations, Canadian armed forces were engaged in a military action not authorized by that body and in direct violation of its Charter. As it happened, one day in March 1999 Canadians woke up and found that they were at war, and that Canadian pilots were bombing Serbia. Yet there was no declaration of war. Neither the Canadian parliament nor the Canadian people were consulted. By taking away the right to declare war, NATO abrogated the ultimate expression of a nation's sovereignty. If it is essential that countries give up some of their sovereignty as the price they pay for membership in global institutions such as NATO, it is surely mandatory, then, that such institutions follow their own rules, respect the rule of law, and operate within the generally accepted framework of the United Nations charter. This NATO did not do. To the credit of Greece, despite its NATO membership, its government refused to take part in any military action against Serbia. The people of Greece from the outset of the bombing made abundantly clear their adamant opposition to the war. This is not the first time in history that Greece has adopted a courageous and heroic stand in the interest of truth.

The ease with which the mainstream media in the West accepted and indeed supported without serious question the NATO military action needs to be examined seriously. None of the major Canadian newspapers or television networks, to my knowledge, expressed concern about the legality of the bombing and – more alarmingly – they seemed almost eager to accept and condone the massive bombing, even when civilian targets in Yugoslavia were intentionally hit. All the atrocity stories related by Albanian Kosovars were accepted at face value and few questioned the canned news stories manufactured by the NATO public relations machine. The reason for this extraordinary media submissiveness can be partially explained by the secretive nature of the NATO decision-making process. Nevertheless, I suspect the paramount reason explaining the reluctance of the media to question NATO aggression was because of a natural hesitancy to challenge a war that allegedly was being fought for humanitarian reasons. Herein lies the danger of the new human rights dogma. In an age of political correctness few are prepared to challenge the appropriateness of bombing people – especially if the bombing is for humanitarian purposes. The Progressive Conservative defence critic in the Canadian House of Commons on the opening day of the attack against Yugoslavia dared to question the validity of the bombing, only to have his leader, Joe Clark, repudiate him the following day. Later the unfortunate man was removed from his position.

Perhaps the most perplexing question about the NATO action against Yugoslavia is why? Why the deep concern about the natural attempts by Serbia to suppress an armed rebellion that was rapidly developing into a full-scale civil war? There were many more appropriate targets if the concern was truly about human rights violations. It is estimated that over three million Kurds have been dispossessed and over 30,000 killed by Turkish military forces. This human rights issue makes Kosovo appear rather inconsequential in comparison. What about East Timor, where for almost twenty-five years the human rights of the East

Timorese were violated by President Suharto's military forces using British aircraft and weapons? It is estimated that Indonesian forces killed 200,000 East Timorese before a peaceful settlement was finally negotiated. Why so little concern about the plight of the Iraqi children suffering as a result of the American- and British-led sanctions against that country? Two successive United Nations assistants under secretaries general have resigned in protest against the embargo. One of these, Hans von Sponeck, in addressing a public meeting in London stated that half a million children had died as a direct result of the sanctions and one out of every five children in Iraq go hungry, yet nobody seemed to care. We have witnessed the reaction of our Western democratic leaders to the frightful humanitarian tragedy in Sierra Leone, where thousands have been killed and many more maimed by the drug-crazed youths of the rebel army: there has been no rush to prevent human rights abuses there. Indeed, U.S. Secretary of State Madeline Albright led a Western imposed peace settlement in that ravaged country that called for the sharing of power with the rebel leader, Foday Sankoh, the man chiefly responsible for the carnage. This is the same Madeline Albright who when asked if she thought the sanctions against Iraq were worth the lives of so many Iraqi children replied in the affirmative. Obviously Western democratic leaders are selective about their human rights concerns. There was no suggestion of intervention in Chechnya – another example of human rights violations on a scale that made Kosovo look like a picnic. Lloyd Axworthy, then Canada's foreign minister answered this charge of inconsistency in a speech at the New York University School of Law by saying, "for those who criticize humanitarian intervention on the grounds that its inconsistently employed, I would ask: if the international community cannot intervene everywhere, does that mean we must not intervene anywhere?" This is too convenient and facile an answer.

If there is to be any sense at all in the framework of international security there must be some degree of consistency and criteria to determine when intervention in a sovereign state is warranted. What exactly are the new ground rules for humanitarian intervention? No responsible body or institution has yet defined them. We do, however, know what the ground rules were before the bombing in Kosovo. These were the rules established by the founders of the United Nations, and they spell out quite clearly that the UN Security Council must give its approval before armed intervention can be taken against a sovereign state. If Security Council authority is blocked by the veto power of one of the great powers then it is still possible to go to the General Assembly, where a two-thirds vote is sufficient to permit intervention. The point is that NATO didn't approach the Security Council before bombing Yugoslavia. It is ironic that, having totally ignored the

United Nations Charter, NATO leaders place so much reverence on some of the subsidiary organs of the UN. The International Criminal Tribunals for the former Yugoslavia and Rwanda receive lavish praise from NATO leaders. So far every attempt by international lawyers to get the tribunal in the Hague to consider charges against NATO leaders has met with no success.

It is because of my experience in Yugoslavia that I am cautious about the so-called new human security agenda. Those who champion human rights frequently do so for the wrong reasons; very often there is a hidden agenda that has little to do with human rights. Furthermore, more often than not, the intervention does more harm than good. The NATO intervention, ostensibly for humanitarian reasons, ended up creating a human rights catastrophe. NATO's action convinced China and Russia that the West cannot be trusted. Even more serious, the high moral ground that had been a proud feature of the Western democracies has been abandoned. We have shown ourselves to be no better than our former communist adversaries – quite prepared to use violence and force to gain our ends, and prepared as well to wrap these ends in the cloak of high purpose and humanitarian principle.

Yugoslavia, as with other Balkan nations, has never been given long enough periods of peace or immunity from outside interference in which to work out its own destiny.[2] The country has never had time to foster and nourish democratic institutions and traditions. Yugoslavia's ethnic differences have been frequently exploited by outside powers and used by them to divide the nation and tear it apart with ethnic hatred and violence. It is wrong to look upon the peoples of the Balkans as bloodthirsty primitives who from time to time set about slaughtering each other. Throughout most of history these ethnic groups – Serbs, Croats, Macedonians, Albanians, Slovenes, Bosnian Muslims – have lived at peace with one another. It is when they become pawns in the game of big power politics that their ethnic differences are exploited and violence ensues. Twice in this century Yugoslavia has been broken apart, and in both instances the breakup occurred either as a direct result of outside intervention or was precipitated by the actions of other states. In both instances the dissolution of the state was accompanied by ethnic cleansing and mutual massacre.

THE SECOND WORLD WAR

To people unfamiliar with Balkan history, the violence and bloodshed that took place in the former Yugoslavia in the 1990s is incomprehensible. How is it possible that such atrocities could occur in Europe on the eve of the new millennium? The answer to this is to be found in the events that took place in Yugoslavia during the Second World War.

Following the invasion of Yugoslavia, the country was dismembered and divided among the Axis powers, Germany, Italy, Hungary, and Bulgaria. Croatia was granted independence as an Axis puppet state and ruled by Ante Pavelic, the Fascist Ustashi leader. Hitler awarded Croatia with all of Bosnia-Hercegovina, with its large Serbian and Jewish population. Pavelic and his Ustashi proceeded with a campaign of genocide directed against the Serbian and Jewish populations of Croatia and Bosnia-Hercegovina in which frightful massacres took place. Ustashi gangs savagely slaughtered tens of thousands of Serbs in Croatia, often forcing them into their Orthodox Churches and burning them alive. Other Serbs were given the choice of conversion to Roman Catholicism or death. Yet others were driven out of Croatia into Bosnia or Serbia. Thousands of Jews, Serbs, and Gypsies were exterminated in Croatian camps. At the most infamous of these, Jasenovac, close to 100,000 victims were killed, not by gas but by bullet, club, or knife. In Bosnia, similar massacres of Serbs took place. The Muslims of Bosnia often assisted the Ustashi killers. Later in the war, the Germans recruited a Muslim ss Division, which gained notoriety for its atrocities against the Serbian civilian population.

After the invasion of Yugoslavia the Italians occupied Kosovo, and when Italy dropped out of the war in 1943 the Germans entered Kosovo and promised the province independence. They raised an ss Division from among the Albanian population: the infamous Skender-berg Division, which set about methodically slaughtering Serbs in Kosovo. As the war progressed Serb guerilla bands retaliated against the perpetrators of these crimes with counter-massacres of their own. The horrors committed in Yugoslavia during the war, where over one million people perished, were not forgotten. In Croatia, Bosnia, or Kosovo, there were few Serbs who had not lost friends or relatives during the Second World War. These nightmarish memories were still very much alive in the 1990s and in large part account for the atmosphere of fear, suspicion, and hostility that rapidly developed in Yugoslavia on the eve of its second dismemberment. Tito's refusal to allow any discussion of these horrendous wartime events added to the sense that the ghosts of the victims remained at large.

THE TITO YEARS AND THE END
OF THE COLD WAR

Tito's communist regime brought unity, stability, and relative prosperity to Yugoslavia. His break with Stalin and the advent of the Cold War placed Yugoslavia in a favoured position between two great powers. Yugoslavia became eligible for loans from the International

Monetary Fund (IMF) and eligible for membership in the General Agreement on Tariffs and Trade (GATT) and entry into association agreements with the European Community (EC) and the European Free Trade Association (EFTA). As one of the founders of the non-aligned movement, Tito's Yugoslavia enjoyed a high level of international prestige. Its citizens were allowed freedom of travel, and in contrast to most of the other countries in the Eastern bloc, Yugoslavs, whether Serb, Croat, Macedonian, or Slovene, were proud of their country's status and achievements. However, things began to go wrong for Yugoslavia in the early 1980s. Tito's death in 1980 coincided with the beginning of a serious economic depression. Throughout the 1970s, Yugoslavia, like many other countries, had borrowed heavily from the IMF and commercial banks. The era of massive global lending came to an abrupt end in 1979. Oil prices rose sharply and interest rates jumped to double digits. Remittances from Yugoslavia's guest workers abroad, which had financed half of the Yugoslav deficit since the 1960s, fell dramatically as thousands of workers were forced to return home. The foreign debt crisis forced the government to introduce harsh austerity measures. Unemployment increased, inflation rose at the rate of 50 per cent per year, and soon the savings of the middle class were wiped out. Food and petrol shortages occurred, and political unrest soon followed. The two most affluent republics, Slovenia and Croatia, began to question the federal government's economic policy. They complained that their revenues were being used to support economically backward Macedonia and the Serbian province of Kosovo. These complaints expressed themselves as claims for more democracy and political autonomy from the central Government.

The vacuum created by the collapse of communist ideology throughout Eastern Europe began to be filled by nationalist and ethnic aspirations. The internal problems experienced by Yugoslavia were compounded by the changes taking place in the international arena. As the Cold War came to an end, so did Yugoslavia's privileged position vis-à-vis the Western powers, especially the United States. In 1989, the U.S. removed Yugoslavia from its list of countries eligible for Western credits. Yugoslavia was no longer important as a buffer between the Soviet Union and Western Europe. It lost its special standing and became just another country of the Balkans.

SEPARATIST MOVEMENTS

By 1990 it was evident the Yugoslav Federal Republic was experiencing serious strain. Both Slovenia and Croatia were moving rapidly towards separation. In Serbia, Slobodan Milosevic had cracked down hard on the Albanian majority in Kosovo and had removed autonomous status from that province and the northern province of Vojvodina. Albanian unrest had been suppressed with violence. Human rights violations increased and the Albanians in Kosovo withdrew from the political and civil life of that province. There was every indication of serious trouble ahead. The first democratic elections in the republics chose leaders who appealed to ethnic passions. Throughout the nation an atmosphere of unrest and fear was evident. Paramilitary groups were forming, and arms were being smuggled into the separatist republics. Civil authority was beginning to break down. The first sign of trouble occurred in Croatia. A change in the Croatian constitution that relegated the Serbian population living there to minority status created fear and distrust among those who recalled the devastating impact of Croatian nationalism during the Second World War. The election of the right-wing nationalist party of Franjo Tudjman, with its anti-communist and anti-Serb campaign, added to their concerns, (Serbs made up a little more than 12 per cent of the Croatian population in 1991). These Serbs began to arm themselves and to demand self-determination. In March 1991 the first armed clashes between Croatian police and Serbian paramilitary groups occurred.

The warning signals that Yugoslavia was beginning to break apart did not at first cause serious alarm among the Western powers. The United States was preoccupied by the Gulf War and more concerned about events in the Soviet Union. Europeans were concerned about the Maastricht Treaty and the fall of the Berlin Wall. It was only when the first armed clashes occurred and it became apparent that Slovenia and Croatia seemed determined to secede from the federation that the West turned its attention on Yugoslavia. That attention proved to be unhelpful and too late. Initially the West's official position was that Yugoslavia must remain united. Both the U.S. and the European Union warned the individual republics that separation from Yugoslavia was unacceptable and any republic that broke away would not be recognized or granted entry into the European Union.

SLOVENIAN INDEPENDENCE

When it appeared possible in June 1991 that Slovenia might in fact declare independence, the U.S. Secretary of State, James Baker, flew to Belgrade and in a one-day marathon session met with the leaders of the six republics. He warned them again that Yugoslavia must stay together and remain united. The last person he met with that day was Ante Markovic, the federal prime minister. Baker told the prime minister, a Croatian, that if the Slovenes took overt action to secede from Yugoslavia, the United States would not object if the federal army was called in to preserve the unity of Yugoslavia. Within a matter of days the Slovenes seized by force the federal customs posts along the Italian and Austrian borders, and Markovic ordered the federal army into Slovenia. Most observers did not expect the Slovenes to resist against the powerful Yugoslav army (JNA), but contrary to all expectations the Slovenes did resist. Armed with German-supplied hand-held antitank missiles the Slovenes destroyed a number of tanks, and in order to avoid further bloodshed, Markovic ordered the army to withdraw. Thirty-seven JNA soldiers were killed in the brief encounter and twelve Slovene Territorial Defense members lost their lives. The media coverage of the "Slovene war" played a major role in shaping subsequent public opinion in the west. The federal forces were from the outset described as the "Serb-dominated" Yugoslav army, and the Western media soon depicted the struggle as one of David and Goliath, with the JNA playing the role of the giant Goliath. Thus from the beginning of the Yugoslav conflict the Serbs were branded as the bad guys even though most of the JNA troops were conscripts from Kosovo or Macedonia.

The federal armed forces withdrew into Croatia, and soon after fighting broke out between JNA troops and Croatian paramilitary groups. The dismemberment of Yugoslavia had begun. The "Slovene War" marked a turning point in the attitude of Western governments towards the possible disintegration of Yugoslavia. Their policy that the nation must remain united changed, and Germany and Austria began to press for the recognition of Slovene and Croatian independence. It is now known that as early as 1990, Croatian and Slovene leaders held meetings with senior politicians from both of these countries urging support for independence. During this time the Vatican was openly lobbying for independence and had particular influence on German politicians in Bavaria.

PREMATURE RECOGNITION

Despite strong pressure from the U.S. and opposition from France and Britain, Germany's determination to grant recognition prevailed. Chancellor Helmut Kohl was able to obtain French and British approval by granting concessions relating to the EC monetary union and Britain was allowed to opt out of the treaty's social charter. Germany also conceded that all six of the Yugoslav republics were eligible for independence. It was also agreed that before independence was granted the republics would have to meet criteria established by the Badinter Commission, a group of European jurists set up by the EU to arbitrate disputes and establish criteria for recognition.

Without waiting for a decision from the Badinter Commission, Germany announced the recognition of Slovenia and Croatia on 23 December 1991. The premature recognition of Slovenia and Croatia guaranteed that the breakup of Yugoslavia would not be resolved by peaceful means. Western intervention had again exacerbated and complicated a serious Balkan problem, and again the German intervention had little to do with the actual problem faced on the ground in Yugoslavia. Kohl's ruling party was under severe pressure politically and he needed an initiative to restore the party's standing. The opposition Social Democratic Party had been advocating recognition and Kohl wished to seize the initiative and capture the issue for his own party. In addition, the foreign minister, Hans Dietrich Genscher, had been criticized previously for reluctant and belated support for the Gulf War. Recognition of Slovenia and Croatia would demonstrate that Germany was capable of taking foreign policy initiatives on its own. Recognition would also change the nature of the struggle in Yugoslavia from an internal dispute to one of a war of aggression against two independent states.

BOSNIA AND HERCEGOVINA

As fighting continued in Croatia, it became evident that the war could spread to Bosnia. The diplomatic challenge for the West was to contain the conflict and prevent bloodshed in Bosnia, which because of the events of the Second World War held the potential for dreadful violence. Thanks to the skilful efforts of the Portuguese foreign minister, Jose Cutileiro, acting under the auspices of the EU, an agreement was reached among the three ethnic leaders of Bosnia that seemed to offer an acceptable compromise aimed at preventing violence. The agreement called for an independent Bosnia divided into three constituent and geographically separate parts, each of which would be autonomous. While not a perfect solution, the agreement was preferable to civil war. In March 1992, each of the three leaders, Izetbegovic for the Muslims, Boban for the Croats, and Karadzic for the Serbs, signed the so-called Lisbon Agreement. Among diplomats in Belgrade there was general relief and for the first time a sense of hope for the future. However, within days of the Lisbon Agreement, the American ambassador, Warren Zimmerman, flew to Sarajevo and met with Izetbegovic. Finding that Izetbegovic was having second thoughts about the agreement he had signed in Lisbon, Zimmerman suggested that if he withdrew his signature, the U.S. would grant recognition to Bosnia as an independent state. Izetbegovic withdrew his signature and renounced the agreement. Within days the war had spread to Bosnia. Ironically, after 200,000 deaths and massive destruction throughout

Bosnia, the Muslims were afforded by the terms of the Dayton Accords less territory than they had been guaranteed by the Lisbon Agreement. There has been a good deal of speculation about why the U.S. chose to intervene in Bosnia and why it influenced Izetbegovic to renounce the Lisbon Agreement. One explanation is that the U.S. wished to demonstrate to the Muslim world that it could support Muslim causes. After the Gulf War, it is suggested, the U.S. was anxious to find a Muslim position with which it could ally itself. The official U.S position for its intervention was that recognition was the only way to prevent the war from spreading to Bosnia! Whatever the reason, it seems evident the U.S. intervention did more harm than good.

KOSOVO

Given the experience of Slovenia, Croatia, and Bosnia, it is little wonder that the Albanians in Kosovo realized the most effective way to gain independence was to take up arms and resort to violence. This had been the formula for success before and there was every reason to expect it would work again. Indeed, given the successful public relations campaign that had been waged against President Milosevic and the Serbs and the record of human rights violations in Kosovo, it was inevitable that Kosovo would be the next part of Yugoslavia to break away. As the KLA escalated its armed attacks on Serbian police stations and stepped up its assassinations of Serbian politicians and Serbian sympathizers among the Albanian population, it could count on Serbian security forces to retaliate with ruthless anti-insurgency tactics. The KLA could also count on the Western media to give full coverage to these heavy-handed measures. By October 1998, the fighting in Kosovo had escalated to the point where the United Nations felt obliged to intervene. A UN Security Council Resolution called for an end to the fighting, a withdrawal of the Yugoslav army to barracks, and the introduction of OSCE observers into Kosovo as monitors on the ground to ensure that both parties kept the peace. Initially the army and security forces complied with the UN Resolution, but the KLA did not stop its campaign of terror and again the army reacted with force. Villages suspected of harbouring KLA activists were burned and their inhabitants dispersed. Many innocent people lost their lives. Unable to stop the violence, the U.S. and EU decided to intervene. The instrument of their intervention was to be NATO.

THE NATO BOMBING

The story of NATO's military intervention in Kosovo is well known. It is a story of unmitigated disaster. None of its policy objectives were

achieved. The long-range consequences of its intervention seriously
damaged the global security structure that was established after the end
of the Second World War. Its intervention violated international law
and its own commitment to using only peaceful means of resolving
international disputes. NATO's bombing of Yugoslavia was done without the involvement of the United Nations. It failed utterly to do serious
damage to the Yugoslav military but tragically destroyed the civilian
infrastructure of Serbia and caused untold environmental damage to
the countries along the Danube River. In the name of humanitarian
objectives it caused a humanitarian disaster. NATO took sides in a civil
war and became the airforce of the KLA to wrest away from a sovereign
state an integral part of its territory.

While the bombing of Yugoslavia was taking place, President Havel
of the Czech Republic visited Canada and addressed both chambers of
the Canadian Parliament. He received a standing ovation when he
declared that the war being fought in Kosovo was the first war in history
not fought for territory but for human rights. Yet the war in Kosovo
took territory away from Serbia and transferred it to the Albanian
population. The war fought for human rights ended with the mass
expulsion of the non-Albanian population from Kosovo, and the UN
and NATO forces have proven unable to prevent murder, arson, and
pillage from occurring throughout the territory. Unfortunately, President Havel got it wrong.

NOTES

1 Some pundits have suggested that the theoretical basis of the new interventionist doctrine had its origins – ironically – in a Carnegie endowment
   for international peace report entitled "Changing our ways: America's
   role in the world." This report argued for the necessity of the U.S. to
   realign NATO and OSCE the Organization for Security and Cooperation
   in Europe, in order to better deal with new security problems in
   Europe. Military intervention for humanitarian objectives was to be
   encouraged. The Carnegie report was published in the summer of 1992
   and is thought to have strongly influenced President Clinton and the
   Democratic Party's foreign policy elite.
2 As far back as 1878, after the Russian armies supported by Serbia and
   Montenegro had defeated the Ottoman Turks, the Western powers
   fearing that Russian Pan-Slav dominance would upset the balance of
   power in the region decided to intervene. Their objective was to revise
   the treaty of San Stefano, which had ended the Russian-Turkish war
   and in effect brought to an end Ottoman power in the Balkans. The

instrument of Western intervention was the Congress of Berlin, which was convened in June 1878. Otto von Bismark, the German chancellor, was chairman. The British prime minister, Disraeli, along with his foreign secretary, Lord Salisbury, attended. The Congress achieved its objective, the San Stefano treaty was undone, and Russian influence in the Balkans was neutralized. One means of doing this was the decision that Bosnia-Hercegovina, formerly a province of the Turkish empire, was to be occupied and administered by Austria-Hungary. The Austrian foreign minister, Count Andrassy, predicted an easy occupation – "a company of soldiers and a brass band" would be all that was necessary. In fact, it took three months of heavy fighting and over 200,000 troops to occupy the major towns, and resistance was never overcome in the mountains and countryside. The Austrian-Hungarian incursion into Bosnia-Hercegovina ended with the assassination of Archduke Franz Ferdinand in Sarajevo in 1914, and the cataclysm of the Great War of 1914–18 followed. Less than twenty-five years later, Germany's unprovoked invasion of Yugoslavia in April 1941 heralded another Western intervention in that troubled nation. The German Wehrmacht was never able to conquer Yugoslavia but the Second World War inflicted a terrible and indelible legacy on the country that was later paid for in the bloodshed and violence of the 1990s.

The Legal Institutions of the New World Order: "Might Makes Right" and the International Criminal Tribunal for the Former Yugoslavia

MICHAEL MANDEL

The fundamental document of the old world order is the Charter of the United Nations. Its central tenets are the equality of states and the prohibition of the use of force in international relations. Violence is only permissible when authorized by the Security Council, an elected body that also includes as permanent members – each with a veto – the victorious Allies of World War II including China (a minor U.S. partner in the war against Japan). The only permissible unilateral use of military force is the strictly limited right of self-defence, temporarily available until the Security Council can deal with the situation.

The triumph of global capitalism, the fall of the Soviet Union, and the emergence of the United States as the world's only superpower – the fundamental building blocks of the New World Order – have caused a radical overturning of the legal order entrenched by the UN Charter. The 1999 war over Kosovo, fought under the legally preposterous claim of unilateral "humanitarian intervention," was soon followed by the mortal blow to the Charter of the 2001 war against Afghanistan, under the equally preposterous claim of self-defence.[1] All this has been accomplished without changing one comma of the Charter. There has been one important legal innovation: the appearance of various international criminal tribunals to try war crimes and crimes against humanity. To date two have been established by the Security Council, for Yugoslavia and for Rwanda. The flagship tribunal was the one for Yugoslavia and it was this one that the United States was keenest to establish.

The establishment of the Yugoslavia tribunal was part and parcel of the very violation planned and executed by the U.S. in Yugoslavia, so it seems natural to try and understand this tribunal. This is especially so since this institution has been celebrated as proof that the New World Order brings a golden age of human rights. In the following pages I outline my own experience with the tribunal and I show how this has led me to believe that it operates to legitimate wars, loss of national sovereignty, and the human suffering that accompanies wars.

It was impossible for anyone to miss the central role played by the International Criminal Tribunal for the Former Yugoslavia ("ICTY"), and especially the Office of the Prosecutor, in NATO's 1999 bombing attack on Yugoslavia. At several key moments the tribunal was front and centre in the mass media, lending crucial credibility to the claims of NATO that it was essentially on a humanitarian mission to defend the helpless Muslim population in Kosovo (and earlier in Bosnia) from Serb criminals. In January 1999, within two days of highly contested American accounts of a massacre at Racak, then Chief Prosecutor Louise Arbour made a dramatic televised appearance at the border of Kosovo, demanding entry to carry out investigations into the event. Racak, of course, was the occasion for a major escalation in NATO rhetoric and it led directly to the talks at Rambouillet where the NATO countries presented Yugoslavia with their ultimatum.

Then, only days after the bombing had commenced, Arbour announced an indictment of the noted Serb paramilitary leader "Arkan" for alleged war crimes in Bosnia, an indictment she had kept secret since 1997. The impression of the centrality of the ICTY was strengthened when Arbour made successive television appearances with British Foreign Secretary Robin Cook and American Secretary of State Madeleine Albright. Cook made a great show of handing over war crimes dossiers that NATO had prepared against Yugoslav authorities and Albright swore undying allegiance to the ICTY and promised it more money. Perhaps the major turning point occurred when, as civilian casualties of NATO's bombing were sickening the world, Arbour announced the indictment of Yugoslav President Slobodan Milosevic for various crimes, including murder, which had occurred during the bombing.

Finally, at war's end, when tribunal investigators arrived with NATO leaders in Kosovo to unearth sites of alleged Serb atrocities against civilians, the point of the whole war (from NATO's perspective) was driven home. And when people started to question the paucity of victims compared to NATO claims, Carla Del Ponte, Arbour's replacement, made a well-publicized and improvised visit to the Security Council – I know it was improvised because she had to cancel a long-scheduled meeting with me to attend – to reassure the world that the victims could yet well amount to what NATO had alleged. So, without questioning (for the moment) the sincerity of the tribunal, we cannot deny its centrality as a legitimation of NATO's war on Yugoslavia.

ILLEGALITY OF THE WAR

The irony of this is that one of the pivotal facts about NATO's war against Yugoslavia is that it was flatly *illegal*, both in the fact that it was ever undertaken and in the way it was carried out. It was a gross and deliberate violation of international law and the Charter of the United Nations. The Charter authorizes the use of force in only two situations: self-defence or when authorized by the Security Council.

Sections 3 and 4 of Article 2, as well as Article 33 of the Charter, explicitly call for the pursuit of peaceful means and the avoidance of force as the paramount policies in matters of conflict. In the case that an amicable agreement cannot be established, Article 37, Part 1 decrees that the matter be referred to the Security Council, who, as stated in Part 2 of this same Article, shall evaluate the threat to international peace and security and decide upon how to proceed further in order to ensure peace on an international level, as articulated in Article 39. As Article 41 proceeds: "The Security Council may decide what measures not involving the use of armed force are to be employed to give effect to its decisions, and it may call upon the Members of the United Nations to apply such measures. These may include complete or partial interruption of economic relations and of rail, sea, air, postal, telegraphic, radio and other means of communication, and the severance of diplomatic relations." Only if such procedures are not successful may the Security Council, under Article 42, "take such action by air, sea or land forces as may be necessary to maintain or restore international peace and security. Such action may include demonstrations, blockade, and other operations by air, sea or land forces of Members of the United Nations."

Furthermore, Article 51 addresses the issue of self-defence, a right that is not infringed upon by the Charter "until the Security Council has taken measures necessary to maintain international peace and security." However, it also emphasizes that not only must all self-defence measures be reported to the Security Council but that the Security Council retains the authority and obligation to conserve peace on an international level, an obligation that is not influenced by the right for individual or collective self-defence.

The jurisprudence of the International Court of Justice is also very clear. For instance, it stated in its ruling against the United States' intervention in Nicaragua:

While the United States might form its own appraisal of the situation as to respect for human rights in Nicaragua, the use of force could not be the appropriate method to monitor or ensure such respect. With regard to the steps actually taken, the protection of human rights, a strictly humanitarian objective, cannot be compatible with the mining of ports, the destruction of oil installations, or again with the training, arming and equipping of the contras.[2]

It should be noted that the preliminary decision of the World Court last year in Yugoslavia's case against ten NATO countries, including Canada, does not in the slightest contradict this statement. The World Court's rejection of Yugoslavia's claim was based solely on a lack of jurisdiction due to various conditions set by the parties on the right of the World Court to judge their disputes. The United States, for example, simply and rather revealingly, has refused to recognize the general jurisdiction of the Court since it lost the Nicaragua case. But while the Court agreed that it had no jurisdiction over the case, it made some important observations that are worth quoting:

16. Whereas the Court is profoundly concerned with the use of force in Yugoslavia; whereas under the present circumstances such use raises very serious issues of international law;
17. Whereas the Court is mindful of the purposes and principles of the United Nations Charter and of its own responsibilities in the maintenance of peace and security under the Charter and the Statue of the court;
18. Whereas the Court deems it necessary to emphasize that all parties appearing before it must act in conformity with their obligations under the United Nations Charter and other rules of international law, including humanitarian law.[3]

To sum up, in the case of NATO's war on Yugoslavia, neither Security Council authorization nor self-defence was even claimed by NATO as justification for the use of force. As a violation of the United Nations Charter, the attack on Yugoslavia also violated the NATO Treaty itself and Canada's own domestic law. The preamble of the NATO Treaty (1949), states that the signers of this document are attesting to their commitment to the premises of the United Nations Charter, as well as their resolve to live amicably with all human beings.

Article 1 of the treaty reiterates the language of the UN Charter in that it deems the peaceful resolution of conflict as well as the refraining from measures of violence that go against United Nations principles as the foremost objectives to be pursued. Article 7 makes clear that the NATO treaty in no way obliterates "the rights and obligations under the Charter of the Parties which are members of the United Nations, or the primary responsibility of the Security Council for the maintenance of international peace and security."

As far as the relevant sections of the Canada Defence Act are concerned, Article 31, Part 1, states that:

The Governor in Council may place the Canadian forces or any component, unit or other element thereof or any officer or non-commissioned member thereof on active service anywhere in or beyond Canada at any time when it appears advisable to do so
(a) by reason of an emergency, for the defence of Canada; or
(b) in consequence of any action undertaken by Canada under the United Nations Charter, the North Atlantic treaty or any other similar instrument for collective defence that may be entered into by Canada.

It should be pointed out that this is a very rare case of scholarly consensus: the war's illegality was not disputed by any legal scholar of repute, even those who had some sympathy for the war, for instance Professor Antonio Cassese, former president and judge of the ICTY itself![4]

HUMANITARIAN JUSTIFICATION

We all know that the leaders of the NATO countries sought to justify this war as a humanitarian intervention in defence of a vulnerable population, the Kosovar Albanians, threatened with mass atrocities. A lot turns on this claim, but *not* the illegality of the war. In fact, the reason why there is such unanimity among scholars on the illegality of this war is that there is no "humanitarian exception" under international law or the UN Charter. That does not mean that there are no means for the international community to intervene to prevent or stop humanitarian disasters, even to use force where necessary. It just means that the use of force for humanitarian purposes has been totally absorbed in the UN Charter.

A state must be able to demonstrate the humanity of its proposed intervention to the Security Council, including, of course, the five permanent members possessing a veto. The Security Council has, indeed, shown itself capable of acting in these situations. It issued numerous resolutions authorizing action in this conflict (Resolutions 1160, 1199, and 1203 of 1998 and Resolutions 1239 and 1244 of 1999, the last of which brought an end to the bombing). The Security Council has also demonstrated its capability of authorizing the use of force, for example its approval of "all necessary means" to restore the sovereignty of Kuwait in Resolution 678 of 29 November 1990, which gave Iraq until 15 January 1991 to withdraw. Bombing by the Americans commenced on 16 January. Indeed, virtually the same words ("all measures necessary") were used in Security Council Resolution 770 of

13 August 1992, which the Americans used to justify their relatively brief 1995 bombing of Serbia prior to the Dayton Accords on Bosnia.

This is not to defend either of these cases of the use of force, but merely to show that the Security Council was far from ineffectual at authorizing it. But NATO did not even move a Resolution before the Security Council over Kosovo. Nor did it use the alternative means of demonstrating to the international community the necessity for its use of force in the General Assembly's *Uniting for Peace Resolution* (1950), which allows the General Assembly to recommend action to the Security Council if two-thirds of those present and voting agree.

There are two basic reasons why these procedures were not utilized by NATO in this case. In the first place, the most plausible explanation of this whole war was that it was, at its foundation, nothing less than an attempt by the U.S., through NATO, to overthrow the authority of the United Nations. In the second place, NATO could never have demonstrated a humanitarian justification for what it was doing, because it had none. In law, as in morals, it is not enough for a humanitarian justification to be claimed, it must also be demonstrated. To use an odious example, but one which makes the point clearly enough, Hitler himself used a humanitarian justification for invading Poland and unleashing World War II: he claimed he was doing it to protect the German minority from oppression by the Poles.

In the case of NATO, what had to be justified as a humanitarian intervention was a bombing campaign that, in dropping 25,000 bombs on Yugoslavia, directly killed between 500 and 1,800 civilian children, women, and men of all ethnicities and permanently injured as many others; a bombing campaign that caused $60 to $100 billion worth of damage to an already impoverished country; a bombing campaign that directly and indirectly caused a refugee crisis of enormous proportions, with about one million fleeing Kosovo during the bombing; a bombing campaign that indirectly caused the death of thousands more, by provoking the violent retaliatory and defensive measures that are entirely predictable when a war of this kind and intensity is undertaken, and by giving a free hand to extremists on both sides to vent their hatred. What also has to be justified is the ethnic cleansing that has occurred in Kosovo since the entry of the triumphant KLA, fully backed by NATO's might, which has seen hundreds of thousands of Serb (and Roma and Jewish) Kosovars driven out and hundreds murdered, a murder rate that is about ten times the Canadian rate per capita.[5]

These results were to be expected and they were predicted by NATO's military and political advisers in their very careful planning of the war, which went back more than a year before the bombing commenced. A humanitarian justification would have to show that this disaster was outweighed by a greater disaster that was about to happen and would have happened but for this intervention. The evidence for this is meagre to say the least.[6] Nobody could seriously maintain that the conditions for a repeat of the Bosnian experience were present, namely an all-out civil war with well-armed parties of roughly equivalent strength on each side and huge ethnic enclaves fighting for their existence. These conditions simply did not exist in Kosovo.

Similarly, the facts do not indicate a humanitarian disaster would have occurred but for NATO's bombing. A total of 2,000 people had been killed on both sides in the prior two years of fighting between the KLA and the Serbs, and violence was declining with the presence of UN observers. The alleged massacre of forty-five ethnic Albanians at Racak must be regarded with the greatest suspicion not only because of the circumstances but also because of the involvement of the American emissary William Walker, with his history of covert and illegal activities on behalf of the Americans in Latin America.

The report released in December 1999 by the Organization for Security and Co-operation in Europe (OSCE) is not of much value in assessing the situation either. It argues that NATO had no choice in the face of mounting Serb atrocities, but the "Acknowledgements" section of the report notes that it was entirely written and paid for by the NATO countries themselves, with no other OSCE countries participating.[7] Even more importantly, the evidence is overwhelming that NATO did not make serious efforts at averting a disaster and was not at all serious about peace.

If we look at the Rambouillet negotiations, a number of questions arise that are impossible to answer if NATO were really interested in achieving peace. For example, why was the irredentist and insurrectionary KLA preferred as the NATO interlocutor to the only popularly elected leader, the moderate Ibrahim Rugova? Why, for that matter was Rugova ignored during the war? Why did the U.S. insist on a secret annex to the Rambouillet Accord (Annex B) that would have allowed it to occupy all of Serbia? Why did the final peace agreement in June look so much like what the Serbs had agreed to before the bombing? Do we really think that NATO could not have put the $10 billion of bombs it dropped to better use, working out and underwriting a peace agreement that would have accommodated and protected all sides if it actually were interested in humanity and not war? Why are NATO countries so unwilling to spend money on the reconstruction of Kosovo, claiming that they have run out of money with less than $1 billion spent?

And where, to resolve these enormous doubts about whether NATO acted out of humanitarian motives this time, is the evidence that these people have *ever* acted out of humanitarian motives before? With such huge holes in its argument, we are entitled to cross-examine the leopard on its spots. What about the failure to intervene with force in Rwanda? What about the United States' own bankrolling of the repressive Suharto regime in Indonesia? What about Turkey's violent repression of the Kurds, a humanitarian disaster that has claimed 30,000 lives, not 2,000?[8] What about the United States itself? It is the richest country in the world, but it has created within itself social conditions so violent and racist that its normal murder rate is in the realm of 20,000 per year, almost as high, per capita, as Kosovo in the fall of 1999. It puts two of its own people to death by lethal injection every week. NATO has no humanitarian lessons to teach the world.

Finally and very importantly, we must ask some serious questions about the way in which this supposed humanitarian intervention was handled. With the Kosovars supposedly in the hands of genocidal maniacs, NATO gave five days warning between the withdrawal of the observers and the launch of the attack. This was followed by seven days of bombing that mostly ignored Kosovo itself. In other words, the bombing was an invitation to genocide that was not accepted; nevertheless, it was guaranteed to produce a refugee flow that would legitimate a massive bombing campaign.

FALSE CLAIMS AND COVERT INTENTIONS

That NATO leaders would lie about their motives should startle no one. They have already been caught out often enough to shatter their credibility. Forget "I did not have sexual relations with that woman." What about the claim by NATO spokesman Jamie Shea that it was the Serbs who bombed the Albanian refugee convoy – until independent journalists found bomb fragments "made in U.S.A."? What about the claim by NATO General Wesley Clark, with video up on the screen, that the passenger train on the Grdelica bridge was going too fast to avoid being hit – until somebody pointed out that the video had been accelerated to three times its actual speed? What about the claim that the Chinese embassy was bombed because NATO's maps were out of date? Mr Clinton (and Mrs Clinton) and Mr Cohen, the Secretary of Defence, claimed that a "Holocaust" was occurring in which perhaps 100,000 Kosovar men had been murdered; when the bombing was over, that number dwindled to 2,108 – and no investigator has yet said anything about who those men were or how they died.

In fact, most people in the world simply did not believe NATO's claim of humanitarianism. A poll taken in mid-April 1999 and published by *The Economist* showed that this was a very unpopular war, opposed by perhaps most of the world's population both within and outside of the NATO countries.[9] A poll taken in Greece between 29 April and

5 May 1999 showed that 99.5 per cent of the participants were against
the war, 85 per cent believing NATO's motives to be strategic and not
humanitarian, and, most importantly, 69 per cent in favour of charging
Bill Clinton with war crimes, 35.2 per cent for charging Tony Blair,
and only 14 per cent for charging Slobodan Milosevic, not far from
the 13 per cent in favour of charging NATO General Wesley Clark and
the 9.6 per cent for charging NATO Secretary General Javier Solana.[10]

Much more plausible than the humanitarian hypothesis is the one
that the United States deliberately provoked this war, that it purposely
exploited and exacerbated another country's tragedy – a tragedy partly
of its own creation (we should not forget that the West's aggressive
and purely selfish economic policies have beggared Yugoslavia over the
last ten years)[11]. NATO exists to make war, not to avoid it. The arms
industry exists to make profits from dropping bombs. (Maybe that's
why they put up a big chunk of the money for the fiftieth anniversary
NATO summit in Washington during the bombing)[12]. And the U.S., by
virtue of its military might, dominates NATO the way it cannot dominate
the United Nations.

The most plausible explanation, then, one brilliantly expounded by
Professor Peter Gowan of Great Britain, is that this attack was not
about the Balkans at all. It was an attempt to overthrow the authority
of the UN and make NATO, and therefore the U.S., the world's supreme
authority, to establish the "precedent" that NATO politicians have been
talking about since the bombing stopped, and to give the U.S. the free
hand that the UN does not give in its conflicts with the Third World
and its rivalries with Russia, China, and even Europe.[13] In other words,
this was not a case of the UN being an obstacle to humanitarianism.
It was a case of using a flimsy pretext of humanitarianism to overthrow
the UN.

Not only was this an illegal war that had no humanitarian justification, it was a war pursued by illegal means. According to admissions
made in public throughout the war (for instance during NATO briefings),
eye-witness reports, and powerful circumstantial evidence displayed
on the world's television screens throughout the bombing campaign
– evidence good enough to convict in any criminal court in the world –
NATO leaders deliberately and illegally designated places with only a
tenuous or slight military value or no military value at all as targets.
These places included city bridges, factories, hospitals, marketplaces,
downtown and residential neighbourhoods, and television studios. The
same evidence shows that, in doing this, NATO leaders aimed to
demoralize and break the will of the people, not to defeat its army.

The American group Human Rights Watch issued in 2000 a lengthy
report documenting a systematic and massive violation of international

humanitarian law by NATO in Yugoslavia.[14] They estimate the civilian victims to be about 500. This figure should be taken as a minimum because it is a number Human Rights Watch says it can independently confirm and that can be attributed directly to the bombing. It excludes persons known to be killed as an indirect result of the bombing. Every benefit of the doubt is given to NATO, a fact exemplified by the report's puzzling, undefended, and, in fact, indefensible distinction between these grave "violations of humanitarian law" and "war crimes." Human Rights Watch also documented the use of anti-personnel cluster bombs in attacks on civilian targets.

One reason civilian targets are illegal is that civilians are very likely to be killed or injured when such targets are hit. All of the NATO leaders knew that. They were carefully told that by their military planners, yet they still went ahead and did it, and without any risk to themselves or to their soldiers and pilots. That is why this war was called a "coward's war." The cowardice lay in fighting the civilian population and not the military, in bombing from altitudes so high that the civilians, Serbs, Albanians, Roma, and anybody else on the ground, bore all the risks of the "inevitable collateral damage." Displacing all the risks onto the civilian population is contrary to the recognized laws of war. Indeed, there is persuasive evidence that, in some circumstances at least, NATO not only knowingly killed civilians but deliberately set out to do so: for example, on the Grdelica and Varvarin bridges (12 April and 30 May 1999) and the NIS marketplace (7 May).[15]

WAR CRIMES CHARGES BEFORE THE INTERNATIONAL TRIBUNAL

So we have an illegal and unjustified war, carried on in plain view by illegal means, yet one whose legitimacy, as we said at the outset, was sought to be enhanced by the actions of the ICTY in charging NATO's enemies with war crimes. It is not surprising, therefore, that, starting in April of 1999 and continuing to the present day, dozens of lawyers and law professors, a pan-American association representing hundreds of jurists, some elected legislators, and thousands of private citizens from around the world have lodged formal complaints with the International Criminal Tribunal in The Hague charging NATO leaders with war crimes.

The logic was inexorable. The NATO leaders planned and executed a bombing campaign that they knew was contrary to the most fundamental tenets of international law and that they knew would cause the death and permanent injury of thousands of civilian children, women, and men. On this ground alone, i.e. the killing of hundreds or thousands of civilians knowingly and without lawful excuse, these leaders were guilty of mass murder. Milosevic and other Serb leaders were indicted in The Hague for the murder of 385 victims. The total number of victims of the 98 people executed for murder in the U.S. in 1999 was 129. NATO leaders murdered at least 500 and perhaps as many as 1,800.

The particular complaint I am involved in was filed with the Hague Tribunal in May 1999 and names sixty-eight individuals, including all the heads of government, foreign ministers, and defence ministers of the nineteen NATO countries (including U.S. President Clinton, secretaries Cohen and Albright, Canadian Prime Minister Chrétien, ministers Axworthy and Eggleton, and so on down the list), and the highest ranking NATO officials, from former Secretary General Javier Solana through generals Wesley Clark and Michael Short to official spokesman Jamie Shea.

Our complaint charges these NATO leaders with the following crimes under the Statute of the Tribunal:

Grave breaches of the Geneva Conventions of 12 August 1949 (contrary to Article 2) namely the following acts against persons or property protected under the provisions of the relevant Geneva Convention: (a) wilful killing; (c) wilfully causing great suffering or serious injury to body or health; (d) extensive destruction and appropriation of property, not justified by military necessity and carried out unlawfully and wantonly.

Violations of the laws or customs of war (Article 3): (a) employment of poisonous weapons or other weapons to cause unnecessary suffering; (b) wanton destruction of cities, towns or villages, or devastation not justified by military necessity; (c) attack, or bombardment, by whatever means, of undefended towns, villages, dwellings, or buildings; (d) seizure of, destruction or wilful damage done to institutions dedicated to religion, charity and education, the arts and sciences, historic monuments and works of art and science.

Crimes against humanity (Article 5): (a) murder; (i) other inhumane acts.

Article 7 of the Tribunal Statute provides for "individual criminal responsibility" in this way: "A person who planned, instigated, ordered, committed or otherwise aided and abetted in the planning, preparation or execution of a crime referred to in articles 2 to 5 of the present Statute, shall be individually responsible for the crime." The same Article provides that this remains valid regardless of the official position of the perpetrator, and also specifies that a crime committed by a subordinate does not exempt the superior of his responsibility if he was aware the deed would be committed and failed to intervene.

After delivering our complaint in May 1999, we were in frequent contact with the tribunal, traveling to The Hague twice (in June and in November 1999) to argue our case with chief prosecutors Louise Arbour and Carla Del Ponte and their legal advisers, filing evidence, legal briefs, and arguments in support of the case. After our last visit, Ms Del Ponte issued a number of statements indicating that her office was indeed studying our submissions and the submission of several parliamentarians to see whether charges against NATO leaders should be laid. She went so far as to tell a reporter from the London *Observer* in late December, "If I am not willing to do that [prosecute NATO leaders if the evidence incriminated them], I am not in the right place: I must give up the mission."

However, this was followed by vigorous denunciations from NATO and the American government, declaring that the mere thought of prosecutions was preposterous. Ms Del Ponte's obsequious and quite absurd response – that there was no "formal inquiry" (whatever that means) and, though they were still studying the case, they had seen nothing yet to justify opening one – was enough to convince us that there was no point in continuing to make submissions to the tribunal. We wrote her that:

We feel we must protest your recent statements and those of your spokesman, which, combined with your failure to act on the thousands of complaints against NATO that have reached your office over the past year, are turning this investigation into more of a farce than a judicial proceeding. We regret to say that, for all the faith that has been put in your Tribunal by the people of the world, it continues to conduct itself as if it were an organ of NATO and not of the United Nations.

This is nothing short of a disgrace. If, despite all the evidence that has been provided to you since the first complaint reached your office in April 1999, followed by thousands more from lawyers, legislators and citizens around the world, you have still seen "nothing to indicate" that even an investigation is required, the only possible conclusion to draw is that you are not serious about your duties, and perhaps never were. If you cannot apply the law to NATO as well as to NATO's enemies, it seems that you are not, in your own words, "in the right place" and should, indeed, "give up the mission."

This was not, of course, the first time that the tribunal had given the world serious reasons to doubt its impartiality. We have already mentioned the dramatic for-the-cameras performance of Arbour at the border of Kosovo after Racak, lending a precipitous and totally unwarranted credibility to William Walker's claim that a massacre of civilians had occurred. Then there was the announcement of the secret indictment of "Arkan." The televised meetings with Cook and Albright all took place after well-grounded complaints of war crimes against them had reached Arbour's attention. But what left little doubt about the nature of the tribunal was the indictment of Slobodan Milosevic and other Serb leaders in the midst of the bombing, on the basis of undis-closed evidence, and for events that had occurred only six weeks earlier in the middle of a war zone, on what, in other words, must have been very flimsy and suspicious evidence. Of course this has to be compared with the inability of the Tribunal to even "open an investigation" after one year of being provided with overwhelming evidence in the public domain of NATO leaders' crimes, which, even using the most conser-vative estimates, resulted in the deaths of far more civilians than those for which the Serb leadership was indicted.

When, at the conclusion of the bombing, Arbour handed over the investigation of war crimes in Kosovo to the NATO countries' own police forces, notwithstanding their obvious motivation to falsify the evidence, we publicly protested. When we returned to The Hague in November 1999, we made the tribunal's credibility a central theme of our submissions:

In conclusion, the Complainants are forced to say that they cannot understand the failure of the Tribunal to act on these and the many other complaints against the NATO leaders. The law is clear. The evidence is overwhelming. More than enough time has passed, especially given the speed with which the Milosevic indictment was issued. The failure of the Tribunal to act is raising strong suspicions of bias and continues to directly contribute to the suffering in Yugoslavia. The Tribunal must act now.

According to the U.S. State Department lawyer who, on Madeleine Albright's instructions, wrote the Security Council Resolution estab-lishing the tribunal, the United States sponsored this tribunal for the purpose of pure propaganda:

[t]he tribunal was widely perceived within the government as little more than a public relations device and as a potentially useful policy tool ... Indictments also would serve to isolate offending leaders diplomatically, strengthen the hand of their domestic rivals and fortify the international political will to employ economic sanctions or use force.[16]

So it is fair to ask why we bothered with such a tribunal in the first place. I cannot speak for everybody who participated in this initiative or the many similar ones, but I can say that, in my own case, the complaint to The Hague was primarily a form of opposition to the war. Ideally, of course, the prosecutor would issue indictments, or at least make a statement telling NATO to stop its law-breaking or face the consequences, but I, personally, always regarded this as a very remote possibility. Not because of the strength of the case, of course. The case is strong. But, in my experience, politics usually trumps law.[17] Nevertheless, given the centrality of the tribunal in the justification of the war, it struck me as essential to demonstrate beyond any reasonable doubt the equal guilt of NATO and thus to deprive them of the powerful ideology that they were white knights fighting war criminals.

On the other hand, we had to face up to the possibility that the tribunal would seek to discredit our case and thus vindicate NATO. This seems to be what is happening now. It would not surprise me if a report was being prepared now to absolve NATO from all liability – though the fact that it has taken so long suggests to me that this is no easy task. Will that end matters in NATO's favour? It depends. If the tribunal makes a persuasive case for not prosecuting NATO leaders despite the evidence, then it will. But I am convinced that it does not have a snowball's chance in July of doing so.

Is it not the tribunal that will have the last word? Perhaps, if the tribunal's role began and ended with punishing Balkan criminals – you could imagine how little it would have the last word if it dared to issue warrants for the arrest of NATO leaders, no matter how well-deserved.[18] But the tribunal's role exceeds merely issuing indictments. It has to legitimate the New World Order, which seems to include the absolute monarchy of the U.S. over international law. Where legitimacy is concerned, though, it is the people of the world who have the final say, not some criminal court set up in an insurance company building in a sleepy little Dutch town.

So I do not regard the tribunal's failure to do its duty as a defeat for global democracy, although it clearly was a stab at it. I will tell you why. At Victoria College of the University of Toronto, where I passed by this morning (30 April 2000), you can read the words "The truth shall make you free" chiseled in stone above a stately portal. "Make you free" is putting it rather high, I thought to myself, but it sure helps.

The fact that the world made an overwhelming case to the Hague tribunal for the punishment of NATO and the Hague tribunal rejected the case constitutes, paradoxically, an important advance for democracy. Why? Because it is an advance in our understanding of judicial institutions and their interrelation with democracy, considering "democracy" in the broadest and most authentic sense of equality of political power. There is powerful propaganda about courts being impartial and above politics. But time and again, courts have proved themselves to be essentially an antidote to democracy, a way in which elites fight the democratic tendencies of representative institutions (like the United Nations, for example). I have always thought that the only point in studying law was so we could lay bare the truth of legal institutions for everybody to see, so they could judge for themselves where to place their allegiance. If we have identified a corrupt institution and, by revealing its corruption, helped weaken it, then maybe something worthwhile has been salvaged from this terrible tragedy.[19]

NOTES

1 I am writing this introduction at a remove of more than a year from when I wrote the original chapter for this collection. On the illegality of the war against Afghanistan see my "Illegal Wars and International Criminal Law," *Third World Association of International Law Journal* (forthcoming 2002).

2 CASE CONCERNING THE MILITARY AND PARAMILITARY ACTIVITIES IN AND AGAINST NICARAGUA [Nicaragua vs. United States of America] *(MERITS)* Judgment of 27 June 1986, *I.C.J. Reports,* 1986, 134–5, paragraphs 267 and 268.

3 CASE CONCERNING THE LEGALITY OF USE OF FORCE [Yugoslavia vs. Canada] International Court of Justice, 2 June 1999.

4 "Ex iniuria ius oritur: Are We Moving towards International Legitimation of Forcible Humanitarian Countermeasures in the World Community?" *European Journal of International Law* 10, no. 1 (1999). See also "NATO, the UN and the Use of Force: Legal Aspects," by Professor Bruno Simma, ibid.

5 Of the many accounts of the effects of the war, see especially the detailed and devastating report by the Federal Republic of Yugoslavia, Federal Ministry of Foreign Affairs, NATO Crimes in Yugoslavia: Documentary Evidence, Vol. I, 24 March – 24 April (Belgrade, May 1999); Vol. II, 25 April – 10 June 1999 (Belgrade, July 1999) and the multi-faceted Selected Research Findings of the Independent Commission of Inquiry to Investigate US/NATO War Crimes Against the People of Yugoslavia, held in New York City on 31 July 1999. The hardly pro-Yugoslav Human Rights Watch Report: Civilian Deaths in the NATO Air Camapaign (February 2000) certifies the FRY volumes as "largely credible."

6 See, generally, Bob Allen, "Why Kosovo? The Anatomy of a Needless War," Canadian Centre for Policy Alternatives, July 1999.

7 "The data gathered by the OSCE-KVM was analysed and consolidated into this publication under the supervision of the OSCE Office for Democratic Institutions and Human Rights (OSCE/ODIHR) in Warsaw, Poland. This publication was made possible by the generous material,

technical and logistical support of the Government of Poland, and the generous financial support of the Governments of Austria, Denmark, Norway, Sweden, Switzerland and the United States of America. Additional logistical support was provided by the Government of Germany. These contributions are gratefully acknowledged. The OSCE/ODIHR is grateful for the advice and assistance of staff of the International Criminal Tribunal for the former Yugoslavia (ICTY) in the development of this report." ("Acknowledgements" in *Kosovo/Kosova As Seen, As Told*).

8 Noam Chomsky makes these points with great force in "The New Military Humanism: Lesson from Kosovo," *In These Times*, 19 September 1999.

9 "Oh what a lovely war!," *The Economist*, 24 April 1999 shows more than a third of the population in Canada, Poland, Germany, France, and Finland opposed, almost an even split in Hungary, an even split in Italy, and a majority opposed in the Czech Republic, Russia, and Taiwan.

10 "Majority in Greece wants Clinton tried for war crimes," *The Irish Times*, 27 May 1999.

11 See Michel Chossudovsky's compelling analysis, "Dismantling Former Yugoslavia, Recolonizing Bosnia-Herzegovina," in his *The Globalisation of Poverty: Impacts of IMF and World Bank Reforms*, Penang: Third World Network, 1997, 243–63.

12 "The event was hosted by a committee of US and multinational companies, which had raised nearly eight million dollars in cash and contributions from its members for the opportunity to mingle with the visiting delegations. Host Committee members (each of whom had contributed $250,000 or the equivalent for the privilege) included many from the world of information technology, communications, the motor industry, financial services, and of course defence contractors such as Boeing, Raytheon, United Technologies and TRW." Nicola Butler, "NATO at 50: Papering over the cracks," *Ploughshares Monitor*, December 1999; *Disarmament Diplomacy*, no. 38 (1999).

13 Peter Gowan, "The Real Meaning of the War over Kosovo," in L. Panitch and C. Leys, eds., *The Socialist Register 2000: Necessary and Unnecessary Utopias*, London: Merlin Press, 1999.

14 Human Rights Watch, *Report: Civilian Deaths in the NATO Air Campaign*, February 2000.

15 See, for example, http://www.grdelica-case.org

16 Michael Scharf, *The Washington Post*, 3 October 1999.

17 See for example, my "A Brief History of the New Constitutionalism, or 'How we changed everything so that everything would remain the same,'" *Israel Law Review* 32 (1998), 250.

18 Deputy Chief Prosecutor Graham Blewitt seems to think they'd be *shut down* if they charged NATO: "If the evidence is there that NATO forces had committed a breach of humanitarian law, we have a duty to act. If it meant the tribunal was wound up because no one would support us, so be it," said Blewitt. Kevin Cullen, "War crimes tribunal wins new esteem," *Boston Globe*, 17 April 2000, A01.

19 In June 2000, well after this article was finished, Carla Del Ponte announced to the Security Council that she had decided not to open a formal inquiry into NATO war crimes on the advice of a committee of her office that she would release in a couple of weeks. If the Criminal Tribunal for the Former Yugoslavia had little credibility before this report, it has none whatsoever afterwards. Even the way Del Ponte announced that there would be no charges against NATO would have embarrassed a serious tribunal: she was not "opening an investigation" because she was "completely satisfied" they were innocent. So how did she satisfy herself if she did not investigate? In reality, the tribunal was so anxious not to offend NATO that it had to deny that there was even an investigation. Fortunately, Amnesty International issued its report two days after Del Ponte spoke to the Security Council. It is hard not to suspect that Del Ponte anticipated her own report (issued ten days later) to try and draw attention away from Amnesty. I challenge anyone to read both reports and not conclude Del Ponte's is a hoax. Amnesty's report is cautious, at times too cautious, establishing clear and admitted instances of what it has no hesitation in calling NATO's "war crimes" that should be prosecuted. It also establishes beyond any doubt that NATO systematically lied. Del Ponte's report reads like it was written by a NATO lawyer. In fact, it was – the report bears the stamp of long-time Canadian army lawyer William Fenrick, Arbour's and Del Ponte's senior legal adviser. It is an amateur work, deliberately misquoting the law and admittedly taking NATO's every word at face value ["It [the committee] has tended to assume that the NATO and NATO countries' press statements are generally reliable and that explanations have been honestly given." (Paragraph 90)]. The only time it does not take NATO's word is where NATO admits to war crimes (as in bombing the RTS television station or the Grdelica bridge for a second time, after the pilot knew a passenger train was on it). It should be remembered that Amnesty is no friend of the Yugoslav government. It was very critical of its actions in Kosovo before and during the war, though it did not spare either NATO or the KLA. And it restricted its charges of war crimes to those which were clear on the record, in other words the tip of the iceberg. Nor did Amnesty take a position on the legality of the war, but as was stated earlier, all scholars of any repute agree the war was illegal. I repeat: killing at least 500 civilian children, women, and men knowingly and without lawful excuse is mass murder.

Neo-Liberalism and the Chilean Model: A Forerunner of the New World Order

J. NEF

For over a decade, mainstream politicians, intellectuals, and media have praised Chile as a model for Latin America, the Third World, and beyond.[1] A major Canadian newspaper went as far as to propose that Canada should follow a similar set of neo-liberal socioeconomic prescriptions.[2] In fact, Chile is nowadays a showcase for the "New World Order." Needless to say, this simplistic but common presentation tends to ignore the complexities of both the process of "transition" going on in that country and the deceiving nature of globalization. Similar paradigmatic claims have been made before regarding Asia's Little Tigers and, closer to home, Mexico, prior to the signing of the North American Free Trade Agreement. Given the lack of analysis and high levels of ideological enthusiasm, subsequent events such as the "Tequilazo," the Chiapas uprising, and the "Asian Crisis" took many pundits by surprise.

Despite such disappointments, and perhaps because of them, the Chilean experience continues to be peddled by free-market ideologues as proof of the validity of their recipes. For the right, Chile is the "solution" for Latin America, very much as Cuba was for the left in the early 1960s. There is a amazing parallelism between the old and the new Manichean worldviews, between those intellectuals who embraced the Cuban Revolution as the only way and those, including several of the same individuals, who today proclaim the universal validity, historical inevitability, and scientific nature of "really-existing capitalism." It is true that with the Latin American continent in socio-political and economic turmoil, today's Chile appears as an island of stability and prosperity. It is one of Latin America's strongest economies, with visibly democratic features and publicized gains in human rights. However, despite its considerable achievements, Chile is and remains on the whole a structurally vulnerable and underdeveloped country that bears the scars of a brutal military regime and lives still under its shadow. Chilean "success" is largely a triumphalistic narrative that hides the reality of a fragile political "normalization," one that has preserved the institutional, economic, and social legacies of a counter-revolution and is pregnant with uncertainties and deep contradictions.

At close scrutiny, even the most talked-about "redeeming features" in the Chilean experiment, such as efficiency, order, stability, and predictability, are – as it is also the case with the Asian "Tigers" – not so much rooted in the intrinsic goodness of economic orthodoxy and the peculiar democratic transition but in long-term developments. They predate both the imposition of neo-liberal policies by the military regime and the subsequent democratic normalization of the 1990s. Since the nineteenth century, most governments have persistently emphasized human resources development, national education, and public health. Since the 1920s, virtually every government has embarked on efficiency- and probity-oriented administrative reforms, while since the late 1930s induced development policies have been vigorously pursued. Structural reforms, such as agrarian reform in the 1960s and 1970s, were thoroughgoing. All these preexisting conditions facilitated the favourable economic upturn of the 1990s.

Furthermore, two important political aspects of the Chilean show-case are often downplayed. The first refers to the nature of the military regime. The 1973 coup that ushered in the sixteen-year dictatorship of General Pinochet was part of the Cold War. It was squarely a transna-tional war waged against the Chilean state and nation by the dominant regional superpower. The ensemble of internal forces clustered around the military had the financial, logistic, and ideological support of powerful external constituencies: the American government, its defence and intelligence apparatus, and large foreign corporations. Recent CIA documents have revealed that the extent of U.S. penetration in Chile's military intelligence and government was much deeper than ever admitted.[3] This reactionary coalition, which had already been involved in trying to prevent a turn to the left and had waged a vicious economic blockade, stood to gain from a drastic change in policies and regime. Its long-run economic project, referred by its supporters as the "seven modernizations," was a blend of unbridled capitalism implemented by means of authoritarianism and repression.[4] Even with the Cold War virtually over, both the transition and the consolidation of democracy in Chile have been far too dependent on the acquiescence of the same players. Thus it is not unreasonable to think that a change in the correlation of forces among external constituencies would continue to have a dramatic impact upon the sustainability of the domestic regime.

The second aspect refers to the nature of democratic politics emerging from the 1988–89 transition. Despite profound ideological differences with its authoritarian predecessor, the three coalition governments elected since 1990 constitute a "new management" of a system whose basic orientation, intellectual "software," and structure – as well as significant members of its personnel and aspects of its rules of the game – have been inherited from the Pinochet era.[5] Furthermore, the agendas and blueprints for the transition from dictatorship to democracy have been cast by the same forces that affected the earlier transition from democracy to military rule.

THE TWO SIDES OF THE ECONOMIC "MIRACLE"

At the moment, Chile is perhaps the Latin American country displaying "best behavior" vis-à-vis the international financial community. Its programs of debt and deficit reduction, structural adjustments, "debt-for-equity" swaps, and free-trade policies have been highly praised in international financial circles, including the IMF and the World Bank. Such strict adherence to economic orthodoxy has resulted in a marked improvement in Chile's credit rating. It has also affected the country's high score among the international business community as relatively corruption-free, being among the top twenty less corrupt countries, just below the U.S. and above a number of Western European states.[6]

For over ten years Chile has exhibited signs of an economic "boom," with indexes of growth of the GNP of 9 and 12 per cent between 1987 and 1991 and between 5 and 4.3 per cent in 1993 and 1994.[7] Even after the 1998–99 collapse of the Asian markets, with one year of negative growth, the Chilean economy quickly returned to a rate of expansion of near 5 per cent. Per capita income in 1999 was about $12,000 (versus less than $9,000 in 1993), the highest in Latin America. The once soaring inflation is under control, from about 18 percent annually in 1991 to 8.9 per cent in 1994 and 2.3 per cent in 1999. Investment is significantly up, while the still massive foreign debt ($1,890 in 1991 per capita terms – among the largest in Latin America) has become manageable. Canadian investment in Chile has grown from less than $500 million in 1989 to nearly $3.7 billion (13 per cent of all foreign investment), making Canada the second largest investor in Chile after the U.S. (75 per cent). Bilateral trade, at a modest $427 million in 1994, grew 23 per cent in just one year. In sum, from a rather conventional point of view, the economy is "doing well."

But there is another, much darker side of the story. Leaving aside the argument of the regressive distribution of such an economic expansion, a long-range view of Chile's economic performance indicates a relatively modest rate of overall real growth, in which significant upturns often occurred at the heels of sharp downfalls. We can mention two such examples in recent history. The first was the period of acute polarization, paralysis, and sheer chaos preceding the 1973 coup. This was immediately followed by the recession induced by the military regime, known as the "shock treatment" (1973–75). In the first year after the coup, the military and its allies waged what they construed as a protective war against "subversion," but simultaneously they carried on an offensive war to destroy the organization of the popular sectors. Dramatic rates of economic decline (-12.5 per cent in 1975 alone) brought down gains sustained by labour in previous years. The shock was also aimed at reverting income distribution. The second example is from the period between 1982 and 1984, under the undisputed helm of Pinochet and his team of neo-liberal economic advisors, when the GNP declined by rates of over 14 per cent. From a comparative perspective, Chile's long-term economic record is far less impressive than that experienced by other Latin American economies,[8] for example, Mexico, Ecuador, Costa Rica, Uruguay, and, most remarkably, Colombia.[9] In the latter case (which few would venture to present as a model to be imitated), and leaving aside the impact of the illegal economy, Colombia's economic performance appears sustained, relatively stable, and with better income distribution. In the case of Mexico, despite corruption, fraud, distributive inequities and intermittent financial crises (1995, 1998), that country's productive transformation has been by far less onerous to its poorer sectors than has the Chilean "miracle."

There is no doubt that for its economic "success," most Chileans had to bear for too long an extremely high and unevenly distributed social and economic burden, as attested by the staggering (and for many years growing) levels of poverty, skewed distribution of wealth,[10] and unprecedented abuse of human rights. It is impossible to separate the "positive" side of the Chilean transformation from its dark side, manifested in the destruction of democracy, persistent violations of human dignity, and creation of a terrorist state. As the late Orlando Letelier put it, economic freedom for a minority and political repression for the majorities are two sides of the same coin.[11] The huge gap between rich and poor continues to expand. Some analysts, including former President Aylwin, consider Chile to have had one of the worst distributional profile in the Americas, second only to Brazil.

THE AGRICULTURAL "REVOLUTION"

One of the most remarkable and hailed features of Chile's productive transformation has been in the agricultural and resource sectors. Though the modernization of the countryside is the most talked about, forestry and fisheries expansion have been equally dramatic. Since the coup and the undoing of the most populist and redistributive features of the agrarian reforms of the Frei and Allende administrations, a thorough agrarian counterrevolution has been underway. It has involved the rapid technification, capitalization, and internationalization of agriculture leading to export-substitution. Agricultural exports, with a heavy incidence of "non-traditional" products such as fruits and wines, today account for about 27 per cent of all exports, second after copper exports.

The Green Revolution with neo-liberalism in the countryside has meant the emergence of new social fractions and the transformation of old ones.[12] For instance, a "rural bourgeoisie" and a seasonal rural "semi-proletariat" has emerged. Most of the old *latifundistas* have mutated into a modern and internationalized agro-business class, strengthening their already substantial linkages with finance capital. Meanwhile, traditional peasants have lost their access to small property (through indebtedness or productive marginalization), becoming instead property-less wage earners. The horizontal and vertical integration of production, the steady decline of agricultural wages, marked seasonality, and the pauperization of the bulk of the population are at the core of this agricultural modernization.

In either case, the prosperity of the few has been financed by the impoverishment of the many, assisted by state repression and anti-labour legislation such as the Plan Laboral of 1979. A similar pattern has emerged in the areas of forestry and fisheries. High technification and vertical integration of production, processing, commercialization, and distribution – even more so than in industry and agriculture – has led to near monopoly situations. As in the other sectors, the agricultural "revolution" is sustained by labour-reserves of cheap, abundant, and non-unionized workers: in short, the low-wage economy.

LABOUR DISARTICULATION

As many industries have been transferred from the public to the private sector and others have been acquired by foreign bidders or have simply disappeared, the very foundations of Chile's patterns of social relations have been altered. Despite a recent reprieve experienced since the inauguration of President Lagos in March 2000, blue-collar organizations have been seriously weakened and fragmented since the military

takeover. Since the return of democracy, the entrenched rightist opposition and its allies in business associations have managed to derail the
enactment of labour laws that simply enshrine minimum international
standards along ILO lines. Both in numbers and in strength, labour
power has declined dramatically from the heyday of unionism in the
late 1960s and early 1970s.[13]

A socio-political consequence of the process of economic restructuring, assisted by an outwardly anti-union legislation, is the growing
number of informal workers, who are only loosely and in a fragmen-
tary fashion integrated into the labour market. They are non-affiliated,
and thus possess a very limited capacity to organize and mobilize. A
large segment of the existing manufacturing sector in today's Chile is
"informal" (that is, it does not conform to norms contained in safety,
health, labour, or environmental regulations) and employs cheaper,
non-union workers. Furthermore, a significant portion of the large
formal industries sub-contract with "informal" suppliers. All this helps
to keep wages exceedingly low, thus allowing significant increases in
business profitability, high concentration of capital and production,
and "international competitiveness."

ELITE RE-ARTICULATION

In contrast, and in a friendlier environment, the already strong business organizations have become even stronger. The main and all-
encompassing business organization is the National Confederation of
Production and Commerce (CNPC, established in 1932). It is the central
umbrella organization, with a distinctively neo-liberal and corporatist
orientation. It includes in its membership all major "functional"
economic associations: agriculture, industry, mining, construction,
commerce, and the financial sector. These are the "owners" of Chile.
Their principal mouthpiece is the national newspaper, *El Mercurio,* a
communications monopoly that is closely intertwined with neo-liberal,
corporatist, and authoritarian personalities in the military regime. It
has also been Chile's principal mechanism for moulding public opinion
and for constructing the elite's hegemonic discourse for over a century.

At the present, the business associations' size, finance, organization,
interlocking capacity, representation in official government agencies,
control over media, and ability to define the "intellectual" agenda of
universities,[14] has created, for the first time in Chilean history, a hegemonic business class stronger than the state itself. The military, as the
only potential power contender to this new arrangement, has been
symbiotically aligned with business in an entangling alliance, which
includes also important external constituencies.

THE "MODERNIZATION" OF THE STATE: AUTHORITARIAN CAPITALISM

Neo-liberalism has provided the blueprint not only for the economy but also to a large extent for the social set-up in which economic life takes place.[15] However, neo-liberal ideas, or the intellectuals espousing them, could not have affected by themselves the course of Chile's development. For this to occur two ideological and socio-political linkages were essential. First, as a consequence of academic repression following the 1973 coup, neo-liberals attained intellectual predominance in university, government, and business circles. With economic nationalists and structuralists on the run, and the business community in search for a new slogan, it was easy for neo-liberals and monetarists to rely on U.S. academic support and gain the upper hand.

Second, an appropriate linkage with the ideologies of the other allied groups of the 1973 elite revolt (namely the Catholic corporatist and integralist right and the military) was developed. Though neo-liberalism and national security may appear antagonistic at first glance, a more in-depth analysis reveals axiological and, most important, deontological compatibilities. This amalgam was greatly facilitated by the ideological intermediation provided by Catholic, corporatist, and integralist thinking of Chilean "revolutionary conservatism." In fact, Chilean fascism constituted the bridge between national security with its interventionist and authoritarian tendencies and economic liberalism with its claim to economic 'freedom'. A liberal-conservative synthesis emerged. This grafting of neo-liberalism, reactionary modernism and national security was the fundamental task of the regime's main ideologue, Jaime Guzmán.

The authoritarian-capitalist state in Chile, imbedded in the 1980 constitution, involves an amalgam of economic neo-liberalism (à la Friedrich von Hayek or Milton Friedman), Catholic and corporatist integrism in the social sphere and National Security in the political realm. The latter in particular has configured a vertical and highly repressive view of the political process. Being the dominant ideology of the security establishment, it has deeply influenced the state officials' views on "internal war," human rights, and the 'appropriate' methodology for handling dissent.

THE REFORM OF THE PUBLIC SECTOR

Beginning with the military regime, and in marked contrast with the past, the public sector has been significantly reduced as far as social, health, educational, housing, and economic functions are concerned.[16]

These were extensively privatized and transferred – at discount prices – to a business community made of the most conspicuous supporters of the military regime. Subsequently, transnational insurance businesses, in alliance with domestic capital, established a firm control over the bulk of pension funds, health care, and the like.[17]

This massive transfer of public monies to private hands occurred with *hardly any real accountability*. In practice, and leaving aside euphemisms, it was by and large an expropriatory takeover of the social savings of workers and employees by the private financial system. Notably, the only exception to this privatizing fever has been the social and health services of the Armed Forces. Social security funds under the Ministry of Defence have retained their autonomy and protection under state authority, which is paradoxical, given the predicated "goodness" of the reforms imposed upon Chile's blue – and white-collar workers.

THE VANISHING MIDDLE CLASS

With the shrinkage of the state's economic and welfare functions, there has been a rapid fragmentation and virtual disappearance of the traditional white-collar bureaucratic and professional middleclasses. Traditionally Chile's middle classes and their political and bureaucratic institutions played an important brokerage and moderating role in the political process. This mesocratic state – referred to by many as "the state of compromise" – provided a cushion to reduce socioeconomic tensions between business and labour. In fact, as Valenzuela has argued, the distinctive democratic style of Chilean politics could be traced back to this institutionalization of class antagonisms through political and bureaucratic bargaining mechanisms. This order of things, already strained by the catastrophic polarization of 1970–73, was purposely eradicated by the military regime. Pinochet's "war on politics" was essentially a war of demolition against this particular form of republican and democratic lifestyle.

In addition to the forceful shrinkage of state corporations and the administrative apparatus of the state, with its political bargaining and patronage, the financial and cultural foundations of Chile's middle classes were purposely undermined. One such policy was the aforementioned privatization of social security funds. This cut deeply into the economic base of old-age security, health care, credit, and housing of all white-collar employees. Another was the dismemberment and privatization of education. Until 1973 Chile had a high quality (and generally free and accessible) public education system, reputedly one of the best in Latin America. When the national public education system was transferred to the municipalities, which were headed by military-appointed mayors, both the quality of education and the economic status of schoolteachers (another important segment of the middle classes) declined considerably.

Instead, and in sharp contrast with the past, quality education was made accessible exclusively to those able to pay for it. In the same vein, university education was distorted with political interference, forceful closures, arbitrary firings (*exoneraciones*), the hiring of "politically reliable" personnel, military rectors, etc., as to leave the university system virtually in shambles. Especially affected in this anti-intellectual crusade was the highly prestigious University of Chile, traditionally the cradle of the country's professional middle classes.

MILITARY GUARDIANSHIP:
THE PARALLEL STATE

Conversely, since the coup, the armed forces have enhanced their role in society. They did so by expanding the economic and cultural basis for their reproduction as a social group. In fact, they turned themselves into the leading and best organized and recognized segment of the middle class[18] as the guardians of an elitist and vertically ordained socio-economic order. In this sense, they became a de facto surrogate political class (as well as a surrogate middle class).

The officer class also radically changed its position and function in society and in the political system. Once a component of the public sector – an armed bureaucracy generally subordinated to constitutional authority – the military evolved not only into a virtually autonomous "state within the state" but into the state itself. Their mission was also radically altered. From a relatively small national force largely concerned with defending the territorial sovereignty of the state from external aggression, the officers mutated into a highly efficient, not to mention exceedingly costly, occupation force of their own society at war with an "internal enemy."

The transformation of the military into a super police force had profound effects on the nature of the state and its relation to the civil society. First, it seriously compromised the real security of the nation, understood as the sovereign pursuit of the "national interest." Second, it created an immediate law-and-order problem by confusing regular policing and crime prevention with the more "glamorous" counter-insurgency. This problem expressed itself simultaneously in a sharp expansion of state-sponsored criminality and an ostensible decline in public ethics. Third, and most grievously, is the irreparable damage to the bond of trust between the military and civil society. All this has weakened the authority of the state and fractured, rather than unified, the nation. Military rule in no uncertain terms induced a process of political de-development and de-institutionalization, whose long-term consequences are still felt.

Either the Pinochet regime counted on the firm support of the U.S. government as it demolished parliamentary democracy, or, at worst, the White House did not pursue an openly and effectively hostile policy towards the regime. Business and military sympathies for the authoritarian regime were persistently high in the United States.[19] Only when an overall policy of "democratic transition" for the entire region was unfolded did Pinochet become an embarrassment. At this stage, a centrist government appeared as the best political alternative.

CIVILIAN SUPPORT
FOR AUTHORITARIANISM

There is a persistent anti-democratic feature of Chilean politics: the existence of a significant constituency, both military *and* civilian, that supports the authoritarian-capitalist model. This constituency is not only important in numbers, but its intensity and resources (especially if bullets are added to ballots, something that democratic governments cannot do) provide a more than adequate level of support. In the years after the coup, the once declining electoral strength of the right rose significantly.

Conversely, the long period of repression, legal entanglements drafted by the military regime, and the almost total prohibition from political activity severely affected the political forces that depended heavily on grassroots voting. The centre, while holding its own, largely stagnated. For the left in general, proscription meant disaster.[20] Not only did their numbers dwindle, but the very nature of the left changed: it became more elitist and had enormous difficulties reaching an atomized labour constituency.

The deflation of the centre and the left translated into an even greater *relative* support for authoritarianism. In the 1988 plebiscite, which Pinochet lost, such support amounted to 43 per cent of the electorate. In the elections of 1989 and 1993, the figures remained at over one-third. The centre-left Christian Democratic-Socialist coalition, which has been in power since 1990, has retained the "moral upper ground" but is internally weak. In addition, it possesses low organicity and has an extremely limited capacity to mobilize support beyond the realm of electoral politics.

There are numerous explanations for the authoritarian tendencies in Chilean society. Most important is the ability of the economic right to control the media. The main newspaper chains, radio-stations, and television stations have remained in the hands of basically the same apologists of the Pinochet regime as during the authoritarian era. Alternative, middle-of-the-road, and leftist publications languish without an appropriate market for their ideas. The climate of uncertainty and fear cultivated by years of military repression also remains. Even today, the Allende years evoke in many an indescribable irrational horror, as something to be prevented at any cost.

There is an entire generation of Chileans – in fact, most of the electorate – that has not yet had democratic exposure. Anti-democratic propaganda has been, and continues to be, very clever and subliminal. Significant numbers of people either deny the atrocities committed or justify them in terms of fear or "necessity." These "authoritarians" are found among the better-off upper and upper middle classes as well as the alienated "popular" sectors. Although those who objectively benefitted from the Pinochet regime are greatly outnumbered by those who experienced deprivation, the ideological illusion of "order" still plays a major role in Chilean politics.

AN ENTRENCHED
COUNTER-REVOLUTION

The historical project developed by the dictatorship and its allies inside and outside Chile was institutionalized and finetuned for nearly two decades. Though since 1990 the country has operated by design and default under elected governments, the economic, social, and political effects of "authoritarian modernization" have been thoroughgoing for the whole of Chilean society. In its most fundamental terms, this project and its procedural mechanisms – including Pinochet's "tailor-made" constitution – have been maintained after the negotiated exit of the general by then President Aylwin in 1989.[21]

Institutionally we can witness the paradox of a legitimate government managing an authoritarian state with anti-democratic "preserves" and exceedingly weak political brokerage. The transition process has been the result of a pact of elites from which most of the civil society has been excluded. In negotiations and pacts the old regime maintained "meta-power" by controlling and redefining the rules of the game, and subsequent democratically elected governments have accepted the constitutional, institutional, and socio-economic order laid out during the previous regime.

THE CHILEAN MODEL IN PERSPECTIVE

The movement from democratic transition to consolidation in Chile has been a painfully slow and frustrating process. Some could argue that what has really taken place since 1990 is the consolidation of the 1973 counterrevolution. Democracy in Chile is still conditional: a concession by the authoritarian regime to those who won in the electoral arena in 1988, 1989, 1993, and, by a pitifully narrow margin, in January 2000. Chile's road to democracy is still sluggish and uncertain.

Perceptive observers of Chilean affairs in the early 1960s, such as Frederick Pike, noted the growing chasm between elites and non-elites in the sharply divided Chilean society. The military regime widened and entrenched this gap. My observations of the patterns of social relations and urban settlement in contemporary Chile lead me to accept the hypothesis of "two Chiles." These two "worlds" are internally heterogeneous, complex, and stratified; nevertheless, they are unified in their separateness.

About one-third of the population comprising a European, affluent, well-educated, well-housed, well cared for, consumption-intensive, upper middle and upper class in Chile. They dwell in neighbourhoods of quality housing comparable to those of the First World, with all the proper amenities, landscaping, and facilities present in cities like Toronto, San Francisco, Sydney, or Amsterdam. They enjoy the benefits of a modern way of life and can expect themselves and their children to live "within the law" in relative – yet eroding – security.

Then there is the other Chile, making up roughly the other two-thirds of the population. It is largely *métis*, poor or impoverished, unemployed, discriminated against, with limited access to educational, health, and mobility opportunities. Despite appearances, it is deprived of effective political representation and is alienated from the channels of power and influence. It makes up the internal "Third World" of labour reserves "below the law," to which growing segments of the white-collar (and allegedly more "European") vanishing middle classes must be now added.

Between these two worlds, there exists a sort of economic, social, cultural, and even racial apartheid, mediated only by the exigencies of a low-wage economy. More often than not, violence, including that of everyday life, fills the void. For many years, a form of top-down – and largely above "the law" – repressive violence maintained this sepa-rateness. But "bottom-up" violence is present in the form of anomic, insurrectional and also purely criminal violence. In my view, this process of national disintegration, combined with an increased process of transnationalization of both the "modern" socioeconomic formations and the state is at the very core of Chile's vulnerability and, conse-quently, insecurity.

As long as these "two solitudes" coexist, Chile will be structurally a stalemate society in which growing frustration, extreme socio-political tensions, and loss for support for *any* government, will be in the cards. Lack of governance breeds ungovernability. At present, neither a dramatic loss of popular support for the elected government nor the fracturing of the centre-left alliance are improbable. Should either of these scenarios unfold, the government will have no recourse but to depend upon the "patriotic" support of the political and social organization of the right and, of course, the armed forces. This could only enhance polarization and shatter the hopes for stable democracy. It would also reveal the intrinsic fallacies extant in the pretended Chilean model.

If the Chilean experience is in any way paradigmatic, it is in pointing out the grave problems and mounting tensions contained in processes of controlled democratic transition that are accompanied by IMF-style "structural adjustments" and transnationalization,[22] leading to restricted democracies and the emergence of "receiver states." The latter act as warrantors, debt collectors, and insurance policies of last resort for an elitist arrangement that is, in theory and practice, unstable. Chile is perhaps the most successful example of the Latin American "liberal-democratic" hybrid, but it still remains an imposition by force of a modus operandi whose effects are less than salutary and unsustainable for the bulk of its people.

NOTES

1 The *New York Times*, editorial, 18 March 1991. Also Jonathan Kandell, "Prosperity Born of Pain," *The New York Times Magazine*, 7 July 1991, 15–16. Similar praises have come from Peruvian novelist and former presidential candidate Mario Vargas Llosa: "Chile será muy pronto un país desarrollado, dijo Vargas Llosa," *La Epoca*, 17 April 1991, 10.

2 See James Whelan, "What Canadians could learn from Chile's strong economy," *The Toronto Star*, Sunday, 2 January 1995, D4, D5.

3 "Chile Security Chief was CIA Informer," BBC *News*, internet service 19 September 2000, 23:24 GMT, 00:24 UK.

4 The "seven modernizations" predicated by the institutional intellectuals of the former military regime constitute the pillars of the project of the so-called "Chicago Boys," along the lines of theories spoused by Milton Friedman and Friedrich von Hayek, who served as mentors of the regime. The modernizations included: 1) new labour legislation; 2) the transformation of the social security system; 3) the municipalization of education; 4) the privatization of health-care; 5) the internationalization of agriculture; 6) the transformation of the judiciary; and 7) the decentralization and regionalization of government administration. See Patricio Silva, "Technocrats and Politics in Chile: from the Chicago Boys to the CIEPLAN Monks," *Journal of Latin American Studies*, no. 23 (1991), 389–96.

5 For a more elaborate analysis of transition, see my piece with
   N. Galleguillos "Chile: Redemocratization or the Entrenchment of
   Counter-Revolution?" in Archibald Ritter, Maxwell Cameron, and David
   Pollock , *Latin America to the Year 2000: Reactivating Growth, Improving Equity, Sustaining Democracy*, New York: Praeger, 1992, 177–93.
6 See Transparency International, "Bribe Payers Index and Corruption
   perception Index 1999," Internet document: http://www.transparency.de
   (20 January 2000).
7 See Canadian Embassy (Chile), Commercial Division, several issues
   of "Chile," 1995–2000; also *The Economist* Intelligence Unit, *Chile.
   Country Report. Annual Survey of Political* and *Economic Back-
   ground*, London: EIU, 1990; also CEPAL, *Anuario Estadístico de
   América Latina y el Caribe*, Santiago: Publicaciones de las Naciones
   Unidas, 1990, 489–90 and Chile, *Boletín del Banco Central*, various
   monthly issues 1984–2000. The inflation for recent years reveal a
   marked declining trend, from about 20 to less than 5 per cent. This
   sharply contrasts with an average inflation rate of over 200 per cent
   for the Latin American continent.
8 See Oscar Altimir, "Income Distribution and Poverty Through Crisis
   and Adjustment," *CEPAL Review*, no. 52 (April 1994), 17.
9 See Michael Mortimore, *Negotiating Dependency: The State and TNCs
   in the Context of the Political Economy of Colombian Development*,
   unpublished Ph.D. thesis, Department of Political Science, University
   of Toronto, 1985, 452–83.
10 See Comisión Económica para América Latina y el Caribe (CEPAL),
   Una estimación de la magnitud la pobreza en Chile 1987, Santiago:
   CEPAL, División de Estadística y Proyecciones, 1990. Using real per
   capita income growth data from UN sources for 1970 and 1987,
   a comparison of trends in income and poverty can be made:

	1970	1987	17-year change	Annual increase
Index of GNP per capita	100.0	105.6	5.6	0.3
Index of poverty	100.0	224.1	124.1	7.2

This means that poverty grew in the period over twenty times faster than income.

11 Orlando Letelier, "The Chicago Boys in Chile: Economic Freedom's
   Awful Toll," *The Nation*, 29 August 1976; also Silva, "Technocrats and
   Politics," 385–410.
12 For a succinct overview of the capitalization of agriculture, see Polo
   Díaz and Tanya Korovkin, "Neo Liberalism in Agriculture: Capitalist
   Modernization in the Chilean Countryside" in N. Galleguillos and
   J. Nef, guest editors, *Chile – Le Chili*, Special Issues of the *Canadian*

Journal of Latin American and Caribbean Studies 15, no. 30 (1990), 197–220.

13 See Javier Martínez and Eugenio Tironi, *Clase Obrera y Modelo Económico. Un Estudio del Peso y Estructura del Proletariado en Chile*, Santiago: PET-Academia de Humanismo Cristiano, January 1983, 241–3; also Fernando Leyva and James Petras, "Chile's Poor in the Struggle for Democracy," *Latin American Perspectives* 13, no. 4 (Fall 1986), 4–21.

14 See J. Nef, "El concepto de estado subsidario y la educacion como bien de Mercado," Revista *Enfoques Educacionales* 2, no. 2 (1999–2000), 89–98.

15 For an analysis of the ideological hybrid of the authoritarian regime, see Renato Cristi and Carlos Ruíz, "Conservative Thought in Twentieth Century Chile," in Galleguillos and Nef, "Chile," 27–76. For a treatment of the subject of "revolutionary conservatism" or "reactionary modernism" in the German context, see Jeffrey Herf, *Reactionary Modernism. Technology, Culture and Politics in Weimar and the Third Reich*, Cambridge: Cambridge University Press, 1984. In Chile, the roots of this ideology go far back to the conservative and protofascist "historical revisionists" of the earlier twentieth century such as F.A. Encina, Alberto Edwards, Mario Góngora, Osvaldo Lira, and others. The late Senator Jaime Guzmán, and founder member of Independent Democratic Union (UDI), was the main intellectual architect of Pinochet's "Authoritarian Republic," expressed in the 1980 constitution. Clearly inspired by corporatism, Catholic integralism, the U.S.-made "national security doctrine" and neo-liberal economic principles, Guzmán's greater task was to provide for a framework to integrate these diverse discourses in one common political "software."

16 A table of government expenses between 1972 and 1988 illustrates this change of priorities:

	1972	1988	Variation
	%	%	Index
Defence	6.1	10.4	+70.0
Education	14.3	12.0	−16.0
Health	8.2	6.3	−23.0
Housing, Social Security, and Welfare	39.8	39.2	−3.0
Economic Services	15.3	11.2	−27.0
Other	16.3	20.9	+28.0
Total Government Expenditure as % of GNP	43.7	33.4	−24.0

Source: The Economist Intelligence Unit, *Chile 1990*, London: EIU, 1990.

17 For a study of the evolution and structure of social security in Chile, see CEPAL, *El desarrollo de la seguridad social en América Latina,* Estudios e Informes de la CEPAL No. 43, Santiago: Naciones Unidas, 1985, chap. 4, "Chile," 99–133. For a "P.R." overview from the perspective of the private managers of Chile's social security funds (AFPS), see "Los nuevos dueños de Chile" and "Un cumpleaños feliz," *El Mercurio,* Sección Economía y Negocios, Sunday, 14 April, 1991, F1, F16. For an uncritical analysis of the social security reform, see a report by Marco Santamaría, reprint no. 20138 of *The Columbia Journal of World Business* (Spring 1992), 39–51.

18 The security establishment of the Ministry of National Defence, includes the army, some 50,000 strong, the navy (30,000), the air force (about 15,000) and the *Carabineros* police (about 30,000). There is no civilian police as such. The figure for 1988–89 includes 33,000 conscripts on a two-year compulsory duty. The length of conscription was increased from one to two years after the 1973 coup. By law, 9 per cent of all proceeds from copper exports goes directly to financing the armed forces (the estimate for 1988 was $200 million U.S.). In addition, Chile possesses a small but active "military-industrial complex" in the form of a number of dynamic enterprises such as the privately owned Cardoen, located in Iquique and the army-owned FAMAE in Santiago. The military has also the de-facto control of numerous "military zones" under their exclusive jurisdiction and outside the effective control of the central government, including an operational nuclear research station in Lo Aguirre, in the outskirts of Santiago. This makes the defence establishment one of the major holdings of real estate in the country. Unless otherwise indicated, data and estimates on armed forces come from the International Institute for Strategic Studies, *The Military Balance 1989–1990,* (London: IISS, 1989, 186–8 and from Ruth Leger Sivard, *World Military and Social Expenditures 1987–88,* Washington: World Priorities, 1987, 46. The figure for 1965 was obtained from the U.S. Arms Control and Disarmament Agency, *World Military Expenditures 1969,* Washington: ACDA, 1969. The figures for 1973 and 1981 came from the U.S. Department of the Army, *Chile. A Country Study,* 2nd ed., (Washington: U.S. Department of the Army, 1982), 151.

19 Some of the best direct sources are the U.S. Senate Special Committee on Intelligence Activities, *Report of the Committee. Covert Action in Chile,* under the chairmanship of senator from Idaho Frank Church, 1976 and the *ITT Papers,* published in Spanish under the title *Los Documentos Secretos de la ITT,* Santiago: Quimantú, 1971. A useful insight is former U.S. ambassador Edward Korry's testimony of 27 March 1973 to the U.S. Senate Sub-committee on Multinational

Corporations of the Committee of Foreign Relations, chaired also by Senator Frank Church, *Multinational Corporations and United States Foreign Policy: The International Telephone and Telegraph Company in Chile, 1970–71*, part 1, 277–318. A longer version appeared in *Penthouse* (May 1977). Also see Victor Marchetti and John Marks, *The CIA and the Cult of Intelligence*, New York: A. Knopf, 1975, 38–43, 330–1, Anthony Sampson's *The Sovereign State of ITT*, Greenwich: Fawcett, 1974, Donald Freed with Fred Landis, *Death in Washington: The Murder of Orlando Letelier*, Westport: Lawrence, Hill & Co., 1980, and Armando Uribe's *The Black Book of American Intervention in Chile*, Boston: Beacon Press, 1975.

20 A thirty year trend of voting preferences illustrates of this decline of the left and the "assisted" recovery of the Right.

Voting Trends

	1957	1965	1969	1973	1988	1989
% population registered						
% registered voters	18.0	34.8		44.5	61.0	59.0
Voting turnout						
as participating	35.9	69.5		81.2	92.1	94.5
% of population	12.3	27.4	20.9	36.3	57.7	55.8
% rightist vote	33.0	12.9	20.9	23.6	43.0	40.7
PDC vote	9.4	43.6	31.3	29.1		26.1
% PR vote	22.1	17.7	13.4	5.5		3.8
% centre: (PDC+PR)	31.5	61.3	44.7	34.6		51.4
% centre left					54.7	57.6
% leftist vote	10.7	23.3	29.4	38.9		5.2

21 For an analysis of the ideological continuities of the institutional intellectuals of both the military regime and the present Christian Democratic administration see Silva, *"Technocrats and Politics,"* 385–410.

22 For a discussion of the contradiction between national development and transnational capitalism, see Osvaldo Sunkel's classical piece, *"Transnational Capitalism and National Disintegration in Latin America," Social and Economic Studies* no. 1 (March 1973), 140–50; also J. Nef and W. Robles, "Globalization, Neoliberalism and the State of Underdevelopment in the New Periphery," *Journal of Developing Societies* 16, fasc. 1 (2000), 27–48.

The New World Order and the Destruction of Public Education: The Case of Canada

JENNIFER SUMNER

We need to remember that the vast majority of our public institutions were once the property of the private sector. They were made public precisely because it was determined through past experience that this was the only effective way to ensure that the institutions would serve the needs of all Canadians, regardless of their individual wealth, on the basis of equity, compassion and human rights.[1]

Public education, like the rest of the public sector, is under siege in Canada. Along with such publicly funded institutions as health care and transportation, education is being slowly starved by deliberate withdrawal of funding, making it ripe for privatization by the corporate market. That takeover would return us, full circle, to the time when education was not a human right but a privilege for those who could afford to pay for it.

The reason education has been targeted for privatization is simple: globally, education is worth $2 trillion annually; in Canada, it is worth $60 billion.[2] But this windfall is inaccessible to private interests as long as it remains within the public sector. Moving it to the private sector can be accomplished with the kind of restructuring that is the hallmark of the New World Order.

THE NEW WORLD ORDER

The New World Order has its roots in the aftermath of the Second World War. In his speech entitled "Whose World Order: Conflicting Visions," Noam Chomsky[3] argues that the United States had an overwhelming share of global wealth and power at the end of the war, and "dominant forces within the state-corporate nexus in the United States planned to use that power to organize the world as much as they could in accord with their own conceptions." Their plan worked so well that by 1991, with the fall of the Soviet Union and the rise of the corporate agenda, George Bush Sr could announce with confidence that a New World Order had arrived.

A euphemism that hides the power of transnational corporations, the New World Order is enforced through a set of policies that ensure corporate dominance. These policies seek to lower corporate taxes and accommodate international flows of speculative capital, deregulate business and secure monopoly private property rights under law, and reduce public expenditures and privatize public services.[4] This last policy mechanism most directly affects public education.

EDUCATION AND THE PUBLIC SECTOR

Education in Canada has a proud history within the public sector, whether through mandatory public and secondary schooling for all children, subsidized higher education, or opportunities for lifelong learning such as distance education, adult education, and extension education. Publicly funded education has also been associated with the notion of the public good, which "refers to actions taken in the interest of all citizens."[5]

A Canadian think tank called the Caledon Institute of Social Policy lists the contributions that public education can make to the public good:

- High-quality public education advances the well-being of all citizens and helps us accomplish some of our most cherished public purposes.
- Public education is necessary to the economic health of both individuals and nations.
- Public education creates informed consumers who can make intelligent choices as to the products they wish to purchase.
- Public education involves the acquisition of moral and spiritual power. It builds the foundation of nations by helping students develop values related to the welfare society – values such as honesty, truth, civility, social justice, cooperation, and a determination to combat violence, racism, gender inequality, and environmental degradation.
- Public education is the great equalizer, with educational institutions being a place where individuals of diverse backgrounds can come together. It is, by definition, an inclusive system. It provides the glue of shared values and history, providing citizens with a sense of what it means to be Canadian.

- Public education is not only the foundation for an informed intelligent citizenry, which comprises the bedrock of democracy, but also a distinguishing practice of a society that can be properly called democratic.[6]

However, the notion of the public good has fallen out of favour in recent years because it contradicts the unfettered individualism that characterizes the New World Order. According to Nef and Robles,[7] the collectivist concept of the public good is to be replaced with a view of the public good as "individual responsibility." This responsibility means that those who are unable to fend for themselves are blamed for their own problems and left largely on their own to solve them.

Through an ideology that demonizes the public sector, the corporate agenda champions privatization as the only "efficient" option for education. But as Susan George[8] points out, privatization simply involves transferring "wealth from the public purse – which would redistribute it to even out social inequalities – to private hands." And it is the transfer to private hands that precludes education working for the public good, that is, in the interest of all citizens.

One of the logical outcomes of such a privatizing transfer is the emergence of education management organizations (EMOS). Modelled on the health management organizations (HMOS) in the United States, these private, for-profit corporations run a school board or a university like a business, looking for the largest output with the smallest input or, in other words, the largest profit for the smallest amount of education provision.

How does the corporate agenda of privatization play out in Canadian education? In spite of the wide variety of educational situations in Canada, the impacts of this agenda are essentially the same across the country. It merely manifests itself in different ways, according to the local context. The impacts follow a familiar pattern: defunding or underfunding, which provokes a crisis in the public education institutions, which in turn engenders a restructuring that either forces them into unequal "partnerships" with private corporations or eliminates them completely. Either way, the public good is replaced by the corporate interest, which benefits a minority of shareholders and top-level managers instead of all Canadians.

PUBLIC AND SECONDARY EDUCATION

The assault on public and secondary education in Canada takes many forms, from teacher bashing and outsourcing to crowded classrooms and narrowed curriculums. Trade agreements such as NAFTA, right-wing think tanks like the Fraser Institute, and business alliances such as the Canadian Council of Chief Executives (formely the BCNI) pressure variously compliant provincial governments into the corporate agenda of privatization. One example of the inroads of privatization is the emergence of the charter school, which represents the application of market principles to education while remaining outside any collective agreements or community control. However, New Zealand's experience with charter schools should provide a warning to Canadians. In that country, every public school was turned into a charter school, which resulted in the middle class "shopping" for schools for their children while the poor and the less mobile were left in ghettoized neighbourhood schools. As a result of this restructuring, 1,000 teachers left the system and one out of every five principals quit.[9]

The United States provides another warning of the privatization of public and secondary education through the example of Education Alternatives Inc (EAI), a corporation that privatizes the management and operation of public schools and only accepts contracts that allow it to use its own employees and curriculum. The American Federation of Teachers produced a scathing report of EAI's management of Baltimore schools, citing staff cuts, increased class sizes, replacement of paraprofessionals with low-paid interns, and diversion of classroom funding for overhead, lawyers, accountants, corporate travel, and profit.[10]

The penetration of the corporate agenda into the public sector is clearly evidenced by the spread of YNN, the Youth News Network, into the public school system. A private commercial news and current affairs network, YNN provides Canadian schools with televisions, audio-visual equipment, and computers in exchange for airing its 12.5-minute "newscast" and 2.5 minutes of commercials in all classrooms for at least eighty per cent of the academic year.[11] The Peel Board of Education in Ontario, for example, has already built YNN into its school classrooms, with compulsory ad-watching, and ad volumes and student attendance enforced by school principals.[12] Although YNN was at first outrightly rejected by the Quebec minister of Education on the grounds that it was contrary to Article 94 of the Education Act ("commercial solicitation contrary to the mission of the school"), the minister was compelled to review the decision, and three schools had YNN by 1999. A number of questions naturally arise in such a situation: Whose point of view is supported in the newscasts? What values are being passed on to school children? What becomes seen as the norm in Canadian classrooms – the caring society or the consumer society? What kind of teaching is put into place to offset the effects of such indoctrination?

While some schools are forced into corporate alliances for survival, others are deemed superfluous and closed. In the province of Ontario, for example, the Conservative government has a policy of closing rural public and secondary schools, declaring them to be "inefficient." Placing money values above life values, it can find no importance in the role these schools play in the web of rural life. There is no recognition of the uniqueness of rural communities or the superior pedagogical outcomes of rural schools.[13]

HIGHER EDUCATION

Higher education is the cream of the privatization opportunities for transnational corporations, representing billions of dollars of profit, ready access to public money, and enhanced prestige through association with university imprimaturs. In the so-called knowledge economy that is part of the New World Order, higher education is touted as the route to prosperity and success.

However, the corporate agenda of privatization has sinister implications for higher education. Canadian academic James Robert Brown[14] describes what privatization and the business model mean to faculty members:

increased dependence on industry and philanthropy for operating the university; an increased amount of our resources being directed to applied or so-called practical subjects, both in teaching and in research; a proprietary treatment of research results, with the commercial interest in secrecy overriding the public's interest in free, shared knowledge; and an attempt to run the university more like a business that treats industry and students as clients and ourselves [faculty] as service providers with something to sell.

From the point of view of the public as a whole, the privatization of higher education has even wider repercussions. Shaker[15] outlines a number of them. First, privatization will result in prohibitive tuition costs. Instead of being seen as a basic human right, education will become an increasingly expensive commodity. Already the tuition fees at private institutions are two to three times the fees at public ones. Second, students attending private institutions of higher learning have higher defaults on loan repayments than those attending public universities and colleges. Third, unlike other OECD countries, Canadian business finds it much more cost effective to simply eliminate on-the-job training and leave it to public education, which in the case of higher education means that the public sector foots the training bill for business. With private institutions, the individual students pay the job-training bill. In either case, the corporations benefit from an education system that is increasingly geared to lower those crucial input costs that will result in higher output. Fourth, existing evidence shows that private institutions stay in business as long as they make money and will cut costs accordingly in order to increase shareholder profits, with little attention to academic quality. When they no longer make a profit, they close or move elsewhere, leaving students who have paid enormous fees without an education. Fifth, regardless of the rhetoric, private institutions benefit from public subsidies because all students can claim 17 per cent of their tuition fees as a non-refundable tax credit, regardless of the amount of those fees.

University research is an indicator of the changes that the corporate agenda is bringing to higher education. Forced alliances with private interests have restructured the research carried out at institutions of higher education. For example, research was traditionally publicly funded at the Ontario Agricultural College at the University of Guelph. In the early 1990s, however, university policy quietly changed and half of all research funding was required to come from private interests. Without the input of private funding, no public funding would be forthcoming. The predictable result is a systematic censorship of scientific research itself. Research that supports corporate interests and produces products or knowledge that can be commercialized and sold by corporations for a profit is selected. Research is not done for the public good (such as precautionary testing of the safety of genetically modified organisms) because no private interest would ever fund such research. In fact, as Noam Chomsky[16] pointed out in his convocation speech after accepting an honorary doctorate from the University of Guelph in 1999, the public good is incidental when it comes to research in the commercialized university.

And while it may appear that corporations revitalize institutions of higher education with their capital inputs for research, in reality that investment is repaid many times over in the form of unlimited access to publicly funded resources such as research grants, laboratories, and highly educated personnel. For example, at the University of Guelph, it is estimated that the roughly $10 million (1998 figures) that industry invests annually to support proprietary research allows it to leverage a healthy chunk of the roughly $250 million taxpayer investment at the university.[17]

One of the spinoffs of the corporate research agenda now controlling universities is closed thesis defences. Traditionally open to the public as part of the pursuit of public knowledge, some thesis defences are now closed to everyone except those who are willing to sign a document promising they will not reveal what they have heard without the express permission of the researcher. This abrogation of the defining tradition of the academy – shared knowledge and open debate – has been permitted because "from time to time a student will develop significant intellectual property in the course of his or her research and wishes, legitimately, to protect that property until it can be patented or published in a particular format."[18] Such a departure begs the question of public ownership of knowledge produced at public institutions. And while some may find it "legitimate" to privatize public knowledge, such privatization not only contravenes the mission of many institutions of higher learning but also contributes to the destruction of public education and undermines the public good.

Brown argues that it will not only take strong leadership in the university to protect research from the eroding effects of commercial concerns but also require massive government protection and promotion of public knowledge: "Patent laws, for instance, must not allow the privatization of the public good. University research must be funded overwhelmingly from the public purse. And the public – rather than corporations or individual scientists (or even secretive governments) – must own the results."[19] Higher education in Canada has often promoted the public good, but the penetration of the corporate agenda into this part of the public sector has forced a restructuring favouring disciplines that directly support corporations over those that do not. Couched in the rhetoric of skills development, development that helps to cut the costs of corporate on-the-job training, government policy skews funding choices away from the humanities and liberal arts. Such choices "miss the real utility of a liberal arts education: the development of general analytic and writing abilities," which is so valuable to industry, government, and the larger community.[20]

When asked where such funding choices left a liberal arts education, Noam Chomsky replied that it came down to a question of values: "Do we want universities to be places where people come to grips with human affairs, cultural tradition, and the problems that people face? Do we want them to be a place for advancing and understanding society? Do we want them to be a place for creative work? Or, do we simply want students to be servants of private power?"[21] In other words, we need to ask ourselves whether higher education should reflect and promote something more than just money values as the "regulating objective of thought and action."[22]

LIFELONG LEARNING

Lifelong learning is the process by which individuals continue to develop their knowledge, skills, and attitudes over their lifetime.[23] Although something of a catchphrase, lifelong learning represents the ongoing thirst for knowledge and dedication to learning that has characterized humans for thousands of years. Lifelong learning is becoming increasingly popular around the world, and Canada is no exception. Within this country, distance education, adult education, and extension education are three significant manifestations of lifelong learning. Each has a history within the public sector, and each is feeling the privatizing pressures of the corporate agenda.

Distance Education

Distance education could be said to be the Trojan horse of the New World Order as it invades public education. Based on a learning experience that can be easily packaged and sold, distance education has a long history of serving corporate interests, from its beginnings in fly-by-night private institutions to its current endorsement by cash-strapped universities.[24] Distance education tends to be content-heavy, top-down, monological, and technologically driven, all of which contribute to its potential for commodification. With millions of students enrolled worldwide and the market for distance learning estimated at US$300 billion,[25] this potential has not been lost on transnational corporations.

For example, huge multinationals like Disney, Microsoft, and Time-Warner are currently exploring links with a number of American education institutions to create teaching materials for distance learning and to supply the technology to deliver them around the world.[26] Thompson, the Canadian electronic publishing group, has recently reached a deal with the eighteen-member worldwide university network, Universitas 21 (which includes three Canadian universities: McGill University, University of Toronto, and University of British Columbia), to deliver e-degrees.[27] A number of American universities involved in distance education are lending their names to private corporations in exchange for revenues from financial speculation in the education industry through stock options and initial private offerings.[28] And Canada's Department of Foreign Affairs and International Trade organized a distance education seminar at a Mexican university to, among other things, "help to develop business opportunities."[29]

Will such corporatized distance education ever have the potential to contribute to the public good, or will it "only represent the educational companion to economic globalization"?[30]

Adult Education

Unlike distance education, adult education in Canada has a long history of working for the public good. Educational experiences such as the

Women's Institutes, the Antigonish Movement, the National Farm Radio Forum, and Frontier College have made Canadian adult education famous around the world.

But the pressures of the New World Order have penetrated the emancipatory vision of adult education, leaving some to speculate whether such pressures are "tying adult education predominantly to vocational and technical matters and requiring it to be a slave to the cash register."[31] Others are even more pessimistic, contending that adult education, outside of those forms needed for market adjustment and maximization, is being left on the sidelines.[32]

The implications of the corporate agenda are far reaching and sinister, with the potential to affect every aspect of adult education.[33] Its role in society would become one of service to the global market. Funding would no longer be the duty of the state but of the individual. Governance would not involve democratic decision-making and popular input, but decision-making guided by market demand. Access would be restricted to those who could pay, while those unable to pay would either go into debt or do without. Adult education curriculum would limit both the choice and range of subjects to those relevant to market demand, with courses becoming vehicles for corporate advertising and course materials covered with corporate logos. Teaching would involve adapting students to the needs of the global market, while learning would narrow to "learning for earning," with no critical or transformative potential. Outcomes would involve quantification and ownership – how little input is required to achieve how much output. Couched in the rhetoric of inevitability, the corporate agenda seems poised to completely engulf adult education in Canada today, sweeping aside its historic contribution to the public good and turning it into one more product for sale in the global market.

Extension Education

Extension education has a long history in Canada because of its farming heritage. Described as "a public investment in the ability of agriculture to voluntarily incorporate public goals,"[34] extension education was originally set up in institutions of higher education as a means of improving the education of rural people. It formed a bridge between institutions of higher education and the community, bringing the results of cutting-edge agricultural research to farming practice.

But like other forms of lifelong learning, extension education is feeling the pressures of the New World Order. According to Lauzon, "the meaning of education has changed from being a *right* that is an inherent part of a civilized and democratic society to being a *product* or *service* to be purchased by a consumer. University extension is not immune from this shift; in fact, it is leading the way in the promotion of marketplace values in the university and in the public arena."[35] As discussed previously, part of that shift is a change in the research carried out at institutions of higher education. The production of knowledge for the public good has historically contributed to the overall fund of public knowledge. However, such "free" knowledge is incompatible with the corporate agenda because private interests cannot compete against this unpriced public good. For this reason, knowledge for the public good is being eliminated and replaced by the production of knowledge that can be privatized, commodified, and sold in the global market.

One of the first casualties of this new research agenda has been extension education, with its transfer of public knowledge from the researcher through the extension worker to the farmer. In Ontario, extension education was completely eliminated in the early 1990s. Its demise has left farmers without a fresh source of knowledge, which leaves them dependent on the propaganda of fertilizer and pesticide corporations – some of the largest transnational corporations in the world. In other provinces, extension education is metamorphosing into professional education and career development,[36] both of which reflect and promote the corporate agenda.

In essence, under the pressures of the New World Order, "university extension as community service simply will not be allowed to survive in the new entrepreneurial university if it refuses to or cannot deliver profits."[37]

RESURRECTING THE COMMONS

With the public sector under siege and education being restructured to serve not the public good but corporate interests, the New World Order seems to be ascendant in Canada. Money, not life, has become the "regulating objective of thought and action," and this value orientation drives the decisions made about the public sector. How can such an anti-life orientation be overcome? The answer begins with the age-old notion of the commons.

As an area of land for use by the public, the term "commons" originated in feudal England, where the "waste," or uncultivated land, of a lord's manor could be used for pasture and firewood by his tenants.[38] However, the commons has a long history in many countries as "nature-given land or resource."[39]

In 1968, Garrett Hardin, a professor of biology, wrote an article entitled "The Tragedy of the Commons," in which he argued that the commons could not work as a concept because of human greed. After projecting the self-maximizing principle of neo-classical economics onto social formations that precisely reject its self-centred value system, he advocated that "the tragedy of the commons as a food basket is averted by private property, or something formally like it."[40]

Philosopher James Robert Brown has overturned Hardin's notion of the tragedy of the commons by arguing that the real tragedy is not the overexploitation of common resources but their privatization – in Brown's case, the tragedy of the commons is the privatization of the university.[41] He, among others, is resurrecting the idea of the commons, discredited since Hardin's neo-liberal dismissal. Allied with notions of the public good, the commons is finally enjoying a long-awaited return, as is shown by this statement from the Caledon Institute of Social Policy: "It is in the public interest to protect the public good. The air and water that comprise the natural commons are essential components of life. Perhaps we need to understand public education as an element of our 'social commons' – as part of the lifeblood of our collective well-being."[42]

THE CIVIL COMMONS

No one has rehabilitated the idea of the commons more incisively than John McMurtry, who has put forward the concept of the civil commons, which he defines as "any co-operative human construction that protects and/or enables the universal access to life goods."[43]

Long with us but unrecognized, the civil commons is "what people ensure together as a society to protect and further life, as distinct from [privately owned] money aggregates."[44] Life-based and life-protective, the civil commons is oriented to life values, not money values. A completely different frame of understanding from the priced consumption of the global market, the civil commons depends on universal accessibility, which means "available without market price or other exclusionary fence to it, where need and choice concur with the common life interest served."[45] Examples of the civil commons include sewage and sanitation systems, water and power installations, sidewalks, bridges, social safety protections, laws, public airwaves, libraries, postal services and social assistance.[46] It also includes public education. In essence, it is "the vast social fabric of unpriced goods, protecting and enabling life in a wide and deep seamless web of historical evolution that sustains society and civilization."[47]

McMurtry emphasizes that "it is important to distinguish between 'the commons' as nature-given land or resource and 'the civil commons' which effectively protects it, and ensures access of all members of the community to its continuing means of existence."[48] In this way, the civil commons is 'civil' "insofar as the common life-good it embodies is protected by conscious and co-operative human agency."[49]

But just as the traditional commons were cleared by acts of enclosure to make way for private profit, so too the civil commons is currently being cleared by the corporate agenda to make way for private profit. "There is now no place in the world, indigenous or industrialized, in which the civil commons is safe from corporate market invasion."[50] One of those sites of corporate market invasion is public education.

PUBLIC EDUCATION
AND THE CIVIL COMMONS

Public education is part of the civil commons because it was created and maintained for the public good by conscious human agency. It is one of those cooperative human constructs that people ensure together as a society to protect and further life. According to McMurtry, "education for all people of a society without barriers of social caste or market cost" is a major institution of a developed civil commons.[51] This means publicly funded education, one that is available to all people. If grounded in life values, "the entire practice of formal education ... can be decoded as the process of judging and enabling more comprehensive levels of thinking across defined breadths and depths of cognition."[52] However, if grounded in money values, these comprehensive levels of thinking are ruled out where they do not result in sustained or increased profit for private corporations. Such grounding in money values is clearly evident under the corporate agenda, where education becomes a business opportunity, not a learning opportunity, a chance to "make a killing," not a chance to increase life capabilities. In the New World Order, education becomes a commodity for sale in the market for those who can afford to buy it – a corporate enterprise instead of a liberating experience.

To counter this *real* tragedy of the commons, we must first of all come to recognize the importance of the civil commons and life values to human and planetary life. Once recognized, they can guide our choices and decisions, and become a touchstone for future action in the world. They can also help us to find our way through the rhetoric and obfuscation that accompany the New World Order, especially the language of inevitability that Canadians seem so susceptible to when it comes to privatizing public education.

Armed with our knowledge of the collective strength of the civil commons, we can refuse to participate in educational experiences that promote corporate interests. We can pressure educational administrators to leave decision-making in public hands, not private ones. We can lobby politicians to keep education as part of the public good. We can wage media campaigns to raise public awareness of the importance of the public sector. We can speak out against lowering taxes, which only drains the public purse that supports the civil commons.

The only way to ensure that our public institutions are equitable, of a high quality, accessible and publicly accountable, is to maintain adequate public funding. We need to ensure the strength and stability of our public educational institutions, not allow a market-based system of education which will by its very nature (and as has been proven by the evidence) reinforce socioeconomic inequities rather than provide a basis from which we can attempt to overcome them.[53]

Above all, we must encourage education that valorizes the public sector, that promotes the public good, and that teaches us to honour the civil commons. It is time to challenge the money values that hold education hostage to a value program that cannot understand the importance of life itself. There is more to living than serving corporate interests, and recognizing our roots in the civil commons is a good place to start.

CONCLUSION

The destruction of public education in Canada is part of the worldwide assault on the civil commons in the New World Order. Just as there has been a long history of relentless expropriation of the natural commons around the world, there is now an ongoing expropriation of the civil commons for private gain through the privatization of explicitly public goods.

As we come to understand the civil commons and its role in the history of human civilization, we can also begin to understand how it is built, and how it is destroyed. Its destruction is not the inevitable expression of "human greed" but the strategically planned outcome of carefully orchestrated media campaigns, policy decisions, and political capitulations to global corporate financial pressures. We have not "lived beyond our means," as we have been so often told, but are being, quite literally, swindled out of our evolved public goods by those who would benefit from their privatization for corporate profit. The corporate agenda is everywhere working to defund and appropriate the civil commons so that we will all be dependent not on the unpriced goods of our shared heritage but on the priced goods of the global market system.

We can see the evidence of this corporate expropriation of public education all around us: crowded classrooms, demonized teachers, narrowed curriculum, logo-infested teaching materials, closed schools, user fees, crumbling infrastructure, ill-paid contract faculty, corporate research, skyrocketing tuition, and privatized knowledge.

The civil commons was expressly built to protect us from the ravages of an unregulated, private-profit economy. Although its expressions can be markedly local, it is a transcultural phenomenon, providing the inherited, shared life-substance of all developed cultures. Public education is perhaps its profoundest expression, as well as its most effective vehicle. It should not be destroyed by the agenda of a global market paradigm that in principle cannot value beyond the corporate bottom line to the well-being and evolving consciousness of life itself.

NOTES

1 Erika Shaker, "Privatizing Higher Education: Profiting from Public Loss," *Ontario Confederation of University Faculty Associations Forum*, Fall 2000, 11.

2 Ibid., 23.

3 Noam Chomsky , "Whose World Order: Conflicting Visions." Speech delivered at the University of Calgary, Alberta, Canada, 22 September 1998. Available at http://www.zmag.org/chomsky/whose_world_order.htm (website of Z magazine).

4 The Globalism Project, Parkland Institute, University of Alberta, Canada, 2001. Available at www.ualberta.ca/~parkland/mcri.html.

5 Sherri Torjman, "Education and the Public Good," Caledon Institute of Social Policy, Communities and Schools Series, April 2000, 1. Available at http://www.caledoninst.org.

6 Ibid., 3–4.

7 Jorge Nef and Wilder Robles, "Globalization, Neoliberalism and the State of Underdevelopment in the New Periphery," *Journal of Developing Societies* 16, fasc. 1 (2000) 38.

8 Susan George, "A Short History of Neo-liberalism: Twenty Years of Elite Economics and Emerging Opportunities for Structural Change." Paper presented at the Conference on Economic Sovereignty in a Globalising World, Bangkok, 24–26 March 1999, 4. Available at http://www.millennium-round.org/Susan%20George.html.

9 Doug Little, "Charter Schools – Making Public Education Private." Global Teach-In: Challenging Corporate Rule. 7–9 November 1997, University of Toronto, Canada.

10 CUPE (Canadian Union of Public Employees), "Corporate Cash-In." Global Teach-In: Challenging Corporate Rule. 7–9 November 1997, University of Toronto, Canada.

11 John Schofield, "Ads Come to Class: Cash-strapped Schools Take a Closer Look at YNN." *Maclean's*, 5 April 1999.

12 Beverley Moore, *The Extent and Impact of Communications Cartels on Public Education: 1980 – 2000*, Ph.D. dissertation, Ontario Institute for Studies in Education of the University of Toronto, 2000.

13 A.C. Lauzon and D. Leahy, "Educational Reform and the Rural Community: An Ontario Perspective." A report prepared for the SRC Research Program, Ontario Ministry of Agriculture, Food and Rural Affairs (Project 023450), 2000, i.

14 James Robert Brown, "Privatizing the University – the New Tragedy of the Commons," *Science* 290 (1 December 2000), 1701.

15 Shaker, "Privatizing Higher Education," 11, 23.

16 Noam Chomsky, Convocation Address to Graduates of the College of Arts, University of Guelph, Canada, 17 February 1999. Reproduced in *At Guelph*, 30 March 1999, 4.

17 Clark, E. Ann, "Academia in the Service of Industry: The Ag Biotech Model." Paper presented at the Canadian Association of University Teachers conference, Universities and Colleges in the Public Interest: Stopping the Commercial Takeover of Post-Secondary Education, Ottawa, Canada, October 1999.

18 Isobel W. Heathcote, private correspondence to author from the dean of the Faculty of Graduate Studies, University of Guelph, Canada, 2000.

19 Brown, "Privatizing the University," 1702.

20 Ibid.

21 Noam Chomsky, "Are Students Servants to a Private Power?" Interview in *Id Magazine*, 25 February – 3 March 1999, 12.

22 John McMurtry, *Unequal Freedoms: The Global Market as an Ethical System*. Toronto: Garamond, 1998, 299.

23 Rosemary Moreland, and Tom Lovett, "Lifelong Learning and Community Development," *International Journal of Lifelong Education* 16, no. 3 (1997), 202.

24 Jennifer Sumner, "Serving the System: A Critical History of Distance Education," *Open Learning* 15, no. 3 (2000.)

25 P. Kingston, "Britain Must Push the Pace," *Guardian Weekly*, 2 May 1999, 19.

26 Ibid.

27 Donald MacLeod, "Cashing in on Clever Business Plans," *Guardian Weekly*, 11–17 January 2001, 24.

28 David F. Noble, "Comeback of an Education Racket," *Le Monde Diplomatique*, April 2000, 15.

29 CanadExport, "Distance Education in Mexico Offers Good Opportunities for Canada," 4 July 2000, 22.

30 Bruce Spencer, *The Purposes of Adult Education: A Guide for Students*, Toronto: Thompson Educational Publishing, 1998, 115.

31 Gordon Selman, Michael Cooke, Mark Selman, and Paul Dampier, *The Foundations of Adult Education in Canada*, 2nd ed., Toronto: Thompson Educational Publishing, 1998, 9.

32 Budd Hall, "Adult Education and the Political Economy of Global Economic Change," in Paul Wangoola and Frank Youngman, eds., *Towards a Transformative Political Economy of Adult Education: Theoretical and Practical Challenges*, Illinois: LEPS Press, Northern Illinois University, 1996, 118.

33 Jennifer Sumner, "Global Dream or Corporate Nightmare? The Privatization of Adult Education in the New Millennium," *Canadian Journal for the Study of Adult Education* 13, no. 2, (November 1999).

34 Peter Bloome, "Privatization Lessons for U.S. Extension from New Zealand," *Journal of Extension* 31, no. 1 (spring 1993, 5. Available at http://www.joe.org (website of the *Journal of Extension*).

35 Allan C. Lauzon, "University Extension and Public Service in the Age of Economic Globalization: A Response to Thompson and Lamble," *Canadian Journal of University Continuing Education* 26, no. 1 (spring 2000), 89.

36 Jane Cruikshank, "Economic Globalization: Implications for University Extension Practice in Canada," *Studies in the Education of Adults* 29, no. 1 (1997).

37 Lauzon, "University Extension," 91.

38 Encyclopaedia Britannica online. Available at http://www.britannica.com.

39 John McMurtry, *The Cancer Stage of Capitalism*, London: Pluto Press, 1999, 204.

40 Garrett Hardin, "The Tragedy of the Commons," *Science* 162, no. 3859 (13 December 1968), 1245.

41 Brown, "Privatizing the University," 1702.

42 Torjman, "Education and the Public Good," 1.

43 John McMurtry, "The Lifeground, the Civil Commons and Global Development." Paper presented at the annual meeting of the Canadian Association for Studies in International Development, Congress of the Social Sciences and Humanities, Sherbrooke, Quebec, 7 June 1999.

44 McMurtry, *Unequal Freedoms*, 24.

45 McMurtry, *The Cancer Stage*, 217.

46 McMurtry, *Unequal Freedoms*, 25.

47 Ibid., 25.

48 McMurtry, *The Cancer Stage*, 205.

49 Ibid., 205.

50 McMurtry, *Unequal Freedoms*, 372.

51 Ibid., 25.

52 McMurtry, *The Cancer Stage*, 163.

53 Shaker, "Privatizing Higher Education," 11.

Women and the New World Order: The "New" Face of the Indian Woman?

MEENAKSHI BHARAT

So free am I, so gloriously free,
Free from three petty things –
From mortar, from pestle and from my twisted lord,
Freed from rebirth and death I am,
And all that has held me down
Is hurled away.
– Therigatha[1]

Money, money, money
Must be funny
It's a rich man's world.
ABBA, lyrics

Things have changed, it is true, and at the dawn of the twenty-first century an assessment of changes becomes incumbent. Hundreds of questions spring up to trouble the mind, each clamouring for immediate attention. One wonders, to start with, whether a New World Order has at all actually come into being? If it has, has it changed the lot of women in the Indian subcontinent? Can "new" be interpreted in its conventional hopeful and promising connotations? If, at the beginning of the twenty-first century, woman is still crying out for freedom from the things that "held [her] down" in the sixth century, can this order really and truly be "new"?

What meaning could a New World Order have for a woman whose primary concern is still escaping "kitchen drudgery" and "the harsh grip of hunger"?[2] In a country where the cultural matrix is such that women's secondary position is not only taken for granted but reinforced with a vengeance, talk of the benefits of globalization seems to be ironically misplaced. The inescapable fact is that the context is one where, even today, the idea of girls wearing jeans can whip up violent fundamentalist strictures from communal, sectarian political parties, as happened recently in Kanpur, an important industrial town. Blinded with ire, these parties seek to enforce a dress code for the inferior sex. Daughters are still unwanted and considered a burden. Female feticide and infanticide are still rampant. Dowry deaths and dowry-related crimes make it into newspapers almost every other day. In fact, Delhi's Tihar Jail has a cell specifically allotted for crimes associated with dowry. The general crime graph against women is rising to alarming proportions. Thus torn apart by these more fundamental battles, the idea of a New World Order is apparently rendered counterfeit with reference to women.

"Drink Pepsi the way the world loves to" screams an advertisement exhorting the Indian to embrace a peculiar global identity, to become part of the New World. But despite seeing the term "New World Order" a hundred times in print, not many have interrogated it in the particular context of women. It is with shock that one realizes that intelligent women, at the supposed thinking vanguard of the many silent million women on the Indian subcontinent and in the developing world, have hardly given a thought to the problem, much less debated it. This shows that no great degree of awareness can be expected of them. A sad comment on the actual situation! Alarming and unsettling reason enough to necessitate a consideration of some aspects of this "new" world situation.

Going by one popularly accepted definition, the "New World Order" is the global political and economic situation that has arisen after the after the cold war, following the break-up of the former USSR. The ensuing ascendancy of the United States of America is probably the most recognizable characteristic of this New World Order. This take-over reveals itself in a comprehensive *global* control that is near total in its ramifications. Small wonder, then, that the process of "global-ization" is the next highlight of the New World Order, the two terms, global and the New World Order, attaining a synonymy. The pleasant idea of the unification of earth in the creation of one global village has allowed the sweeping winds of globalization the run of the world. Whether they are warm, balmy breezes or angry, unkind gales remains to be understood. The dream of this globalizing urge is the foundation of a world in which everybody and everything is inter-linked, but whether this has become a positive reality is uncertain.

Needless to say, the New World Order has had an impact on women, who represent roughly half the population of the world. This impact has been hailed in some circles as the release from feudalism, colonialism, and other oppressions, and the assertion of the cardinal codes of free-dom, equality, and fraternity. Mind-boggling developments in the fields of science and technology have opened new avenues for the material betterment of humanity. The new apparatus of speedy Internet links, an efficient cellular telephone system, and a wide all-encompassing media network have fostered twenty-four-hour marketing and trading. These real time markets have given the centre of the stage to what the 1999 UNDP *Human Development Report* calls the "new actors": the "World Trade Organization (WTO) with authority over national governments, the multinational corporations with more economic power than many states, the global networks of non-governmental organizations (NGOs) and other groups that transcend national boundaries."[3] Privatization and liberalization are two significant adjuncts to globalization, and the combination of the three, it goes without saying, has had far-reaching effects on women.[4]

The first visible effects can be seen in the upper strata of urban society. Here the induction of some degree of gender equality can be noted. In many ways it is here that globalization has visibly brought Indian women more power and therefore more gender parity. They are now able to follow in the footsteps of their confident, assertive Western counterparts. Jet-setting women executives fly all over the world working for their multinational firms; net-savvy, dot-comming women are reaping the material benefits of the "infotech" revolution. Indian women are becoming international celebrities: women directors (Deepa Mehta), actresses (Shabana Azmi), and writers (Arundhati Roy) are making waves around the globe. These are surely the beneficial spin-offs of this globalization. There is no gainsaying the fact that this has done wonders for our sense of self-worth and has fostered a confidence to stand up to global challenges.

Yet, notwithstanding this psychological advantage, even in these quarters the ugly underside of globalization is present. The glitz of global beauty contests, significantly held at "Third World" venues, ensures the commodification of women as objects of beauty. Somewhere along the line, along with global recognition, the Indian woman has also become a sexual specimen to be ogled at in beauty pageants, as were one-time Miss Universe Sushmita Sen, Miss World Aishwarya Rai and now the reigning queen Lara Dutta. Even Arundhati Roy, author of a Booker Award-winning novel, needed to be interviewed on the idiot box lounging provocatively on her bed, hugging a cushion. The latest to join this clique is the attractive Pulitzer-winning author Jhumpa Lahiri, whose photographs were quickly splashed in the media. This is the face of the New Woman of substance, aired to the whole world on a global media network.

But the predicament of women of the working class in urban areas is quite distinct from that of upper middle class and rich women who have reaped the advantages of globalization. Social scientists like Sujata Ghotoskar[5] talk of how women are being pushed out of the organized industrial sector. As if in corroboration, Australian Paul McCarthy in his incisive critique of postmodern Indian society in *Postmodern Desire: Learning from India*[6] describes how women workers were laid off from a garment manufacturing unit that was booming under the impetus of a globalized economy. The lay-offs were made on the basis of reports made by a male supervisor, despite the fact that women worked better at comparatively reduced wages. Obviously, the male worker has hogged all the advantages of this New World Order, thus perpetuating the discrimination of pre-boom times.

President Bill Clinton was bowled over by his experience of India. One of the things that intrigued him was that Indians were watching HBO. While it may be gratifying to be thus placed on a global map, the erosion of values engendered by this global television network is irreversible. "Santa Barbara," one of the first American serials to be aired, caught the fancy of Indian viewers immediately. The most dogged viewers are housewives and young female students. The programs are aired at times specially slotted for their convenience, that is, after housework and school or college are done. The spate of Western TV serials that have followed have vitiated the situation even further and fostered homegrown clones. These television programs have been seen as major contributors to a laxity in moral standards and a rise in teen pregnancies, rapes, and divorces. The New World Order thus spells mischief even as it purports to give new freedom to women.

So, lamentably, despite the general intellectual acceptance of the ideal of equality between men and women, women's movements that have been launched to achieve socioeconomic equality and justice have failed to realize their dreams. Big promises are being handed out to the chant of the mantras of globalization, privatization, and liberalization. Unfortunately, one of the results is the organized, concerted erosion of all vestiges of political and economic sovereignty of developing nations. A couple of decades ago the Indian government said no to multinational corporations. Today, they have been invited in, and the government seems unmindful of any dangers that this entry could portend and thoroughly befuddled about strategies for harvesting the benefits. The effects on the condition of women have not remained hidden, and the pitfalls, as it is already clear, are even more conspicuous in the case of women from weaker sections of society. As has also been already noted, the benefits of globalization seem to have reached only the smart, educated, urban rich. The economic potential of information technology and high-flying executive positions in multinational concerns are the much-touted gains of this New World Order, but these elude the average woman from developing countries altogether. While a Pepsi and a Coke may be available even in the hinterlands of these nations,[7] they do precious little to ameliorate her position in society. LPG (liberalization, privatization, and globalization), by opening the doors to the multinational, has created a surge of unprecedented consumerism. The desire has been stoked, but the *inability to buy* has harsh reverberations for women. Even if there were enough money available to buy, in this markedly male-dominated society the males in the families would first be granted the privilege. The presence of Coke, Pepsi, or any other such consumer item in the market feeds her desire but the inability to buy increases her frustration, which destabilizes and eats into the core of the social fabric. Consumerism sidles in as an insidious canker, forcing women into the pursuit of unhealthy means of realizing their desire to acquire. This sinister impact is never talked about, except sometimes at women's forums, academic gatherings, and in specialized journals.

Once again, McCarthy's thesis seems to corroborate this fall-out. He pinpoints the characteristic problem of Indian society as the rise of what he terms "postmodern desire," which breeds cravings that can neither be fulfilled nor pacified. This complex new middle-class desire, born of the New World Order, finds an outcome that only exacerbates the situation and expresses itself in communalism and fundamentalism. Quite often, women are at the receiving end of this reaction, as the Kanpur jeans episode illustrated. Levis are only allowed as a liberation for males. Women *ought not* to even dream of any such concessional benefit of globalization!

Statistics too give the lie to the promises of this New World Order of LPG. With the profit motive running amok, unequal and inequitable distribution of wealth and resources gives rise to instability and marginalization. Poverty has increased; the disparity between the rich and the poor has widened to a chasm. This process marks the emergence of a new class of people, that of the global elite. The masses still continue to be poor. The riches are vested in the affluent nations and this global elite. The 1999 UNDP report recognizes this aspect of globalization as the most salient attribute of the world today. The exchange of more than $1.5 trillion every day in the world markets naturally accents the fact that the seedbed of globalization is economic. *Money,* or rather the green of the arm-twisting dollar, is the singular, dictating attribute of the New World Order, as expressed in the lyrics from the film *Cabaret:* "Money makes the world go round, the world go round / With a clinking clanking sound." In tune with the new economic ethos, the rich rule, becoming richer by the day. Others try to become rich, and the poor languish. But by far the most horrifying fact is that this poverty has a female countenance. At the

Fourth World Conference on Women in Beijing in September 1995, the finding was that 70 per cent of the world's 1.3 billion women were absolutely poor, and women in poor countries are the most poverty-stricken. Indian women, on the mere basis of population statistics, become the most representative of this harsh fact of the New World Order.

The resulting destabilization and social tensions reveal themselves in increasing criminal activity. We now talk of global fundamentalism and global terrorism, forces that have rent the very fabric of humanity. If cricket has become a signifier of globalization (many people, many nations share a passion for it, lovers of the game travel across the globe to watch a match live, millions watch it on television) match fixing, cutting across nations and nationalities, is the dark underside of this globalized identity. An Indian bookie working from the UK can approach a team or a player from South Africa, India or any other country, to "globally" control and vitiate this global sport. The Internet has become an easy mode for the global trafficking of women for sexual exploitation. "Mail-order brides" and the flourishing business of sex tourism are readily accessible through this medium. Hand in hand with other crimes like drug and arms trafficking and money laundering, the situation burgeons to heinous proportions. This is the terrifying hydra of globalization that characterizes the New World Order for developing nations. "Globalization for the rich is globalization of markets, for the rest of the world it is globalization of poverty and deprivation, of violence and strife."[8]

The women from affluent sections of society, then, hardly seem the rightful focus for a study like this as, to an extent, they too manage to cruise along the waves of the successes of the New World Order. The increase in poverty and the related social problems already mentioned have the maximum effect on women who occupy the lowest rungs of the socioeconomic hierarchy. If multinational consumables have found their way into their worldview, so have Western marketing and production norms. To illustrate this point, India is one of the largest producers of milk in the world. Furthermore, in India, there is no subsidy to milk production. The opening of trade barriers with liberalization has allowed milk-surplus countries to export about 16,000 tonnes of skimmed milk powder along with milk products to India. Incomprehensibly, this import is highly subsidized.[9] This has had a crushing effect on the 80 million odd people who are members of the milk co-operatives in India. Notably, the majority of these people are women. President Clinton's two-hour visit to a women's cooperative in Nayala, Rajasthan, when he danced and chatted with women members, only served to show the sidelining of women. Was any new, exciting economic turnabout promised as a result of this "global" attention? The press reported little on this aspect of the visit, but rather focused on extra-issue elements like how it was a feather in the cap of the Indian government. The press frittered precious news space on cartoons and innuendoes regarding the president and women.

The situation in the agrarian sector is particularly distressing because in developing countries this sector is still the most important occupation. Under the entire process of globalization, self-sufficiency is no longer the criterion for food security. As in the case of milk, barriers have now been lifted to allow for the import of cheaper food. In developing countries like India, the landholding size is particularly small: a mere quarter hectare to the 800 hectares of American farms. Indigenous production cannot expect to match the competition of the industrialized agricultural production of the West. This has destroyed the security of livelihood, pushing able-bodied men to migrate to urban, industrial centres and leaving women behind to till the land alone.

Moreover, vital agricultural land has been taken from farmers with small holdings, rendering many landless and jobless so that huge multinational corporations can establish factories and offices, as for Pepsi Foods in the Punjab and Enron in Maharashtra. Even where the farmer has managed to retain his hold on his land, agriculture has become economically unviable and unattractive. Sometimes, the only option for survival is that the men start working for these corporations, in turn providing, by world standards, unbelievably cheap labour for the multinationals. It goes without saying that women bear the brunt of the effects of all these various inroads of globalization. As I have described, as men move to more lucrative jobs with multinational concerns, women are left to of till the land. Alone, abandoned, and impoverished, then find that, more often than not, the going becomes difficult, sometimes even impossible. At such a time, research bears out, women are quite often forced to sell themselves. The rise in the number of women prostitutes is thus one direct outcome of the New World Order. The epidemic of HIV/AIDS has spread within rural India. "With 95 per cent of the 16,000 infected each day living in developing countries, AIDS has become a poor person's disease."[10] Once again, it is the woman who suffers most, both in terms of the numbers contracting the disease and in having to bear the economic repercussions of losing men who succumb to it.

These circumstances highlight the two most noticeable developments in the socioeconomic scenario: *the feminization of agriculture* and *the feminization of poverty*. These features of the globalized world have a bleak prognosis. The World Bank has forecast that by 2010 the rate of migration in India will be twice the combined population of the UK, France, and Germany. Globalization will hasten this fivefold, according to agricultural economists like Devinder Sharma. Obviously, in a country where the rural population is almost 80 per cent of the total population, this feminization of agriculture has far-reaching implications.

Moreover, women have traditionally been entrusted with the unwritten task of protecting the biodiversity of the nation. India is a gene-rich country and one of the ways in which diversity is maintained is the practice of growing several crops on a landholding. But with the development of global biotechnology, Western notions of monoculture and monopolization of patents has assaulted and destroyed the old diversity. Women have thus been shorn of their traditional role. In the denial of the right to nurture and protect and of the economic power to do so, the character of India traditionally figured as *Bharatmata*, the "Mother of the nation," has been grotesquely altered and the woman's position irreparably weakened.

Also, caring and nurturing, which hold societies together all over the world, has conventionally been placed almost wholly on the shoulders of women. This is even more applicable in a country as steeped in tradition as India is. The UNDP report points out that two-thirds of women's work time is spent in unpaid activities, as compared to one-quarter of men's time. Women predominate in caring professions and domestic service. The competitive global market of today has seen a rise in the participation of women in the formal labour market, yet they have not been relieved of any of the burden of care. The amount of unpaid work still remains high. It is significant that a cartoon originally printed in the *Christian Science Monitor* that was included *twice* in the LPG issue of *Women's Link* shows "the world according to Nike." The cartoon is in two parts. In the U.S. half, a young boy with his hands in his pockets leans against a wall, with "NO WORK" and $150 shoes. The Asian half shows a girl of the same age at a sewing machine, making shoes ("LOTS OF WORK") but wearing none herself. While highlighting the supremacy of the dollar, it draws attention to the feminization of poverty and the cheap female labour market that is the direct result of the New World Order. As Jayati Ghosh says, this is a spin-off of "the macro-economic policies and processes which simply push women into the labor market without ensuring social provision of these requirements."[11]

No wonder that, with little social or economic security, quite often the woman has had to step out of the protective environs of her home to work. The new woman has become constantly hard-pressed for time, reeling under the pressure of having to manage both work *and* home. The sociocultural code has hardly changed to cater for these new developments. Gender biases continue and the patriarchal grasp is as strong as ever. Trying to cope with these in the context of this demanding New Order leads to psychological disorientation and large-scale psychiatric disorders amongst women.

The fourteenth-century devotional poet Janabai seems to have something pertinent for the psychologically stressed woman of the New World Order:

> Cast off all shame,
> and sell yourself
> in the marketplace;
> then alone
> can you hope
> to reach the Lord.
>
> Cymbals in hand
> A *veena* upon my shoulder,
> I go about;
> Who dares to stop me?
>
> The pallav of my sari
> Falls away (A scandal);
> Yet will I enter
> The crowded marketplace
> Without a thought.
>
> Jani says, My Lord,
> I have become a slut
> To reach Your home.
>
> (translated by Vilas Sarang.)[12]

The New World has indeed become a "crowded marketplace," but does the woman have to sell herself to reap the benefits of the New World? As the 1999 *Human Development Report* insists, what we need is "globalization with a human face."[13] While asserting that "globalization offers great opportunities for human advance," it also adds the important qualifier "but only with stronger governance." One feels compelled to add, especially where women are concerned.

NOTES

1 Therigatha Mutta, "The Songs of the Nuns, 6th Century B.C.," translated by Uma Chakravarti and Kumkum Roy, in Susie Tharu and K. Lalita, eds., *Women Writing in India: 600 B.C. to the Present, Volume I: 600 B.C. to the Early 20th Century,* New Delhi: Oxford University Press, 1993, 68.

2 Sumangalamata in *Women Writing in India*, 69.

3 The tenth *Human Development Report*, published for the United Nations Development Programme (UNDP), New York: Oxford University Press, 1999, 1. Many of the data and facts quoted in this article are from this source.

4 The effects of the nexus of liberalization, privatization and globalization is debated at length in *Women's Link* 3, no. 4 (October-December 1997), New Delhi, India.

5 Sujata Gothoskar, "Pushing Women Out: Declining Employment of Women in the Organized Sector," *Manushi* 65 (July-August 1991), 10–20.

6 Paul McCarthy, *Postmodern Desire: Learning from India*, New Delhi: Promilla, 1994.

7 Interestingly, one of the many popular advertisements of Pepsi featuring the sports icon cricketer Sachin Tendulkar, shows *village* children wearing Sachin masks, guzzling Pepsi with their hero.

8 An unpublished report entitled "World March of Women 2000 Maharashtra" by the Maharashtra Women's Group for the Campaign against Globalization, launched on the occasion of International Women's Day, 8 March 2000, headed by Kiran Moghe, secretary of the Maharashtra Rajya Samiti of the Akhil Bharatiye Janwadi Mahila Sanghatana, Pune.

9 Devinder Sharma says that at $1,400 a tonne there is a subsidy of over $1,000, competition that the local produce can never match.

10 *Human Development Report*, 4.

11 Jayati Ghosh, "Gender and Macro-Economic Policy in India Since 1991," *Women's Link*, 11.

12 Janabai (ca 1298–1350) in *Women Writing in India*, 82.

13 *Human Development Report*, 1.

Kenyan Women's Fight for Fertility: Globalization from Above and Reappropriation from Below

TERISA E. TURNER
AND LEIGH S. BROWNHILL

In late 1999 an unprecedented alliance of diverse insurgent forces challenged the World Trade Organization in the now historic "Battle of Seattle." The corporate meeting on "globalization from above" was shut down by an international alliance asserting "reappropriation from below." The main features of corporate globalization are well known.[1] The features of a people's world order, on the other hand, are emerging through countless sites of struggle.[2] One site of this contention is rural Kenya where the courage and creativity of peasant women posit a "life economy" in place of the "death economy."[3] Sir Roger Swynnerton was a colonial agricultural planner based in East Africa in the 1950s. In a 1985 interview he testified, from his imperial perspective, to the tenacity of this "life economy" in Kenyan peasant women's insistence on growing food, not cash crops. According to Swynnerton,

In Kenya twice a year we called our provincial agricultural officers together for a conference to discuss programmes ... About the middle of the 1950s, one of our subjects of discussion was whether we should push for crop specialization in different areas of the country ... leaving food crop areas to produce the subsistence requirements of the cash crop areas. One very experienced provincial agricultural officer said this just would not work. The African was so inured to securing his food supplies that when the first rain started pattering on the roof of his hut, the wife in her sleep would reach over on one side and pick up a hoe, the other side to pick up a bag of seed and in the middle of the night she would go out and start planting food. In no way would she stop doing that whatever the cash crop being grown."[4]

One way to conceptualize capital's attempt to assert a "New World Order" and popular resistance to it is as a *fight for fertility*. The focus in the fight for fertility is for control over the processes and results of fertility: the capacity to reproduce and sustain life in all its forms, especially people (or labour power) and food. Land and labour, as well as the knowledge, bodies, and time of women, are central to the process of enacting or realizing fertility.[5] Much of animal husbandry, agricultural production, and food processing is women's work. In Africa women do some 80 per cent of all farming. Women give birth and nurture people worldwide. Women therefore have a special stake in exercising control over their own fertility. They contend for control with their own menfolk, and with capital, foreign and local. The three parties to this struggle over control of the production of life are (1) women themselves, (2) their own menfolk and (3) local and international capitalists.

The *subsistence political economy* includes not only food production for local consumption and regional trade, but a host of activities and sets of social networks whose main aim is to support and enhance human existence. Subsistence production, or what we alternatively refer to as the subsistence political economy, "includes all work that is expended in the creation, re-creation and maintenance of immediate life and which has no other purpose."[6]

Subsistence is life-supporting activity in which use values predominate. That is, people produce primarily for use, and while they may trade items or services, the production is not primarily for exchange and for the making of money. A subsistence way of life may be precapitalist or it may co-exist in the interstices of the capitalist political economy. Depending on the power relations that exist, the subsistence political economy may be more or less subsumed by the commodified political economy or autonomous from it. Those producing sustenance have an interest in working to make society sustainable through conservation, restitution, relative regional autonomy, and planning.

Capitalists operating nationally and internationally directly contribute to the destruction of the subsistence realm as they construct commodified social relations.[7] In the *commodified political economy*, life sustaining activities are supplanted by profiteering and speculation – the turning of money demand into more money demand.[8] Commodification is central to capitalist industrialization. It is inherently global and enforces an extreme division of labour. It also structures and inflames divisions amongst labourers, for instance through constructing difference as

divisive. Bennholdt-Thompsen and Mies note that within the commodified political economy "life is, so to speak, only a coincidental side-
effect. It is typical of the capitalist industrial system that it declares
everything that it wants to exploit free of charge to be part of nature,
a natural resource. To this belongs the housework of women as well
as the work of peasants in the Third World, but also the productivity
of all of nature."[9]

In the fight for control over fertility, many men, and in particular
kinsmen, act as intermediaries between women and capitalists. These
peasant or waged men may enter into what we call "*male deals*" with
capital. They channel resources and women's labour into the commodified realm to make profits for capital and minor earnings for the
(nevertheless exploited) men themselves. In contrast, some men break
with the male deals and join women in *gendered class alliances* for the
defence and elaboration of the subsistence political economy, against
the incursion of capitalist commodified relations.[10]

Mies and Bennholdt-Thompsen define "housewifization" as the process by which "women's work under capitalism is universally made
invisible and can for that reason be exploited limitlessly."[11] This
concept of the invisibility of women's work "applies not only to
'housewives' in the narrow sense in the industrial countries but also
to the work of the women who do home work, to farm labourers,
peasants, small traders, and factory workers."

Much work in the subsistence economy is exploited by capital,
which, for instance, depends on "free" housework and food production
for the daily reproduction of labourers. But capital also "housewifizes"
waged and contracted labour in the production of commodities. Profits
in Kenya's coffee and tea growing zones depend crucially on housewifization. First women were denied land titles at independence in 1963.
Then, the men who got the titles took loans to grow coffee for export
on their small farms. They paid back the loans with interest from
harvest proceeds. Husbands expected wives to cultivate and weed the
coffee. Wives expected to have a food garden. If prices fell, husbands
could decide to put some of the wives' food plots under coffee. Some
men would simply keep the money for themselves. Women's work was
housewifized in that their publicly recognized rights to land were
curtailed.[12] This meant financial dependence on kinsmen and loss of
autonomy. Women's work was "invisible" and uncompensated.

In this work, we examine three moments in this fight for fertility in
post-colonial Kenya. All three cases are struggles by some of the
world's most exploited people against the capitalist New World
Order.[13] The first upsurge is Maragua women coffee farmers' flight
from coffee between the mid 1980s and the mid 1990s. Those men
who were able to disengage from the corporate agenda cooperated

with their wives in gendered class alliances with the aim of replacing coffee with bananas and other food crops for consumption and trade.

The second insurgency is a 1992 hunger strike at Nairobi's "Freedom Corner," carried out by mothers of political prisoners. These women fought for the liberty and rights of their children – the fruits of their own fertility. They confronted a state that was in the process of attacking urban and rural people and evicting them from their land. These land wars resulted in part from the World Bank privatization drive of the 1990s and the increasing resistance by subsistence producers to the neo-liberal structural adjustment program.[14] The women at Freedom Corner were protected by particular men from police attack. Together the women and men secured the release of fifty-one political prisoners.

The third insurgency is the large-scale reappropriation of land by landless people across Kenya in the new millennium. Women, who lack secure access to land, have a tremendous stake in the outcome of this direct redistribution of the prerequisite to self-provisioning and social security. A key question is the extent to which women's subsistence interests will be served in this new battle in the ongoing fight for control of fertility in Kenya.

Why were these three struggles chosen to illustrate the fight for fertility? They build on each other in that the high point of one struggle is the starting point of the next.[15] That is, there is a strong historical continuity that, rather than being linear, manifests an incremental building with respect to the geographical scope, political conceptions, and capabilities of the participants. The insurgencies illustrate some of the methods of fighting used by each of the three major contenders in the struggle to control women's agricultural and domestic labour. The upsurges are at once intensely local and international. As such they provide various insights into the interpenetration of global hierarchies and community democracies. The battles reveal some environmental consequences of profit-oriented versus subsistence agriculture. They reveal details about the gender relations that characterize struggles over the control of fertility. Finally, they suggest how international struggles "circulate," stimulating more resistance elsewhere and consciously coordinating joint actions.[16] Grassroots 'reappropriation from below' is organized by and against corporate globalization from above.

HISTORICAL ANTECEDENTS TO THE FIGHT FOR FERTILITY

The three instances of overt struggle for the fruits of women's labour that we examine here are all from Kenya's post-independence period. A brief note on the struggles of the colonial period is necessary to contextualize our case studies. Prior to independence in 1963 there were major upsurges in the fight for fertility in the 1920s and again in the 1940s, leading to the Mau Mau war for "land and freedom" (1952–60). In 1922 a Kikuyu woman, Mary Muthoni Nyanjiru, used a customary "curse of nakedness" to lead a bid by several thousand Nairobi Africans to free a political detainee, Harry Thuku.[17] This "chief of women" was jailed for resisting the forced labour of African women on colonial agricultural estates and public works. The 1920s insurgency continued with the formation of an independent African church and school network. These institutions contributed to the organization of Mau Mau, which fought a war to expel the colonial occupiers in the 1950s.[18]

In the 1940s rural women repeatedly challenged British efforts to cull cattle, seize land, and restrict Africans to native reserves and "settlement schemes" as virtual debt peons. This challenge led directly to British counterinsurgency.[19] It escalated into the Mau Mau war, during which the British, with "male dealer" support from African Home Guards, crushed and dispossessed small peasants carrying out subsistence agriculture and trade. The British imposed capitalist farming, and Home Guards and those Mau Mau who surrendered the fight became proprietors of export crop small holdings. Their wives were turned from food to export crop production and the husbands kept the cash income. In this process of housewifization, rural women lost much of their power to control land, crops, the labour process (which was collective), markets, surpluses of many kinds (including time), and community social relations. However, many engaged in holding actions such as funnelling coffee money, where possible, into strengthening the subsistence economy and into educating their children.[20] When export crop income faltered in the late 1970s, they were well-positioned to reassert the subsistence economy. But this required that women confront tremendous opposition from husbands, the government coffee buying cooperatives, and international firms backed by governmental organizations including the World Bank.

FROM COFFEE TO BANANAS: MARAGUA PEASANT WOMEN REPLACE EXPORT CROPS WITH LOCAL FOOD CROPS (1980–2000)[21]

In her study "Gender and Command Over Property," Bina Agarwal came to the conclusion that dispossessed women need independent rights in land.[22] This is our starting point. How have women cultivators organized to gain rights in land? Are there lessons to be learned and

applied elsewhere? We worked closely with women in Kenya throughout the 1990s and learned about their efforts to reclaim and reshape
customary rights to their husbands' land.[23] Their struggle provides
insight into the gendered character of the process of reclaiming land
and social relations for subsistence.

"Every woman belongs to at least one woman's group," Alexiah
Kamene told us as if it were the most obvious fact of life. Kamene is
a widow who lives in Maragua and grows bananas and vegetables on
her one-acre (0.4 ha) farm. She works part-time for a hotelier as a
domestic servant and seasonally hires herself out with a group of other
women to weed or harvest in the gardens of farmers with larger
holdings. "Banana money is better than coffee money. Men do still
take the money from women. Single women manage better. You will
find that banana traders are mainly divorced or widowed women."

Kamene described the situation in Maragua as she sees it. It is not
a utopia for landless women. But it is better than it was fifteen years
ago, when dutiful and unwaged women picked coffee that fetched
incomes for their husbands, state officials, and international merchants.
Beginning in 1986 Maragua farming women have taken steps towards
a new organization of society in which they, as producers, manage
resources, outputs, and incomes.

Maragua is a rural farming community in the area surrounding
Mount Kenya. It lies in the middle of a coffee zone, about eighty
kilometres northwest of Nairobi, Kenya's capital. Maragua Location,
a part of Kigumo Division, covers about 220 square miles. Some
100,000 people live there.[24] Husbands own most of the small, one- to
five-acre (0.4–2 ha) farms in Maragua. Technically and legally, their
wives are landless. In practice, peasant women in central Kenya have
customarily had the right to work on their husbands' farms and control
the use of foodstuffs they themselves produced. Coffee production
since the 1960s has slowly intruded into women's food gardens. This
has been a source of conflict within families. Women cultivators have
historically belonged to collective work groups that applied themselves
to large tasks on each other's food plots. However, these groups never
worked on men's cash crop plots since the income from cash crops did
not cater for women's needs. Wives worked individually, with children
or with casual labourers, on husbands' cash crop plots, but did not
control the yield. When women's food plots shrunk, the time they had
to work collectively with other women also diminished.

At independence the government lifted colonial restrictions on coffee
growing by Africans. In the 1960s and the first half of the 1970s,
coffee production on small holdings provided farmers with substantial

incomes and provided the state with more foreign exchange than any other commodity. In the last half of the 1970s coffee began to lose its attraction to producers. State corruption swallowed sales income so producers were not paid fairly or promptly. Between 1980 and 1990 real international prices for Africa's coffee exports fell by 70 per cent.[25]

By 1986 Kenyan farmers had faced ten years of declining income from coffee. Increasing numbers of women coffee cultivators received nothing from the coffee payments that the government remitted to male landowners. Oral testimony and direct experience confirm that more and more women threatened to stop caring for their husbands' coffee. Some men responded by declaring that if their wives would not work, they would chase the women away from the farms.[26] Government chiefs intervened to mediate between embattled wives and husbands. The chiefs sought to preserve both the marriages and the coffee production, and thereby safeguard the profits on which government revenues depended and on which were premised debt repayment and continued good relations with the International Monetary Fund IMF and Paris Club of donors.

By 1986 the conflict between female coffee workers and male coffee farm owners contributed to a situation of declining overall production.[27] In response to lower coffee export earnings the World Bank and IMF provided funds to increase coffee production. The government raised coffee payments to encourage husbands to defend the industry by forcing recalcitrant wives back to work in coffee. The IMF introduced cost-sharing in health and education, which created a greater need amongst producers for cash. This need constituted a coercive incentive to resume the production of cash crops. In effect, the IMF mounted formidable obstacles to women's efforts to refuse coffee production by introducing incentives in the form of conditional loans to the state, and by requiring the state to pay higher coffee prices to men.

Despite the harsher discipline faced by women in their households, many of those who refused to produce coffee resolved to stay with their husbands and preserve their marriages. But the women planted beans between the coffee trees, contrary to restrictions against intercropping with coffee. They thus provided their families with food and began the tedious process of renourishing the chemically damaged soil. However, their husbands and state officials continued to stand in the way of women's needs to produce food and secure cash income. Finally the women took drastic action. In Maragua and elsewhere in Kenya, women uprooted coffee trees and used them for firewood. The penalty for damaging a coffee tree was imprisonment for seven years. By late 1986 most women farmers in Maragua had planted bananas and vegetables for home consumption and local trade instead of coffee for export. This pattern was repeated to varying extends throughout Kenya and the East and Central African regions as a whole.

By and large, in Maragua in 1986, the typical working man "secured his food supplies" by participating in his wives' rejection of coffee. Husbands recognized that their wives' resistance contributed funds and organizational militancy that allowed men to hold onto their land in the midst of expanding and accelerating large-scale enclosures. Not only did Maragua women cultivators plant food, they also reinstated producer control over land. And they reestablished and strengthened their collective women's work groups that form the basis for many activities such as savings and credit "merry-go-rounds" (*esusu* in Ghana, *susu* in Trinidad and Tobago). In the merry-go-rounds, each woman in the group contributes a small sum of money into a "pot" every week and every week, a different member receives the pot. She typically uses her share to pay school fees or to buy household utensils or a goat.

In 1996 the IMF loaned 12 billion Kenyan shillings (U.S. $218m/CA $299m) to the government. In October 1996, Kenyan president Moi launched an agriculture policy paper aimed at "enabling the sector to run as a fully commercial enterprise,"[28] with emphasis on export crops. Though Maragua farmers escaped the exploitation of the coffee market, the alternative they built exists within the framework of an increasingly privatized and commodified society. The state and multinational corporations continue to regulate working women's labour by giving credit to (male) title deed holders to encourage horticulture. Foreign and local capitalists entice landowning men in Maragua into labour intensive and chemical dependent export production. Husbands of women who have rejected coffee may view horticulture as a means to reassert command over women's labour. Such is the temptation of the male deal. Meanwhile, the state upholds laws that favour men. Into the new millennium, the constitution of Kenya allows discrimination based on sex. This legal framework works in favour of the corporate agenda in that it limits women's subsistence choices.

The relations of production imposed upon producers by capital and the state have organized dispossessed women to resist. They began by refusing the discipline meted out by husbands who sought high returns on the crops women produce. While the IMF is stepping up pressure to privatize state assets, including coffee marketing bodies, women producers are creating an alternative to corporate takeover. Through reviving self-organized and autonomous customary work groups the women have begun to reconstruct subsistence society, for instance through rebuilding a regional trade system.

In sum, the women's dramatic attack on the coffee trees broke and restructured longstanding social relationships at three levels. First, the Maragua insurgents shifted effective control over resources from their husbands into their own hands. Second, they broke their relationships of debt peonage and subjection to the state coffee apparatus and established an alternative self-regulated banana trade. They also contributed to forcing the single-party state to legalize opposition parties.[29] Third, the Maragua women extracted themselves from state-mediated relationships with foreign suppliers of agro-chemical inputs and a global coffee trade that enriched commercial traders at the expense of producers.

THE 1992 "FREEDOM CORNER" HUNGER STRIKE BY MOTHERS OF POLITICAL PRISONERS

Maragua women fought their husbands, the state, and multinational corporations for land. At Freedom Corner, women fought the police, the state, and their corporate sponsors for their sons. Most Freedom Corner women were relatively free from housewifization. They were divorcees, widows, and wives of the disappeared. These independent though poor women did not have kinsmen standing between them and the state. On the contrary, the state stood between the women and their sons. Most of these sons had been imprisoned for trying to "set the country right." Their mothers wanted them out of jail so that they could continue in that vein, especially in securing land so that the men could take care of their aging mothers.[30] In this upsurge in the fight for fertility women fought to regain land and their children.

On 28 February 1992, eight African women met with Kenya's attorney general, Amos Wako, and presented him with an open letter protesting the "continued incarceration by the Kenya Government of scores of political prisoners."[31] Seven of the women were the elderly mothers of imprisoned men. The eighth was the prominent environmentalist Dr Wangari Maathai. All were involved in a newly formed lobby group, Release Political Prisoners (RPP). At the end of the two-hour meeting, the attorney general took the matter of the political prisoners "under advisement." The eight women joined four others who had waited outside the attorney general's chambers. The twelve marched a few blocks to Uhuru Park, across from the Parliament buildings, near the centre of Nairobi city. At "Freedom Corner," the twelve women began a hunger strike to pressure the attorney general and the president to release their sons and all political prisoners in Kenyan jails. Within two days, thousands of people from a cross-section of Kenyan society had come to Freedom Corner to contribute spiritual, material, and physical support to the hunger strikers. On the fourth day, police and security officers beat the mothers with clubs and dispersed their sympathizers with tear gas, batons, and guns.[32]

Hunger striker Ruth Wangari wa Thungu, seventy, provided the following account of this harrowing attack:

We were beaten with teargas, clubs, and the whole area was sealed off by policemen and security officials.

But me because of the experience I had in the forest during the Mau Mau war where we were beaten with teargas and faced with other problems, we had been taught how to defend ourselves.

People fainted. Like Wangari wa Maathai and many other women. But me, when I saw that we were going to be beaten severely, I took a blanket and soaked it in water and covered my head plus some other young men who had not been affected by the tear gas.

When the effect of the tear gas subsided and I took off the blanket, I only saw people lying down immobile – I saw Wangari Wa Maathai was unconscious and was just throwing kicks and also Wa Gakonya and many other people in the same state and they looked like they were dead.

After all this, I tried to think what I would do next. I then stripped my clothes and remained stark naked and started fighting with the policemen, because I saw a young man called Kanene who was one of us and is one of us in RPP struggling with a policeman who wanted to shoot him. I came in between them and stripped off my clothes. When the young people saw me naked, they stopped fighting with the police and ran away.

And we were left with only four policemen whom I know were Kalenjins and they were old men. We fought with them and God helped. At that time the members of the public were in large numbers and there were many motorists who had a chance to pick up the unconscious people and rush them to various hospitals. The people who managed to run away ran and I was left with the four policemen.

We stayed and at last calmness prevailed. And we now put on our clothes and stayed there even though they pulled down the tent and took it with them plus our other belongings.[33]

The customary act of defiance that Ruth Wangari employed was *guturama n'gania* (Gikuyu), or the "curse of nakedness." When women, especially old women or groups of women, expose their genitals to people who have offended or threatened them, they are saying, in effect, "This is where your life has come from. I hereby revoke your life." Those so cursed believe that they will lose their virility. They believe that their land will lose its fertility and they as individuals will be outcasts from society.[34] The four policemen who did not run away were old men of another ethnic group who felt immune to Ruth Wangari's curse. But they did not shoot. They gathered up all of the women's belongings, including a tent that had been donated and erected at the site for the women by four Asian women and men. The police then arrested the women who remained at Freedom Corner and drove them back to their home villages. Within days, all had returned to Nairobi. They resumed their hunger strike in the basement of a church adjacent to Freedom Corner. A year later, having effected the released of fifty-one of the fifty-two men they struggled to liberate, the women ended their vigil and remained linked through the group, RPP.

Peoples' defence of the subsistence economy was given centre stage by the mothers of Freedom Corner in 1992. A public address system was donated anonymously, and the old women defended this open mike. Through it, the most dispossessed and silenced people in the country were able to voice their diverse demands. The coalescence of this cross-section of subsistence defenders so threatened the state that police tear-gassed and beat the mothers on day four of the hunger strike. The beatings enraged the public. Ruth Wangari's employment of the *guturama n'gania* against the police marked a turning point in the fight for fertility. Peasant women in the remotest corners of East Africa were emboldened by their recognition that an old Mau Mau fighter was prepared to die for her cause. Wangari literally used her own productive power as a weapon in the struggle to control the life-and-death decisions of the police.

Thousands of people mobilized to support, defend, write for, speak to, pray with and urge on the mothers of Freedom Corner for a full year. This mobilization did not disappear when the women left the church. It coalesced into dozens of organizations with a multitude of specific demands. These groups expressed the resurgence of the "civil commons."[35] They came together to support one another in times of need. Release Political Prisoners defended Mungiki, a neo-Mau Mau mass movement in 1994. Muungano wa Wanavijiji, an organization of squatters, enlisted the assistance of RPP when, on 5 May 1998, a forty-four-year-old woman, Salome Wacera Wainaina, was murdered by police while defending her land in Kamae. The groups strengthened each other while simultaneously practising highly diverse styles of struggle in pursuit of prisoners' rights, women's rights, law reform, housing, culture, and virtually every aspect of a humane existence. Each organization has a position on land redistribution.

During and after the Freedom Corner event, the state continued to wage war against subsistence advocates by supplying arms and transport for killers, rapists, arsonists, and looters. They targeted the farms and families of specific women involved in the Freedom Corner action. Refugees from the land war streamed in to join the vigil. The women's success in liberating political prisoners established a foundation upon which refugees and other landless people formulated their demands for secure entitlements and a redistribution of life sustaining resources.

THE NEW MILLENNIUM LAND INVASIONS

The pent-up demands for land exploded early in the year 2000.* In a fast-moving and well-organized bid, various grassroots groups and communities reappropriated land not only from white settlers but also from African landholders and the government. The following Kenya newspaper account conveys a sense of the furor:

In Laikipia East, MP Mwangi Kiunjuri threatened to lead squatters to occupy degazetted forest areas in his constituency if genuine cases are not considered first. And in Cherangany, MP Kipruto arap Kirwa told the Marakwet youths occupying a 14,500-acre Agricultural Development Corporation farm to defy the District Commissioner's order to vacate. [Two days earlier] armed Marakwet youths barred a surveyor and a chief from entering the ADC farm. The youths, who carried arrows, swords and machetes, confronted the deputy district surveyor, Mr Naphtali Kinoti, and Kaplamai chief Michael Arusei, who fled. The 400 youths surrounded the officer's vehicle and pushed it off the road, saying the two had been sent to parcel out the land to top government officials.[36]

Barely a month after Zimbabwe's land invasions began in February 2000, certain Kenyan members of Parliament were calling on the landless to take over land owned by multinational agribusiness.[37] In Kenya, as in Zimbabwe, the logic of the maxim "willing buyer – willing seller" is being questioned by politicians for reasons of political expediency and rejected outright by landless peasants who have engaged in a series of land invasions throughout both countries.[38]

The occupations respond to government efforts to violently impose capitalist social relations in the countryside. The Maragua-style resurgence of subsistence is linked to the Freedom Corner protest through the strengthening of women's autonomous trade and social networks. These bind together urban and rural squatters and peasants. Women's networking and their alliances with men who are willing to challenge housewifization were integral to the land invasions in 2000. The state responded throughout the 1990s to the increasing presence of the

---

*This analysis was written before the exponential increase in reappropriations after the election of a new president, Mwai Kibaki, in December 2002. The new government has begun a process of repossessing illicitly "grabbed" land, buildings, and other resources. Popular reappropriations are being undertaken on an even wider scale.

subsistence political economy by mounting what it termed "ethnic clashes,"[39] beginning in 1991. These attacks amounted to eviction of rural subsistence farmers and the creation of a massive internal refugee population, which by 1998 exceeded 300,000, most of whom were women and children.

In the midst of a tremendous burst of organizational activity after 1992, much attention has been given to the proliferation of non-governmental organizations, which supposedly replace the social service provision cut by the state under the imperatives of structural adjustment. Opposition political parties and aspirant political parties in the formal electoral arena have also received attention. But much more significant in the fight for fertility are the militant organizations of the dispossessed, which incorporate millions of members whose livelihoods have been attacked by the onslaught of commodification. We consider two such organizations here.

Members of Muungano wa Wanavijiji (Kiswahili for Organization of Villagers), locate their struggle in the urban streets, slums, and stalls of markets, where they persist in defending a sustenance market presence for African women and men against the highly commodified, globalized market in the region. This group arose when slum-dwellers began to organize to defend themselves and their homes and businesses in the face of an onslaught of privatization-related slum and market demolitions, beginning with Nairobi's Muoroto village in March 1990. The multi-ethnic group, in which young and old, single, divorced, and widowed women predominate, was bolstered in its earliest days by the Freedom Corner vigil, which some of them joined. Though focused on gaining secure communal title deeds to urban residential space, Muungano wa Wanavijiji also includes in its struggle "the liberation of people."[40] This involves caring for orphaned children, battered women and prisoners.

Mungiki (Gikuyu for "Multitudes") is another of the most important organizations to expand dramatically after the Freedom Corner mobilization. They organized and defended victims of state-sponsored violence (the "ethnic clashes") and vocally supported some of the land invasions of 2000.[41] Mungiki claims to bind more than five million Kenyans into a disciplined, multi-faceted organization with the capacity to defend the subsistence economy. In early 2000 Mungiki carried out a daring attack on a police station to release members of the group from jail. Both Mungiki and Muungano are direct successors to the Mau Mau Land and Freedom Army of the 1950s in that members include large numbers of elderly Mau Mau fighters as well as their children and grandchildren. Further, both groups claim to be the inheritors of the Mau Mau legacy to defend entitlements to land and subsistence.[42]

Kenyan newspaper reports provide some indications of the scope of the millennial land "jubilee" and its link to the Zimbabwe invasions. On 18 April 2000, anti-riot police dispersed thousands of squatters who had invaded Brooke Bond Kenya Limited land in Buret District. In Eldoret, Nandi leaders urged the then-president Moi to follow the lead of his Zimbabwean counterpart, Robert Mugabe, by allowing them to invade East African Tanning and Extract Company land, which was up for sale. *The Daily Nation* reported that "Nandi community leaders, under Mzee Elisha arap Sang, 70, and Mr William K. Serem, said that, allowing the community to invade the farms which they believe formerly belonged to them, would help eradicate poverty. The group called on community members 'languishing in poverty in places like Tanzania, Uganda, Laikipia, Maasai, Pokot and even in Congo to claim their pieces of land from those who stole from them.'"[43] Meanwhile, Attorney-General Amos Wako said the constitution guaranteed the right of protection of private property, that land invasions violated the constitution, and that such cases "will be dealt with."[44]

On 21 April 2000, MP Stephen Ndicho described himself as "just a spokesman for those millions of Kenyans without land" and reiterated his call for the invasion of white-owned land. In an open letter to the attorney general, Ndicho invited prosecution: "When I call on the white man to now leave these lands for repossession by native Africans, and you threaten to arrest and charge me with incitement, it goes down very badly as far as the millions of landless poor Kenyans are concerned." Ndicho called for a new pan-Africanist movement aimed at reclaiming all the African land still under the ownership of whites on the continent "because land ownership is not an exclusively Zimbabwean issue."[45]

In May Ndicho launched what he called the Pan-African Movement Over Ancestral Land (Pamoa), aimed at seizing farms from white settlers. Ndicho said that Moi was trying to divert attention by saying that the call would amount to tribal clashes. He said: "We are interested in white-owned land and not African."[46] Many of the large estates in Kenya are owned by black people. In fact, African land has been invaded. *The Daily Nation* of 31 May 2000 reported that "[t]he latest wave of ranch invasions follows a series of incursions on farmland in the district between October last year and January. The President's Kabarak Farm at Laikipia's Segere Location was one of those affected. Other ranches invaded also belonged to prominent Kenyans."[47]

More than 11,000 cattle have died due to drought in Laikipia district, where some 200,000 people were said in 2000 to be in urgent need of relief food out of a population of about 300,000. The invading pastoralists, who claimed that the ranches were part of their ancestral land, were reported to have told the district commissioner that they would "rather die together with their livestock than leave the ranches before the rains came." The Lokdong'oi ranch manager, Lance Tom Harrison, said he feared his 5,000 beef cattle reared on the farm "could die of starvation as about 8,000 cattle, which had moved onto his ranch with herders, would exhaust his pasture if not evicted within a week."[48]

As tensions rose around the Zimbabwe land invasions, the British high commissioner in Nairobi warned Kenyans that foreign investors were being scared off by the calls to take over white-owned land. However, he stated that "British-Kenyans who own land here have no reason to panic at all."[49] Foreign partisans and commentators have been virtually unanimous in decrying the supposed negative environmental impacts of small subsistence holdings and their alleged inability to provide sufficient food.[50] These prejudices ignore the ample evidence that demonstrates that Kenyan Africans' indigenous farming approach maintains substantial advantages over the monocropping and heavily petro-chemical-dependent methods of commercial farmers and over the seed varieties the colonialists imported and popularized.[51]

The Kenyan land invasions of the new millennium differ from the Ugandan Idi Amin-style massacre and eviction of Asians in Uganda in the 1970s in at least the following three ways. First, the thousands of hectares of land being occupied by the landless are capable of directly sustaining thousands of people who will grow their own food and reestablish regional trade networks and social patterns of mutual support. This differs sharply from the expropriation of Asian firms and Amin's practice of handing them out to his cronies who quickly milked them dry.

Second, the land reappropriations in Kenya have so far shown that white-owned farms are not under special attack. In fact, all large landholdings are subject to invasion, whether owned by Del Monte, Brooke Bond, local white families, or the president. Also subject to invasion are government farms in process of being privatized, degazzetted forest land and urban commons. The land invasions in Kenya,[52] are motivated by the extreme inequality in distribution of resources and incomes between the wealthy and the dispossessed. Africa's land invasions are primarily class warfare.

Third, because the land invasions of the new millennium in Kenya are aimed at the dispossession of large landholders, they are distinctly set apart from state-sponsored violence in the land wars of the 1990s. In these, the government orchestrated the massacre and eviction of smallholding peasants.[53] The beneficiaries were members of the African elite along with foreign firms in agrobusiness or real estate speculation.

CONCLUSION

The land invasions of the new millennium find their organizational and philosophical groundings in the feminist actions in Maragua and Freedom Corner, which were aimed expressly at the elaboration and defence of subsistence economies and social relations. Maragua women demonstrated that a certain type of reappropriation of the means of production has been possible, especially when men joined in women's plans to replace coffee with food crops. The reappropriation by peasants of subsistence production *on the land that they already owned* in Maragua foreshadowed the more difficult reappropriation by the dispossessed of *land owned by others*, notably transnational capital and the neo-liberal, privatizing state. The millennium invasions built on the explicit reestablishment by the women of Freedom Corner of open confrontation between the dispossessed and the corporate-sponsored state. This confrontation had been muted and pushed underground since the Mau Mau war ended in the 1960s.

Three lessons that might be taken from the experience of women cultivators in Maragua are, first, that capital organizes women to break exploitative relationships with men and then to join with other women to pursue common class objectives that are shared by people of different ethnicities. The emphasis in structural adjustment program on increased coffee exports meant that husbands pressured women to divert more land and labour away from food production. Corrupt government officials and husbands appropriated most of the coffee money. As a result, very little reached the women producers, who were therefore unable to feed and educate their children. On the other hand, women and their families belonged to coffee cooperative societies. Women's affiliation in the co-ops laid a basis for the development of a common response to their exploitation. Together, women intercropped, refused to work on coffee, and finally uprooted the trees. When women replaced coffee with bananas, they broke an individualized labour process organized by husbands and reestablished a collective production process organized by their own work groups. Resistance against the coffee industry, as manifest in women's work groups in Maragua, cut across ethnic boundaries.

The second lesson relates to the fragility of men's alliances with state officials and international capital. When wives refused to produce coffee, the fragile "male deal" between husbands, the state, and capital dissolved. The myth of the male breadwinner was exposed. The Maragua study suggests that working-class men's abdication of domination over women workers and wives not only extends the scope of all workers' initiatives to control resources but also breaks hierarchical relationships that keep women and men producers hungry, enslaved to capital, and repressed by dictatorship. In repudiating the "male deal," peasant men positioned themselves to work in a gendered class alliance with women in their mutual interests.

The third lesson involves the movement of women cultivators into direct confrontation with international capital. Our analysis confirms the insight that neo-liberal government functionaries predicate their structural adjustment programs on the effectiveness of husbands' discipline over wives' labour.[54] Those women who reject this discipline do so through a transformative process that starts by satisfying the needs of the dispossessed. This undercuts a crucial source of ethnic antagonisms: competition amongst factions of the exploited for resources that are dominated by capital. In repudiating gendered exploitation, women cultivators in Maragua, Kenya go beyond neo-liberalism and the ethnicized violence through which it is imposed.

What capacities do the invaders have to survive counterinsurgency on behalf of local and foreign capital? Colonial capitalists employed African accomplices or "male dealers" in the alienation of Africans' land and in the virtual elimination of many ecologically and nutritionally beneficial indigenous agricultural practices. These male dealers acted as Home Guards or armed defenders of British colonialism against the Mau Mau in the 1950s. Women and dispossessed men then faced an independent African government dominated by Home Guards after 1963. This state organized armed attacks on subsistence defenders beginning in 1991 and continuing throughout the 1990s. These attacks produced a refugee population of some 300,000, and encouraged the growth of groups such as Mungiki and Muungano wa Wanavijiji, aimed to defend subsistence farmers and traders.

In 1998 the Kenyan government purchased riot control tanks from South Africa and used them on the streets against protestors. More generally, the threat of international intervention, overtly or covertly, through counterinsurgency strategies is heightened as multinational corporations and European farmers are targeted for dispossession. In 1999 Susan George quoted "the man who used to be charged with thinking about future warfare for the Pentagon" as stating that "[t]he de facto role of the U.S. armed forces will be to keep the world safe for our economy and open to our cultural assault. To those ends, we will do a fair amount of killing."[55]

We identify the growing internationalization of resistance, typified by the Zapatistas' employment of the internet to build support and defence, as a process of *globalization from below*. It attacks and replaces corporate globalization from above. Cross-border coordination of resistance has been elaborated in Africa through the internet as well as through personal contacts and many informal channels. Peoples in Zimbabwe and Kenya share similar histories of settler colonization by the British, armed anti-colonial struggles and neo-colonial "willing seller – willing buyer" land policies instead of redistribution to small farmers at independence. Groups within both countries now have occupied land to resolve their impoverishment by local and multinational capital. As corporations compound the global range of their control, they impose increasingly similar conditions on more and more of humanity. In saying "no" to corporate globalization, diverse social actors establish mutual awareness of each other's struggles and demands. These build on each other in the practical process of the circulation of struggles. Protestors in Seattle in December 1999 and in Washington D.C. in April 2000 *called for* the reappropriation of what capital has alienated. In the year 2000, Zimbabweans and Kenyans *actually* dispossessed capital by invading land. And like the banana growing women of Maragua, the land invaders, in effect, repudiated debt by refusing to allow the cultivation and export of luxury cash crops that deprive people of food in order to generate foreign exchange to service government loans. The anti-export crop farmers and land invaders in Kenya have advanced the intercontinental resistance to neo-liberalism by strengthening the organizational, spiritual, and material foundations upon which further resurgence of the subsistence economy is being built. This creative process poses a range of challenges to corporate globalization. One challenge lies in its potential to link strikes by producers with boycotts by consumers of corporate commodities. Such a link squeezes the "money sequences" and profit-takers from all sides.[56] It also constitutes an organizational framework for alternative "fair trade" exchanges of self-valorized use values.

The concept of a fight for fertility helps us move away from the constructed, false, and disempowering image of the poor (and especially poor women) as passive, incapacitated victims who accept being consigned to the category of what Susan George calls "the outcasts, people who are not even worth exploiting."[57] In contrast, the fight for fertility conceptualization provides us with analytical tools to excavate and render visible the actually existing alternatives to what John McMurtry calls the death economy.[58] The actually existing subsistence political economy in Kenya emerges as a strong node in an international array of more or less connected subsistence solutions to the problem of unbridled drives for ever higher money returns. The capacity of subsistence workers to withstand counterinsurgency (disguised as "ethnic" conflict) has much to do with international movements drive to reappropriate land and the fight for fertility from below. This elaboration of a new international economic order expresses a human need to survive the economy of death.

NOTES

1 Speaking in Seattle, at a forum on "The WTO and the global war system," during the build-up to the closing down of the World Trade Organisation on 28 November 1999, Susan George of Amsterdam's Transnational Institute identified three effects of globalization: "One, it pushes money from the bottom to the top. Wealth moves upwards, towards those who already have wealth. All over the place inequalities are growing and wealth is moving towards the top. Two, globalization moves *power* from the bottom to the top, and concentrates it in the hands of very few people. In particular, it concentrates it at the international level where there's no democracy and no way for citizens to get a handle on what is happening. Three, globalization is creating a myriad of losers. It is creating a slice of people who are not useful to the global economy either as producers or consumers. We're creating through globalization a three-track society in which there will be the exploiters, the exploited and the outcasts, the people who are not even worth exploiting. This is clearly a scenario for tremendous instability." Susan George, "The Corporate Utopian Dream," in Estelle Taylor, ed., *The WTO and the Global War System,* Vancouver: International Network on Disarmament and Globalization (405–825 Granville St., Vancouver, BC V6Z 1K9, ph. 604–687–3223, www.indg.org), 28 November 1999, 1–2.

2 Tony Clarke, "How to take advantage of the WTO's "crisis of legitimacy," *The CCPA Monitor* 7, no. 2 (June 2000) 1,6. The *CCPA Monitor* is published by the Canadian Centre for Policy Alternatives, #410–75 Albert Street, Ottawa, ON KIP 5E7, Canada. ccpa@policyalternatives.ca; http://www.policyalternatives.ca.

3 John McMurtry, *The Cancer Stage of Capitalism*, London: Pluto, 1999, 171–8; Terisa Turner, Leigh S. Brownhill and Wahu M. Kaara, "Gender, Food Security and Foreign Policy Toward Africa: Women Farmers and the Sustenance Economy in Kenya," in Rosalind Irwin, ed., *Ethics and Security in Canadian Foreign Policy*, Vancouver: University of British Columbia Press, 2001, 145–176.

4 D.F. Bryceson, "African Women Hoe Cultivators: Speculative Origins and Current Enigmas," in D.F. Bryceson, ed., *Women Wielding the Hoe: Lessons for Feminist Theory and Development Practice*, Oxford: Berg Publishers, 1995, 17.

5 The "New World Order" is based on a new international division of labour as capital flees the high-cost, militant labour sites of the north to the "housewifized" south. According to Caffentzis and Federici, the global spread of female "shadow work" represents capital's flight from "the First World feminist revolt against reproductive labor work." The transnational explosion of the sex trade, pornography industry,

mail-order-bride business, and baby adoption market all represent "enormous quotas of reproduction work which capital has exported in the same way that there has been a strategy of exporting part of the manufacturing process with the free enterprise zones." George Caffentzis and Silvia Federici, "Modern Land Wars and the Myth of the High-Tech Economy," in Cindy Duffy and Craig Benjamin, eds., *The World Transformed: Gender, Labour and International Solidarity in the Era of Free Trade, Structural Adjustment and GATT*, Guelph, Ontario: RhiZone, 1994, 144, cited in Nick Dyer-Witheford *Cyber-Marx: Cycles and Circuits of Struggle in High-Technology Capitalism*, Urbana and Chicago: University of Illinois Press, 1999, 135–6.

6 Veronika Bennholdt-Thompsen, and Maria Mies, *The Subsistence Perspective: Beyond the Globalised Economy*, London: Zed Books, 1999, 20.

7 Against the social Darwinism of Rostow, which poses ineluctable "stages of growth" or "catching-up development" from traditional (subsistence) to modern (industrial) societies, we pose industrialization and technology as capitalist weaponry to break up not only worker solidarity but also peasant social relations of self-reliance and sustenance. Walt W. Rostow, *The Stages of Economic Growth: A Non-Communist Manifesto*, Cambridge: Cambridge University Press, 1960. In this vein Harry Cleaver argues that to combat communist insurgency in Asia, U.S. development agencies sponsored new plant stocks and agricultural techniques aimed at breaking down the traditional village structures. This was intended to eliminate the communities within which "guerrillas moved like fish in the sea," and to foster a proletariat for industry that could be fed from rural production. The Green Revolution, argues Cleaver, "provided agricultural technology as the civil side to counterinsurgency warfare." Harry Cleaver, "Technology as Political Weaponry," in Robert Anderson, ed., *Science, Politics and the Agricultural Revolution in Asia*, Boulder, Colorado: Westview, 1981, 276, cited in Dyer-Witheford, *Cyber-Marx*, 70.

8 McMurtry, *The Cancer Stage of Capitalism*.

9 Bennholdt-Thompsen and Mies, *The Subsistence Perspective*, 20–1.

10 Terisa E. Turner, Wahu M. Kaara, and Leigh S. Brownhill, "Social Reconstruction in Rural Africa: A Gendered Class Analysis of Women's Resistance to Cash Crop Production in Kenya," *Canadian Journal of Development Studies* 18, no. 2, (1997), 213–38.

11 Bennholdt-Thompsen and Mies, *The Subsistence Perspective*, 11.

12 Two reductions in women's entitlements to land, introduced with colonial capitalist agriculture are, first, the suppression of the practice of widows "marrying" another woman and thereby becoming a husband with all the land rights of their deceased husbands; and second, the

failure or impossibility of husbands allocating to their wives plots of land on which to grow food crops. This second curtailment arose both because of land shortage as the rich accumulated huge tracts and because peasant land was being used for export and cash crops. See A. Fiona D. MacKenzie, *Land, Ecology and Resistance in Kenya, 1880–1952*, Portsmouth, N.H.: Heinemann, 1998, on "female husbands."

13 Kenya has the world's second highest rich-poor gap, after Brazil. In the 1990s Amnesty International included Kenya in the list of ten most repressive, torture-ridden countries in the world. Torture and state-sponsored terror have persisted since the 1950s British war, which quelled the Mau Mau Land and Freedom Army. African men who fought on the side of British colonialists through their Home Guard people the ruling party and its forces of repression.

14 Leigh S. Brownhill, Wahu M. Kaara, and Terisa E. Turner, "Gender Relations and Sustainable Agriculture: Rural Women's Resistance to Structural Adjustment in Kenya," *Canadian Woman Studies/Les Cahiers de la Femme* 17, no. 2 (Spring 1997), 40–4; George, "The Corporate Utopian Dream," 1–2.

15 In this chapter we employ a feminist Marxist perspective that is grounded in C.L.R. James and Selma James' work on revolutionary insurgency and the centrality of the "invisible," "housewifized" women to capitalist exploitation and to the process of social transformation. In 1947 C.L.R. James wrote of the movement of history that "[a]t a certain stage a developing contradiction, so to speak, explodes, and both the elements of contradiction are thereby altered. In the history of society these explosions are known as revolutions. All the economic, social and political tendencies of the age find a point of completion which becomes the starting-point of the new tendencies." C.L.R. James, "Dialectical Materialism and the Fate of Humanity" (1947), in Anna Grimshaw, ed., *The C.L.R. James Reader*, Oxford: Blackwell, 1992, 153–81.

16 Dyer-Witheford outlines the conception that "workers' struggles provide the dynamic of capitalist development" and capital seeks to free itself from the working class through imposing "successively wider and deeper dimensions of control – toward the creation of a social factory" in which the reproduction of labour power plays a crucial but invisibilized role. Waged men command unpaid labour time outside the workplace in the form of housework. The social factory includes peasants and other unwaged people subject to capital's exaction. "If capitalist production now requires an entire network of social relations, these constitute so many more points where its operations can be ruptured." C.L.R. James pointed to the complexity of the exploited with each faction expressing specific demands and organizational forms. For Dyer-Witheford, recognition of this "variety within labor" leads "away from

vanguardist, centralized organization, directed from above, toward a lateral, polycentric concept of anticapitalist alliances-in-diversity, connecting a plurality of agencies in a *circulation of struggles*." Dyer-Witheford, *Cyber-Marx*, 68.

17 Terisa E. Turner and M.O. Oshare, "Women's Uprisings Against the Nigerian Oil Industry in the 1980s," *Canadian Journal of Development Studies* 14, no. 3 (October 1993), 329–57; Audrey Wipper, "Kikuyu women and the Harry Thuku Disturbances: Some Uniformities of Female Militancy," in Terisa E. Turner, ed., *Mau Mau Women: Their Mothers, Their Daughters, A Century of Popular Struggle in Kenya*, forthcoming.

18 Leigh S. Brownhill, "Struggle for the Soil: Mau Mau and the British War Against Women 1939–1956," unpublished major paper, Master of Arts Program, Department of Sociology and Anthropology; International Development Studies, Guelph: University of Guelph, December 1994.

19 Ibid.

20 Terisa E. Turner, ed., with B. Ferguson, *Arise Ye Mighty People! Gender, Class and Race in Popular Struggles*, Trenton, New Jersey: Africa World Press, 1994. See especially chap. 2.

21 A more detailed account is available in Leigh S. Brownhill, Wahu M. Kaara, and Terisa E. Turner, "Gender Relations and Sustainable Agriculture: Rural Women's Resistance to Structural Adjustment in Kenya," *Canadian Woman Studies/Les Cahiers de la Femme* 17, no. 2 (Spring 1997), 40–4. (York University, Ontario, cwscf@yorku.ca, http://www.yorku.ca/org/cwscf/home.html).

22 Bina Agarwal, "Gender and Command Over Property: A Critical Gap in Economic Analysis and Policy in South Asia," *World Development*, 22, no. 10 (1994), 1455–78.

23 We conducted interviews throughout the 1990s as part of a small international group of participant researchers called First Woman (East and Southern Africa Women's Oral History and Indigenous Knowledge Network). All interviews are cited as "First Woman," followed by the date.

24 Republic of Kenya, *Murang'a District Development Plan, 1994–1996*, Rural Planning Department: Office of the Vice President and Ministry of Planning and National Development, 1993, 1, 12.

25 World Bank, *Adjustment in Africa: Reforms, Results and the Road Ahead*, Washington D.C.: World Bank, 13 March 1994.

26 First Woman interview, Reverend Samwel Theuri, Tumutumu, 2 January 1997.

27 Catherine Mgendi, "Reasons for Decline in Agricultural Production," *Daily Nation*, Nairobi, 3 October 1996, 1; Catherine Mgendi, "Sector Records Negative Growth Rates," *Daily Nation*, Nairobi, 13 December 1996, 4.

28 "Government Plans Fundamental Reforms For Agriculture," *Daily Nation*, Nairobi, 3 October 1996, 1–2.

29 In the town of Sagana, near Maragua town, small-business women refused to deliver coffee to government buyers and simultaneously demanded that the KANU regime repeal section 2(A) of the Kenya constitution, which outlawed opposition political parties. When the coffee industry collapsed, the Paris Club of donors, in 1991, ordered Kenya's President Moi to legalize multi-party democracy. He complied in 1992. First Woman interview, Zawadi Women's Group, Sagana, 7 October 1996.

30 First Woman interview, Beldina Adhiambo, Nairobi, 27 July 1997.

31 *Daily Nation*, 28 February 1992, 2.

32 First Woman interview, Wahu Kaara, Maragua, 12 May 1996; First Woman interview, Ruth Wangari wa Thungu, Nairobi, 29 May 1996; First Woman interview, Ruth Wangari wa Thungu, Nairobi, 24 July 1996; First Woman interview, Wanjiru Kahiga, Nairobi, 4 September 1996; First Woman interview, Elizabeth Wanjiru wa Gatenjo, Nairobi, 15 January 1997.

33 First Woman interview, Ruth Wangari wa Thungu, Nairobi, 29 May 1996.

34 Turner and Oshare, "Women's Uprisings."

35 John McMurtry defines the "civil commons" as any cooperative human construction and agency that enables the access of all members of a community to life goods. The civil commons has innumerable expressions, from vernacular language itself to public health care, regulated clean air and water, universal education, public art and architecture, open environmental spaces, nutritious food, adequate shelter, and affective interaction. *Unequal Freedoms: The Global Market as an Ethical System*, Toronto and Westport, CT: Garamond Press, 1998 and Kumarian, 1999.

36 *Daily Nation*, Nairobi, 21 May 2000. www.nationaudio.com/News/DailyNation

37 Kenyan member of Parliament and member of the then ruling KANU party, Mr Kipruto arap Kirwa said in Parliament on 11 April 2000 that the "Nandi MPs were serious in their claim that the East African Tanning and Extract Company land be returned to its original owners – the Nandi. ... He said the community would reclaim 24,000 hectares and another 30,000 hectares in the Nandi tea zones." Around the same time, MP Stephen Ndicho began a vocal campaign of encouraging Kenyans to invade white-owned land. He called for the invasion of land owned by three multinationals in Central Province – Del Monte, Kakuzi, and Socfinaf. *Daily Nation*, Nairobi, 13 April 2000, www.nationaudio.com/News/DailyNation.

38 Terisa E. Turner, "Land to make a living," *Guardian Weekly*, 8–14 June 2000, 13 (gwsubna@time.ca http://guardianweekly.com).

39 The so-called "ethnic clashes" in Kenya are part of an international pattern of counterinsurgency against indigenous resistance to corporate takeover of local economies. First, the subsistence, mixed and national economies are destroyed by neo-liberal policies enforced by the World Bank and IMF. Then resistance is crushed through state-sponsored terror, passed off to an international media audience as tribal atavism, and hence not worthy of the concern of especially Western citizens. Michel Chossoduvsky has documented this pattern in eleven countries in *The Globalization of Poverty*, London: Zed, 1998. The Peace Research Institute in Oslo, Norway has found that of the ninety-eight major wars in the years 1990 through 1998 there were five commonalities: (1) cash-poor agriculturally based economies; (2) high levels of land degradation, low fresh-water availability, and high population density; (3) a high rate of external debt; (4) a falling rate of export income from primary commodities; and (5) vigorous intervention in the economy by the IMF. Most of these were wars taking place within the borders of a country. Susan George has argued that a high degree of mercenary intervention and covert operation by the United States military in escalating civil wars are established givens ("The Corporate Utopian Dream").

40 First Woman interview, Muungano wa Wanavijiji members, Nairobi, 25 July 1998.

41 *Daily Nation*, Nairobi, 19 April 2000 www.nationaudio.com/News/DailyNation.

42 First Woman interview, Women of Mungiki, Nairobi, 23 July 1998; First Woman interview, Men of Mungiki, Nairobi, 23 July 1998; First Woman interview, Women elders of Mungiki, Nairobi, 24 July 1998; First Woman interview, Muungano wa Wanavijiji members, Nairobi, 25 July 1998.

43 *Daily Nation*, Nairobi, 19 April 2000, www.nationaudio.com/News/DailyNation.

44 Ibid.

45 *Daily Nation*, Nairobi, 22 April 2000, www.nationaudio.com/News/DailyNation.

46 *Daily Nation*, Nairobi, 8 May 2000, www.nationaudio.com/News/DailyNation.

47 *Daily Nation*, Nairobi, 31 May 2000, www.nationaudio.com/News/DailyNation.

48 Ibid.

49 *Daily Nation*, Nairobi, 17 May 2000, www.nationaudio.com/News/DailyNation.

50 An indication of the threat that the subsistence economy poses to the commodified economy is provided by Fraser Thornburn, who wrote that "George Monbiot argues that land redistribution in Zimbabwe 'would enable the poor to produce staple crops for the landless.' It is precisely the severe population pressures in Zimbabwe that make productive commercial farms essential. Even without the current crisis, successful resettlement would demand training and support, costing as much, perhaps, as the purchase of the land itself. Simply buying up the land and dividing it up among the poor would create new communal lands, over-grazed and under-utilized." Fraser Thornburn, "Laying Claim to Zimbabwe's Land," *Guardian Weekly*, 11 May 2000, 13 (*gwsubna@time.ca* or http://guardianweekly.com). In a similar vein, a Kenyan editorial stated, concerning Zimbabwe's landless, "To the landless poor, neither the adverse economic implications of the subsequent land fragmentation, nor the threat of shrinkage in food production owing to envisaged employment of *rudimentary subsistence farming techniques*, make any difference. All they want is land and they want it now, not tomorrow. Half a loaf to them is a lot better than none, and it is big enough to kill for (emphasis added)." *Daily Nation*, Nairobi, 8 May 2000, www.nationaudio.com/News/DailyNation.

51 The advantages of indigenous crops and practices range from the nitrate-storing capacity of pigweed, which Kikuyu farmers did not weed out from their millet plots, to the high calcium, magnesium and protein content in indigenous millet, and the drought,- pest,- and disease-resistance of indigenous millet, which colonialists almost completely replaced with maize, of far lower nutritional quality and far higher negative impact on the environment. The indigenous practice of intercropping was found to provide more food than monocropping or any other system, protect soil from rain and sun, provide a constant insurance against locust, and produce fodder for cattle and goats. Indigenous methods of storing seed in wood ash can prevent weevil damage for at least twelve months. These subsistence crops and techniques substantially enhanced women's control over production. In contrast, European capitalist market-focused agriculture has meant that the control over production and income has moved from women's to men's hands. Export-oriented agriculture has increased soil erosion through the enforcement of practices such as "clean-weeding," which removes protective covering from around crops; terracing, which increases "raindrop erosion;" "deep-tilling," which disturbs the soil integrity; and "pure cropping," which exhausts the soil fertility and rules out the continuous ground cover effected through intercropping. "Pure cropping" or monocropping leads to greater vulnerability to pests and disease. See MacKenzie, *Land, Ecology and Resistance in Kenya.*

It is not the "rudimentary subsistence agricultural techniques" that have lead to the elimination of the "enormous quantities" and "inexhaustible supplies" of "sweet potatoes, yams, cassava, sugar cane, sorghum and millet" from Kenya's Central Province. In fact, those techniques *created* the vast surpluses noted by early European missionaries and explorers. Instead, the colonialists' and neo-colonialists' prioritization of export cash crops over provisioning of local communities has lead to the large-scale conversion of African agriculture from millet to maize, from vegetables to coffee and tea, and from cattle and sheep to wheat, pyrethrum, and sisal. In addition, the colonialists' establishment of tribal reserves, which survive into the new millennium, has meant that far too many people are confined to areas that are far too small, leading to soil erosion and hunger. Outside the reserve, multinationals and local capitalists utilize enormous tracts of land for export crops, chemically damaging the soil and laying ruin to soil fertility. Environmental alarmists who believe that subsistence farmers who invade land will "over-graze and under-utilize" that land are stuck within the premises of the continued existence of the "tribal reserve" where overcrowding results from fixed boundaries and gross inequality in the distribution of non-reserve land. Land may well be under-utilized from the perspective of profit-making while simultaneously be fully utilized with respect to the life-sustaining value of that production.

52 See www.cosatu.org.za for a cautious and non-committal statement from the Congress of South African Trade Unions on the Zimbabwe land invasions. In contrast to the South African President Thabo Mbeki's condemnation of the occupation of agro-industrial establishments in Zimbabwe and his call for a give-back, the powerful trade union confederation poses questions about land redistribution in Zimbabwe. In South Africa land invasions have taken place since the Zimbabwe movement began. For instance, black African farmers in the eastern Cape have occupied land they long claimed as theirs, citing their impatience with the interminable delays of the virtually ineffective government land adjudication board.

53 In 1992, Moi was, like Mugabe in 2000, organizing to win votes. But Moi did so by attacking those who might vote against him and clearing the lands they occupied to make way for local and foreign private agrobusiness and profiteering. Mugabe took a different approach: he sought to reward in advance those who were expected to vote for him with permission to occupy thousands of hectares of land. Mugabe may well maintain his power base, but at the same time, he has put his supporters, the land invaders, in the line of fire of the commercial farmers and the covert guns of the CIA and South African mercenaries.

54 Mariarosa Dalla Costa and Giovanna F. Dalla Costa, eds., *Paying the price: women and the politics of international economic strategy*, New Jersey: Zed Books, 1995.

55 Susan George, "The Corporate Utopian Dream," 1–2.

56 McMurtry, *Unequal Freedoms*, 102–3.

57 George, "The Corporate Utopian Dream," 1–2.

58 McMurtry, "The Economics of Life and Death," unpublished paper presented at the World Congress of Philosophers Conference, Boston, MA, August 1998.

Cuba's Encounter with the Changing Faces of Imperialism

KEITH ELLIS

With the Monroe Doctrine of 1823 the United States announced its intention to be the imperialist power of the Western hemisphere. Its intervention in 1898 in the Cuban War of Independence from Spain marked the beginning of the process of putting the intention into practice, and in the ensuing five years that culminated in the 1903 signing of the Platt Amendment to the Cuban Constitution of 1902, the U.S. demonstrated the domineering and coercive attitude that would henceforth characterize its relations with the Latin American and Caribbean countries. This attitude to Cuba, which all along was met with resistance from Cuban patriots, has become heightened since the triumph of the Revolution in 1959 and has necessitated new, and now national, ways of resistance.

When on 12 May 1989 the then U.S. president George Bush, in an address at Texas A & M University, declared his willingness to welcome the U.S.S.R. into a New World Order, his gesture initiated a process that would make global the reach of U.S. policies. Bush's successor, Bill Clinton, frequently insisted on countries worldwide adopting what he called free-market democracy. This requirement of the New World Order in fact emphasized the measurable corporate benefits of the free market and of privatization rather than democracy, with all the potential hazards in its definition. The term "free-market democracy" is a definition of democracy tailored to the New World Order and suited to the controllers of capital. Privatization, from Russia to Argentina, has brought such mammoth personal benefits to the political and business elites at the expense of the rest of the population as to make these elites unscrupulously enamoured of this form of democracy. Smaller countries have usually responded to these developments in a way that suggests they have accepted the insistent admonition coming from newspaper columnists, orthodox academics, and the principal lending institutions that there is no alternative. Some industrialized countries, Canada among them, follow with apparent enthusiasm the U.S. lead and become proselytisers for the doctrine, in Canada's case particularly in Latin America and the Caribbean. Cuba, however, has found in its history and its culture ample and secure grounds for resistance and for restoring and strengthening its ties to Latin America and the Caribbean with an economic system that represents a challenge to the New World Order. It articulates this challenge in various fora, attracting supportive intellectuals of the highest international repute.

In 1891 José Martí, the great Cuban patriot who is regarded as his country's national hero published an essay entitled "Our America." The essay was the culmination of ideas he had been developing over the previous decade and which stemmed from a dual preoccupation. On the one hand, he observed the failure on the part of the Latin American countries (his "our America") to break decisively with their colonial past in order to become societies based on their true identities and to bring those sectors of the population that were especially mistreated during the period of Spanish domination (the aboriginal populations and those forcefully brought to the Americas) into a state of real redress. At the same time Martí believed that the somnolent continuation of the habits of the colonies in the nominal republics kept those countries weak, making them vulnerable to a new peril related to the old colonial one. Martí resorted to allegory to illustrate this concern:

It was imperative to make common cause with the oppressed, in order to secure a new system opposed to the self-interests and governing habits of the oppressors. The tiger, frightened by gunfire, returns at night to the site of his prey .... He cannot be heard coming because he approaches with velvet-covered claws. When the prey awakens, the tiger is already upon it. (Martí 2: 523)[1]

He later added:

The disdain of our formidable neighbour who does not know us is Latin America's greatest danger; and since the day of the visit is near, it is imperative that our neighbour know us, and soon, so that it will not disdain us. Through ignorance, it might even come to lay greedy hands on us. Once it does know us, it will remove its hands out of respect. (Martí 2, 526)

Martí's alertness to the new peril was exceptional among Spanish American and Caribbean thinkers of his time. It is true that more than

sixty years earlier Simón Bolívar, while insisting on the right and indeed
the necessity of the Spanish American countries to create their appropriate forms of government, had condemned and predicted the persis-
tence of negative U.S. behaviour toward Spanish America. He had
written: "The United States seems destined by providence to plague
Latin America with misery in the name of liberty."[2] But none of Martí's
predecessors or contemporaries approached the perspicacity and acute-
ness with which, even while acknowledging the industrial prowess of
the United States and the attractiveness of some of its writers, he
exposed by word and by actions the machinations with which that
country was attempting to structure formal imperialistic relations with
Spanish America. Having been banished from Cuba and living in the
U.S., he sought out opportunities to intervene in defence of his vision
of an independent Spanish America in Panamerican conferences organized by the U.S., and he gladly served as the delegate to such conferences for any Spanish American country that would so appoint him.
He was also recognized as the person who had initiated the transformation and elevation of Spanish American literary expression, and
prizing journalism above all his other forms of writing – poetry, fiction,
drama – which he practised with exceptional skill, he contributed
prolifically to the best Spanish American newspapers, *La Nación* of
Buenos Aires, for instance, in an age when newspapers aspired to be
constructive in the national interest.

   In addition to knowing the U.S. well, Martí had always shown a
strong aversion to exploitative relationships. The son of a Spanish
soldier who had gone to Cuba to enforce colonial authority, Martí
from his childhood manifested his abhorrence of slavery and vowed
to end it. From the second decade of the nineteenth century, the most
outstanding Cuban intellectuals – some Jesuits prominent among them
– began to press for the independence of Cuba and of all Spanish
American countries, as well as for the abolition of slavery. They
encouraged the practice of thinking of Cuba as a nation guided by
uplifting social ethics and by developmental economics based on education in the arts as well as the sciences. These thinkers had a precarious
existence in slave-holding colonial Cuba, and in the face of hostility
from the state and the official church that supported it, several of them
were obliged to flee Cuba, including the most lastingly influential,
Father Félix Varela, who died in 1853, the year Martí was born. Martí
absorbed the legacy of these thinkers, holding that the *sine qua non*
for a just, decent, and dignified Cuban society was its enjoyment of
independence. When on 10 October 1868 Carlos Manuel de Céspedes
in eastern Cuba freed his slaves and declared Cuba's independence,

thus starting the War of Independence against Spain, the action was swiftly and popularly supported, particularly in the eastern section of the island, with the black population participating eagerly. The principal factor that had been inhibiting this step, the fear on the part of some whites of a free black population now comparable in size to the white population, was giving way to a growing sense of nationhood. José Martí, then fifteen years old, supported the war effort with such zeal that the Spanish authorities imprisoned him at age seventeen, and, a year later, banished him to Spain. There he continued in his writings to denounce Spanish colonialism, and he urged the Spanish people to have their regime bring it and its cruel concomitants in Cuba to an end.

The independence fighters faced enormous odds. With the victory of the independence movements on the American continent by the third decade of the century, Spain could concentrate its forces, some 250,000–300,000 well-armed troops, in Cuba, the jewel in a rapidly dwindling empire. The colony continued for some seven decades after the continental colonies were freed and slavery continued until 1886, more than five decades after slaves in the English-speaking Caribbean were emancipated. The enormous toll suffered by the independence fighters, who often answered guns with machetes at best, and the various lethal forms of punishment inflicted on their sympathizers amounted to a significant decline in the population, to approximately 1.5 million by the end of the war in 1898. It is estimated that one repressive measure alone, the placing of rural families in urban concentration camps, accounted for at least 150,000 civilian lives in 1896–97.[3] The first phase of the war ended inconclusively after ten years, in 1878, with the Pact of Zanjón, which was denounced by the black rebel general Antonio Maceo, who complained that the twin evils of colonialism and slavery still prevailed in the island. His reaction, known as the "Protesta de Baraguá" had deep resonance in oppressed sectors of the Cuban population, and their resentment grew in response to the intensified repression that marked the ensuing period.

In an unshakeable alliance with Maceo, Martí, who had been allowed to leave Spain but not to return to Cuba, worked assiduously in Spanish America, in the Caribbean, and among the many exiled Cubans in the United States, not only to pursue a war that would bring about an independent, sovereign Cuba but also to design that future Cuba. He formulated the constitution of a cooperative republic by drawing up the bases and statutes of the Cuban Revolutionary Party, a party that he envisaged governing a substantially unified Cuba. The chief obstacle to be overcome in the pursuit of unity were the annexationists, who proposed a close alliance with the U.S.. For Martí they

were decisively undermined by influential newspapers in the U.S. that
were frank in their disrespect for Cubans and in their covetous desire
for Cuba's sugar and tobacco. Martí was energetic in targeting and
condemning these attitudes.[4]

The war's second phase, which Martí planned with Maceo and the
Dominican Republic's Máximo Gómez, began in 1895. Martí returned
to Cuba to participate in the fighting, and two months later, on 19 May
1895, he was killed in battle. On the night before his death, he wrote
to his Mexican friend, Manuel Mercado: "I am in daily danger of
giving my life for my country and for my duty; for I understand that
duty and have the courage to carry it out – the duty of making Cuba
independent and thereby effectively preventing the United States from
spreading through the Antilles and with that additional strength over-
power the lands of Our America" (Martí 3: 576). Martí emphasized
to the last the peril of a looming U.S. imperialism and envisaged his
independent Cuba as presenting it with its biggest challenge in the
Americas.

In the following year Antonio Maceo was also killed in battle, as
subsequently were several of his brothers. Their mother, Mariana
Grajales, regarded as the mother of the Cuban nation in present-day
Cuba, encouraged the zeal with which they gave themselves to the
cause of independence. Without Martí and Maceo, the leadership of
the independence forces showed the same aims, courage, and ethics
those two had shown, but they lacked the discerning knowledge of the
United States that Martí had derived from having lived in that country
for many years: "I have lived in the monster," Martí had written, "and
I know its entrails; and my sling is that of David's" (Martí 3: 576).
There was abundant evidence from both government and media
sources that the U.S. did not consider Cubans to be fit for independence
and would not easily countenance an independent Cuba. Besides, the
opinion began to be openly voiced that a war would be good for U.S.
morale and prestige, to show that the United States was ready to be
an imperial power in competition with the European powers and ready
to comply with the full implications of the Monroe Doctrine of 1823.
Spain, weakened by so many wars in the nineteenth century, would be
a good target. Sectors of the U.S. press took advantage of atrocities
committed by Spain during its war in Cuba to stir up considerable
feeling against that imperial power. The United States promised aid to
the independence fighters, and the sinking of the battleship *Maine* in
Havana harbour provided the dubious pretext for intervention. This
was their first organized overseas expansionist military venture; their
previous ones had been against Mexico and Canada countries that are
on their borders.

In the conduct of their intervention in the Cuban independence war, the United States displayed disdain for their professed Cuban allies at every turn. Cuban independence fighters who had engaged the Spanish forces in order to facilitate the landing of U.S. troops in Santiago were promptly prohibited by the Americans from entering armed into Santiago. The reason given by the Americans for their prohibition – that the Cubans would engage in looting – added insult to the injury. The conduct of the diplomatic exercises at the end of the war brought much more enduring humiliation to the Cubans. In a flagrant show of imperialist manners, Cuba was given no voice by the Americans in negotiating the terms of the Treaty of Paris that ended what for them was the Spanish-American War. The Americans also supervised the constitution of the Cuban Republic and the implementation of its electoral system, giving the U.S. a continuing interventionist right to protect their interests in the country.[5] Further, by an amendment to the constitution, the Platt Amendment, the U.S. gave itself the right to occupy militarily and in perpetuity the part of Cuba known as Guantanamo Bay for the purpose of refuelling ships.

The first Cuban Republic was thus launched in May 1902, with institutions fashioned by the United States so as to serve the purpose of continuing U.S. control. The fate Martí had feared for Spanish America and the Antilles, and had tried to avert by making Cuba independent, had befallen Cuba itself. Cuban writers felt the cruel irony. In poetry and prose they decried the prevalence of a second flag on the island. They applied parody and sarcasm to the socio-political situation that Jorge Mañach, a prominent essayist, characterized as "that mockery of a Republic, that illusion of nationality in a colonized, humiliated people."[6] The recrudescence of racism, combined with a divisive electoral system, led to a conflict in 1912 in which more than 10,000 blacks were killed. And in the Platticized republic the system of ownership and employment was marked by unrestrained penetration of U.S. entities into lucrative and influential sectors of the economy. It was a system that had as its concomitant a callous indifference to the well-being and personal development of workers, the bulk of them seasonal, who occupied the lowest socio-economic stratum. The poet Nicolás Guillén encapsulated this situation in his poem entitled "Sugar Cane," from his book *Sóngoro cosongo* (1931):

The black man
next to the canefield.
The Yankee
over the canefield.
The land

under the canefield.
Blood that goes out from us!

The police and the military, armed by the U.S., were the bulwark of
this structure. In the period following 10 March 1952, when Fulgencio
Batista as head of the armed forces seized control of the government,
they were rampant in spreading terror. On 26 July 1953 Fidel Castro
led an attack on a stronghold of the repressive forces, the Moncada
military barracks in Santiago de Cuba. His sense of history was shown
in the inspiration he derived both from the fact that 1953 was the
centenary of Martí's birth and from Martí's intellectual and personal
guidance in beginning the Cuban revolutionary movement. Castro also
alluded to a painful episode in Cuban history when, on the triumph
of the revolutionary forces in January 1959, he declared that no one
was going to prevent those forces from entering Santiago de Cuba as
the Americans had done to the Cuban independence fighters in 1898.
The declaration was an early indication that Cuba had finally won the
sovereignty for which it had been struggling on a grand scale since
1868 and, as Castro was later to say, that was an aspiration from the
time the first palenque or freed enclave was set up by maroons or
escaped slaves in the sixteenth century. The dichotomies of sovereignty
or slavery, homeland or death, became watchwords of revolutionary
Cuba.
   This meant that the United States would have to recognize Cuba's
sovereignty and stop treating Cuba like a colony, or it could strive to
overturn Cuba's government and reinstate the institutions and systems
that would facilitate the penetration of U.S. economic and ideological
control. By imperialist habit, the U.S. has chosen the latter course and
has employed the full gamut of subversive devices that its powerful
economy can afford in its quest to dominate Cuba. Cuba has revealed
that the direct acts of violence alone perpetrated since 1959 by people
directed or supported by the U.S., including the Bay of Pigs invasion,
have resulted in 3,478 Cuban deaths and 2,099 permanently incapacitated Cuban citizens. This does not include the effects of sabotage on
the Cuban economy admitted by the CIA, such as the introduction into
the country of African swine fever in an attempt to destroy the pork
industry, a mainstay of the Cuban food supply. And above all, the
embargo in force since 1961 has made trade expensive when not
impossible for Cuba. The brutal opportunism of the embargo was
evident in 1981, for instance, when a strain of hemorrhagic dengue,
unknown except in laboratories, appeared in Cuba in epidemic proportions, causing hundreds of deaths. Cuban scientists determined that
the vector was the *Aedes aegypti* mosquito; they made arrangements

to purchase insecticide for control of the mosquito from a Mexican company and in the crisis sent air transport to collect what they thought they had purchased. But the Americans discovered that one of their companies owned a part of the Mexican company, and on this basis the sale was cancelled. In the course of the years the Americans have been contriving ways to tighten the embargo and to insist on its observance by subsidiaries of U.S. companies operating in other countries, and the pressure has led even some non-U.S. companies to comply. But even those countries that make spirited protests against the embargo, introduced by the Toricelli-sponsored Cuban Democracy Act of 1992 and subsequently tightened by the Helms-Burton Law of 1996, are not concerned with an aspect of this latter law that goes to the core of persistent U.S. aims and against Cuba's most profound principle – the clause that states that the embargo will not be lifted until the U.S. Congress approves of the form of government in place in Cuba. For all the hardships involved, Cuba has made it clear that, at that price, it will live with the embargo, despite the loss of its principal trading partners by the disappearance of the European socialist world.

Notwithstanding the hardships imposed by the forty years of U.S. hostility, Cuba has demonstrated, contrary to the dictates of the New World Order, that sovereignty is the necessary condition for the development of its people. Even in the times of greatest distress they have put their economy at the disposal of their people, by maintaining education, health care, culture, and sports and by continuing the commitment made by the revolutionary leadership from the earliest days of the movement to transform and elevate appreciably all these areas of national life. Education for all is the foundational base upon which all the other spheres have been structured. Its initial stage featured what was very likely the most successful national literacy campaign in world history. The upgrading of literacy has been accompanied by a progressive heightening of standards for teacher training and of performance at primary, secondary, and tertiary levels. UNESCO in 2001 evaluated primary school students throughout Spanish America for their performance in mathematics and language skills. Headquarters in New York did not believe the results their team of testers brought back from Cuba because the island's students had so clearly outperformed the other Spanish American students. A new team verified the findings, among them that the weakest 25 per cent of Cuban children performed better than the average student in the rest of Spanish America and, overall, the Cuban children's performance was twice as good as the average performance of the children in the rest of Spanish America.[7] Cuba further supports its people in these times of cutbacks elsewhere in

health care, culture, and sport by leading the world in the per capita
provision of doctors, art teachers, and sports technicians. The goal of
rebellious nineteenth-century Jesuit priests of having parallel and equal
emphasis on the arts and the sciences, with the sciences playing an
important role in sustaining independence, has been realized. The goal
was well articulated and practically defined in keeping with developments of his time by José Martí, particularly in a series of articles he
published in 1883, beginning with one titled "Scientific Education."
Scientific education, nationally instituted since 1959, has been the key
to providing the infrastructure to support a biotechnology industry, an
important landmark of which was the creation in 1986 of the Centre
for Genetic Engineering and Biotechnology.

Within the short period of seven years, the centre produced more
than 150 biotechnology items destined primarily to serve the nation's
health care. Other centres were built in Camagüey and in Sancti
Spiritus, to be mainly devoted to the veterinarian and the agricultural
sciences respectively. The distribution of such high-level centres of science and technology throughout the country, more than sixty of them
now devoted to biotechnology (*Granma International*, 20 December
2001), is for the population a semiotic index of the national importance
of science. But there are clear benefits to be had from a concentration of
research institutes and production plants, and in the vicinity of the
Centre for Genetic Engineering and Biotechnology in western Havana
can be found the new Finlay Institute, the National Centre for Scientific
Research, the Centre for Medical Surgical Research, the Immunoassay
Centre, the Ozone Centre, the Centre for Molecular Immunology,
several other biomedical research centres, and eight hospitals, as well
as research centres in other fields such as the Central Institute for
Digital Research, whose work in cybernetics aids many fields of scientific endeavour; all of the centres are involved in research and
production that compete at world levels. These centres have brought
a new level of scientific architecture to Cuba, the Caribbean, and Latin
America. The proliferation of Cuban research and production centres
in the biomedical field since 1986 has contributed to the addition of
diagnostic and therapeutic agents that are playing a strong role in
Cuban public health. They are an important factor in the island's high
life expectancy of seventy-five years, eight years higher than the average
in the rest of Latin America and the Caribbean. They are also a factor
in the record low infant mortality rate of 6.2 per 1,000 live births,
achieved in 2001, a rate that is not only far below that of all other
Latin American and Caribbean countries but is lower than that of the
United States, the richest country on earth, which in the same year
had a corresponding mortality rate of 7 for every 1,000 live births.

This achievement, within the decade in which Cuba lost its European socialist partners and Torricelli and Helms-Burton attempted to tighten the embargo to the point of strangulation, reflects the country's attitude to public health in general and in turn is an index of the profound humanist orientation of the Cuban system. A health care worker commenting on the high (14 per 1,000) infant mortality rate prevailing in Bedford Stuyvessant, New York said: "Whenever you find rising infant mortality it means there are a host of problems that need to be addressed" (CNN, 2 April 2000). Conversely, the steady fall of the rate in Cuba from an estimated 60 in 1958 (there was an absence of organized medical services in much of the countryside and very incomplete statistics) to 45 in the mid-sixties, 28 in 1974, and 17.3 in 1983,[8] to its present impressive levels speaks to a genuine, active, and efficient concern for the primacy of human life and human development. The fall of the mortality rate in Cuba also reflects the non-discriminatory access the people have to health care resources which include not only the highest per capita number of doctors and other medical personnel in the world but also the excellent distribution of these practitioners throughout the island;[9] the people's respect for and involvement in their institutions; the importance of universal literacy and the ability to read critically; the absence of a health-imperilling drug culture; and the openness to and ready implementation of constructive new ideas.[10]

Cuba was for many years visited by epidemics of meningitis, and the disease remained uncontrolled after most of the traditional contagious diseases had been quelled. Scientists at the Finlay Institute, named for Carlos J. Finlay who in 1881 discovered the vector for the yellow fever disease epidemic, a discovery that was ignored by the then colonial regime, took up the challenge and in the late 1980s invented the world's first and still the only genetically engineered vaccine against meningitis B. The vaccine has not only put an end to the epidemics in Cuba but is proving an indispensable shield in other countries, particularly Brazil, Argentina, Chile, and Ecuador, that have suffered from similar epidemics; this in spite of sedulous efforts on the part of established suppliers of vaccines to keep the invention from the market. Indeed, so irresistible has the product become that in July 1999 the U.S. government acquiesced in the arguments put to it by one of its leading pharmaceutical companies, Smith, Kline, Beecham, and, the Helms-Burton law notwithstanding, granted permission for the company to test and market the vaccine. A Toronto company, York Medical, formed by one of Canada's leading investment houses to commercialize Cuban biotechnology products in the industrialized world, is submitting several other products for regulatory approval.[11] Thus products invented in response to local needs are finding a growing place in foreign markets, and scientists are having the additional satisfaction of justifying economically and in good time the substantial outlay allocated to building the sector. Scientists also have a breadth of interests that reassures the population with the alternatives they offer. Traditional herbal medicine, sometimes sanctified by religious beliefs, acupuncture, and homeopathy are all within their investigative scope, and while the Finlay Institute produces genetically engineered vaccines, it also studies aroma or floral therapy. By all these means scientists enhance their stature and that of science in their society.

While medical care, like education and social assistance is guaranteed free of charge to the entire population, the Cuban government is quick to recognize developments that place its citizens in jeopardy. For example, in the process of recovery from the economic crisis of the first half of the 1990s it became clear that a sector of the population faced perilous poverty. The Cuban government is attempting to ameliorate the condition of these people – some pensioners living alone, low-income single mothers, the handicapped – by opening a country-wide chain of restaurants, 1,500 of them by the beginning of 2000, where these people's diets can be supplemented by a full and balanced daily meal costing one peso, the equivalent of $.05 U.S.[12] Such measures violate the precepts of free-market democracy and therefore will not win plaudits from promoters of this ideology, but they fit well within the broad scope of human rights that Cuba insists on observing.

Science has also had a bearing on one of the salient aspects of Cuban life, the development of the island's culture. Education for all is the broad base on which this achievement has been built, and "all" includes the 47 per cent of the population in the Cuban countryside who were illiterate in 1959 (11 per cent were illiterate in the cities, for an island-wide rate of 23.4 per cent). As well, the global curiosity of the country's leader, the rigour and consummate articulateness with which he addresses national issues and links them to international ones from a consistently ethical standpoint, provides enormous stimulus to intellectual activity. Teamwork and the sharing of specialized knowledge are widespread among Cubans. The ease with which they converse about a wide range of subjects at a sophisticated level is remarkable, and they set themselves the highest goals in their fields of cultural performance. In all areas of literature, music, dance, the visual arts, and sports, the island-wide opportunities for schooling and the skilful methods of teaching have resulted in a constant stream of the younger rapidly approaching the performance levels of the older, with a resultant steady rise in standards. The degree of helpfulness artists show to each other in rehearsal or practice is unusual. Their generosity and warmth in their public performances is special, and they are received joyfully by audiences.

The scientists who are doing world-class work in the research centres and the young musicians who make up one of the few national youth symphonic orchestras in the world both derive from the new Cuba. They reflect the composition of the population, except that already in 1993, 56 per cent of these scientists were women.[13]

A necessary condition of the quest for excellence on a world scale is information, and strategies ranging from an ever-increasing number of scholarly journals, to radio programs of serious academic content, to the institution of the nationally transmitted "University For Everyone" television programs and now a third television channel exclusively for education, to the hosting of numerous international conferences and colloquia in fields of interest to Cubans, all ensure access to up-to-date information.

The need to share scarce resources strengthens the ethos of cooperativeness that is a feature of Cuban society. Those who visit the island often are struck by the civility, good manners, and grace shown in general by a population that in its disciplined methods and dignified exuberance seems to have taken to heart Martí's advice: "Ser culto es el único modo de ser libre"[14] ("To be cultured is the only way to be free"). As Nicolás Guillén has written, "te lo prometió Martí/ y Fidel te lo cumplió"[15] ("Martí promised it to you/ and Fidel carried it out). The hallmark of Cuba at the present stage of its development is a humanitarian concern that has at its service the cultivated and freed intelligence of the people.

In the spirit of its national hero and in emulation of his concern for the poor and the neglected everywhere, Cuba, even as it struggles to regain its economic footing and is grateful for good-hearted help it receives, has been showing wondrous generosity to suffering people: to the 14,000 children it has treated in Cuba whose health has been affected by the Chernobyl nuclear disaster, to the more than 15,000 African students who have studied on full scholarship in the island, to the people in some thirty-eight countries who are being attended by Cuban doctors. Cuba is well aware of the devastation natural disasters can cause. In the 1960s it suffered terrible losses of human and animal life and other destruction to hurricanes such as Flora, and it sought ways of minimizing such losses in the future, by making an island-wide study of dangerous locations for housing, by building dams, and so on. At the approach of hurricane Georges in 1998, half a million people were moved to more secure areas, but this couldn't prevent five lives from being lost. The Cuban leaders, who had supervised the safety measures, explaining with cautionary intent how the victims died, gave their addresses to the nation, encouraging letters of condolence. When Georges struck the neighbouring Dominican Republic, people in the interior of the country were not made aware that a hurricane was approaching. More than 2,000 lives were lost. Cuba sent help to the injured and homeless survivors. The sympathy was even greater for the victims of the massive devastation wrought by hurricane Mitch in Honduras and Nicaragua. Cuba was one of only three countries in the world and the only one in this hemisphere to forgive the debt of any of those countries, Cuba forgiving a debt of $51 million U.S. owed to it by Nicaragua, notwithstanding the notorious hostility of the incumbent leader of that country to Cuba. Cuba also sent doctors and medicines and decided to establish in Cuba a Latin American School of Medicine for students from Latin American countries to study on full scholarship. The school started functioning in 1999. When President Clinton eventually visited Nicaragua and Honduras in response to requests for debt forgiveness, he promised to do his best to get the U.S. Congress to approve aid and urged those countries to continue to favour the free market. Castro is a constantly alert advocate for the people of poorer countries, expressing as he did in September 1999 in the Cuban parliament his dismay that the selfishness, injustice, and indifference of the developed countries leave virtually no possibility for third world countries to improve their situation. He observed that the aid promised by the richest countries for development has been reduced to 0.23 per cent of their gross domestic product from the 0.7 percent earlier agreed. The concern Cubans show for others at home and abroad is a factor underlying the exceptional civility visitors to that country usually observe.

It is to John Diefenbaker's lasting credit that, knowing the United States as he did and judging Cuba's revolutionary government on the basis of its relations with Canada, he ensured that Canada resisted the pressure the U.S. began to exert in the early sixties to break the diplomatic relations it had established with Cuba in 1945. Of all the independent countries in the hemisphere, Canada was joined only by Mexico in defying U.S. pressure in that regard. Throughout the last forty years, prime ministers Lester Pearson and Pierre Trudeau also demonstrated the understanding that our respect for Cuba's national rights has been a measure of our respect for our own legitimate national rights. In fact, whenever we have been hostile to Cuba to the extent of taking punitive action, we seem to have done so as a result of seeing Cuba through a prism borrowed from our powerful ally and our action has seemed morally skewed. For example, in 1976 Angola was invaded by the fascist and racist apartheid South African regime. This was not just one of the frequent border incursions; the invasion was threatening the capital, Luanda, itself. Angola asked Cuba for urgent help. Cuba responded, limiting its role to joining the Angolans in defence of their territory. Jesse Helms and others whose keen support for the South

African apartheid regime was influential in Washington complained noisily about the Cuban action, as did the Cuban-American leadership. Even the Trudeau government was pressured into departing from its principled position and withdrew financial support from Canadian NGO projects in Cuba.

The fact that the U.S. was clandestinely allied to the South Africans in the enterprise and had indeed instigated the apartheid state's aggression[16] should not have been reason enough for Canada's compliant stance. And Canadian intelligence should have been sufficiently alert as to have been aware of the veracity of information provided by Cuba at the time and that is now generally corroborated: that Cuba was by no means acting as a surrogate of the Soviet Union when it responded to Angola's plea. On the contrary, Cuba, by its moral force, obliged a reluctant Soviet Union to provide material support for its intervention.[17] The series of Cuban-Angolan victories over the U.S.-backed South African, Mobuto, and CIA-recruited international mercenary troops that culminated after thirteen years in the decisive triumph over the South African forces at Cuito-Cuanavale in 1988, a crucially important factor in the liberation of southern Africa, were due not simply to Cuban military skill. Cuban fighters could find in their own national history wells of empathetic motivation. They could also derive satisfaction from the moral rectitude of their undertaking. On the other hand, the U.S.'s superior military strength was undermined by a moral indefensibility that made it inopportune for the authorities to communicate to their citizens the aims and means of their intervention in the African country. While those authorities whispered to friendly countries their entreaties for collusion, the CIA surreptitiously carried out in the Angolan field activities that often involved the torture and murder of innocent civilians.[18]

In more recent times, we have been witnessing another period of moral unreliability in our government. A process of bonding seems to have taken place with leaders in the cruel war perpetrated against Yugoslavia. A Caribbean aspect of this development was Canada's acceptance during that war of the U.S. invitation to carry out target bombing on Vieques Island, precisely at a time when the inhabitants of that tiny island and other citizens of Puerto Rico were and still are appealing to the U.S. and to the world for the end to this blatant violation of their human rights. This violation is made worse by the low life expectancy of residents of Vieques relative to the rest of the Associated State and by the fact that the U.S. has used depleted uranium casings in some of the weapons exploded there. There are other troubling signs that the Canadian government, abetted by our media, which has become almost anarchistic and apparently intent on subverting the public's intelligence, is becoming less circumspect about the directions in which the U.S. wants to lead it. Our government follows, seemingly careless of the fact that U.S. policy toward Cuba is usually generated by the nexus of its own backward imperialist drive and by the futile annexationist ambitions of a ruthless sector of the Cuban-American community that is adept at fabricating distortions of Cuban reality. This sector also shows great savvy in apportioning electioneering funds to both U.S. political parties and to such figures as Al Gore and Dan Burton, Jesse Helms' partner in fashioning legislation hostile to Cuba.[19] As for Helms himself, all they have had to do to keep his malice at fever pitch is to exaggerate the number of blacks in Cuba.

In this period the Canadian government has again tried to punish Cuba. It has adopted the U.S.'s professed indignation over the fact that four of the U.S.'s Cuban collaborators were found by Cuban courts to be engaged in activities that flagrantly contravened Cuban law and were sentenced to up to five years' imprisonment. Canada has adopted the U.S. categorization of the sentences as human rights violations. Puerto Rico has never attempted to overthrow the government of the United States; there have been no invasions causing thousands of deaths, no blowing up of any passenger airliner, no biological warfare, no crop sabotage, no bombing of hotels, no persistent and ingenious attempts to assassinate its leader or to discredit its institutions, all actions perpetrated against Cuba from U.S. soil. Yet when Puerto Rican men and women faced charges in U.S. courts similar to those the Cuban agents faced in Cuba and when these Puerto Ricans received sentences of up to ninety years in U.S. prisons and averaging seventy-five years, there was no complaint from Canada. Our country, though, reacted to the sentencing of those who were judged to have colluded with the Americans and imperilled Cuban security by again lessening NGO support, freezing the exchange of visits between delegations of ministers and parliamentarians, denying the opening of a consulate in Vancouver, and, saddest of all, withdrawing from a project, initiated by Cuba, to help Haitians. Cuba has been troubled by the infant and maternal mortality rates in Haiti, where the infant mortality rate was 120 per 1,000 live births, compared to Cuba's 6.6 per 1,000 in 1999. Cuba proposed to Canada that they form a partnership to help Haitian women: Cuba would send doctors and Canada would supply medicines. Cuba calculated that some 28,000 lives per year could be saved. Canada's initial reaction to the proposal was very favourable, but it soon withdrew from the project without any adequate explanation. Cuba has proceeded despite this setback and has been instrumental in reducing Haiti's infant mortality rate in 2001 to 74, with a corresponding reduction in the maternal death rate.[20]

There can be little doubt that the pressures of the U.S.-led New World Order have heavily influenced Canadian behaviour. In a paradoxical manner Canada seems to want to assert its independence by anticipating U.S. wishes and acting in accordance with them so that they will have the semblance of authentic Canadian initiatives. But we are in danger of eroding the goodwill and the regard accumulated for us by the sovereign acts of Diefenbaker, Pearson, and Trudeau. The decline from those times in the value of our currency is one symptom of that danger to which our political economists should pay attention. As for Cuba, we should come to appreciate its Martí-like determination to defend its hard-won independence and sovereignty, to ensure that national dignity continues to occupy the place formerly occupied by national humiliation, and to protect its people from the degradation that is being visited on so many countries by the implementation of policies inspired by the ideology of neo-liberal globalization, the newest face of imperialism.

NOTES

1 This and the following Martí quotations are my translations of passages from José Martí, *Obras escogidas en tres tomos*, La Habana: Editorial Política, 1981, 2 vols.

2 Translated from I. Lavritski, *Simón Bolívar*, Moscow: Editorial Progreso, 1982, 185.

3 Oscar Loyola Vega in Francisco López Civeira, Oscar Loyola, Arnaldo Silva León, *Cuba y su historia*, La Habana: Editorial Gente Nueva, 1998, 101.

4 See, for example, Martí's essay "A Vindication of Cuba" (25 March 1889), which is an indignant response to an editorial in the Philadelphia *Manufacturer*: "Do We Want Cuba?" (16 March 1889), both published in *Our America: Writings on Latin America and the Struggle for Cuban Independence*, Philip S. Foner, ed., New York: Monthly Review Press, 1977, 228–41.

5 For a serious history of the electoral system in Cuba and a detailed study of the present electoral process, see Canadian scholar Arnold August's *Democracy in Cuba and the 1997–1998 Elections*, Havana: Editorial José Martí, 1999. August's study, based on exhaustive historical research and on his detailed eye-witness observations of the 1997–98 election process at all levels, is an extremely valuable contribution to the understanding of a creative approach to the goal of democratic representation. All but the laziest political scientists will find little satisfaction with the electoral process prevailing in the republics and other

countries of this hemisphere. The process is undermined by what candidates in U.S. presidential campaigns have habitually recognized as corruption: that is, the crucial role of campaign funding that makes political parties beholden to large contributors and makes a mockery of the vote of the less affluent. Recognition of the importance of money also leads parties even in the wealthiest of these countries to illegally accept foreign donations. In turn, the wealthiest country shows no reluctance to finance and direct campaigns of favoured parties in countries where campaigns are often a mixture of untidy carnival and low-level civil war, leading to governments whose policies are largely determined by external dictates. The electoral process in these countries is also undermined by the often large numbers of illiterate and semi-literate participants. August clearly conveys a picture of a viable and dignified democratic process that is framed by Cuban history, that has evolved with the aim and effect of strengthening democracy and is subject to further evolution to that end.

6 This quotation may be seen in its fuller context in my book *Cuba's Nicolás Guillén: Poetry and Ideology*, Toronto: University of Toronto Press, 1985, 24–45.

7 See Christopher Marquis, "Cuba leads Latin America in Primary Education, Study Finds," *New York Times*, 13 December 2001; and Orlando Oramas León, "Dialoga Fidel con estudiantes de universidades norteamericanas, *"Granma Internacional*, 26 January 2002.

8 Robert N. Ubell, "Twenty-five Years of Cuban Health Care," *New England Journal of Medicine* 309, no. 23 (December 1983), 1468–72.

9 Cuba's performance in this sphere is outstanding worldwide and particularly in the context of Latin America and the Caribbean. As reported by CANA news agency, 10 April 2000, the International Labour Organization in a recent number of its magazine *World of Work*, revealed that, in Latin America and the Caribbean, 140 million people – one of three – still lack access to health services, while 218 million are excluded from social security systems.

10 For instance, in 1995, in the depths of the economic crisis, a public health official in Santiago de Cuba told me of a dietary iron deficiency that was showing up in some pregnant women. A study was promptly made of available unutilized natural sources of the mineral and conferences were organized in different parts of the island to expand on the study and circulate the new information as part of a national nutrition campaign.

11 It is Cuba's policy to retain control of the marketing of its biomedical products to non-industrialized countries so that these countries may have the benefit of lower prices or, in some cases, donations.

12 See Patricia Grogg, "Cuban Programs Assist the Poor," *Pride*, 23 March 2000, 8.

13 Conversation in 1993 with Rosa Elena Simeón, then head of the Cuban Academy of Sciences and now minister of Science, Technology and the Environment.

14 José Martí, *Obras completas*, La Habana: Instituto del Libro, 1965, 8: 289.

15 Nicolás Guillén, *Obra poética 1958–1972*, La Habana: UNEAC, 1972, 139.

16 This is confirmed by both Pik Botha, the South African foreign minister of that time, and by John Stockwell of the CIA's Angola Task Force in interviews broadcast by CNN in its Cold War series on 14 May 2000.

17 This is confirmed by Anatoly Dobrynin, the ex-Soviet ambassador to the U.S.A., in the same CNN program.

18 Note in the above CNN program the testimony concerning torture and murder given by British mercenary Dave Tomkins.

19 See the item by Robert Windrem, an NBC news producer, entitled "Burton, Gore reap Florida riches: Campaign donations may help explain stands on case of Cuban refugee boy" (MSNBC 01/11/00), in which it is revealed that Indiana senator Burton received a major part of his election campaign funds from Florida and that Gore was more dependent than any other presidential candidate on funding from Miami.

20 Despite its early independence, at the turn of the nineteenth century, or perhaps because of it, Haiti has suffered greatly at the hands of imperialist forces. Whereas relations between the United States and Haiti have been calm during dictatorships such as those of Papa and Baby Doc Duvalier, they have been especially tense when there have been democratically elected Haitian governments. The elections of May 2000 were judged to be fair by the International Coalition of Independent Observers. They were won by the party led by Jean-Bertrand Aristide. The well-known Jesse Helms immediately spearheaded a drive to invalidate the elections, claiming that seven senators were improperly elected. The U.S., which had never intervened against the Duvalier dictatorships, imposed economic sanctions on Haiti, blocking all aid, including $500 million in loans. Haiti is one of the poorest countries in the world. A crucial part of the blocked $500 million loan is $146 million targeted at the desperate health care and education conditions in the country. What is more, Haiti is obligated to pay interest on these loans despite not having access to them. It hasn't mattered that the seven accused senators have resigned; the sanctions continue, with hardly any doubt that the underlying reason for this is that President Aristide is perceived as resistant to the New World Order. Such cruelty has an effect not only on Haiti. It also frightens loan seekers and trading partners dependent on the United States into conformity with U.S. directives. (Much of the information in this note is from "Haiti/Economic Sanctions," Human Rights in the Americas, americas@derechos.net).

The Latin American Song
as an Alternative Voice
in the New World Order

MARÍA FIGUEREDO

Que se levanten todas las banderas
cuando el cantor se plante con su grito
que mil guitarras desangren en la noche
una inmortal canción al infinito
Si se calla el cantor ... calla la vida.
(Horacio Guaraní)

May all flags be raised
when the singer stands firm with a strong voice
May a thousand guitars bleed into the night
an immortal song to eternity
If the singer falls silent ... so does life.

Music, particularly songs that are engaged in social commentary and originate from the popular traditions, express the cultural and life-affirming necessities of every society in development. At times, the expression of those cultural imperatives is contentious because it flows against currents that organize the world order. Music, especially that which is sung, becomes an alternative voice in the dialogue between international and regional balances of power if its message, whether explicit or implicit, strikes a chord in a community and lies beyond the imperatives willed by the governing bodies. The capacity of music to reflect ethical positions and values is particularly evident when political, social, and economic tensions are polarized, as occurred during military dictatorships in Latin America in the twentieth century when the New World Order was evolving. We will discuss in this essay how musical expression can influence world relations and how it has done so in Latin America.[1] We will pay particular attention to the post-World War II period, when the United States assumed a more defining role in international relations and thus became a determining factor in Latin America's search to define its voice in the world.

MUSIC AS A VOICE FOR LIFE-AFFIRMING VALUE SYSTEMS AND THEIR SURVIVAL IN LATIN AMERICA

One of the fundamental roles of culture is to manifest the identity of a community. Music is one of the most powerful vehicles of identity. Given its power of simultaneity, it can mobilize large numbers of people, engage various levels of experience, and lead us to receive its message(s) in ways we may not be fully analytically aware. Borrowing from Paul Ricœur's hermeneutic concept, we can say that music is a "way of being," a means by which we experience our world and then give expression to our interpretation of it, so as to enter into dialogue and connection with others. This occurs in such a profound and intense manner that the power of music as a force in society can reach formidable proportions. If this music carries with it messages that sustain a "life code of value" (McMurtry), it does so by positing interconnection, collective good, and liberty as the pillars for its foundation. These core values support the healthy functioning of a society and of its relations to other societies, and seek to create a way of being for the majority of the population.

In questioning or affirming values and beliefs, the capacity of songs is especially poignant, and even challenging to those who fear its hidden, or not so hidden, messages. This is because it links our physical grasp of the world to our intellectual understanding in ways that can surpass any abstract imperative that comes from outside ourselves. As Edward Rothstein suggests, "[t]he power of music, and its threat, does not depend upon understanding [its message]. We do not dissect music, but rather feel and experience the effects of its meaning with a sensual force that no simple argument can equal."[2] The power of music rests in the way it communicates and expresses its structure through complex relationships between composer, interpreter, listener, and society as a whole. These complexities need not be overtly understood for them to be effective. Thus, music as a force for social change is linked to the merging of action and perception, without having to pass through an intense analysis of the complex relationships it encapsulates. According to Michael Chanan, "music is always – among other things – an expression of actual or ideal social relations"[3] How music interacts with society is also explored by Theodor Adorno, a German philosopher, sociologist and trained musician, who draws a parallel between musical and social structure: "Musical forms are interiorizations of social structures [... and] social circumstances are expressed concretely in the 'topos' of music."[4]

We shall see this in the experience of various Latin American countries, although we must of course confine our discussion to certain key examples and events, given the constraints that any work of this nature implies. This essay examines some of the musical forms prevalent in the second half of the twentieth century to see what they reveal about Latin American communities and about how they interpret their society and their place in the world order.

THE ORIGINS AND DEVELOPMENT
OF LATIN AMERICAN MUSIC

The music and songs of Latin America are born from the integration of European, Native, and African influences. Music, melodies, and rhythms were conjugated to particular instruments in each region to give such forms as zamba, samba, son, guaracha, bambuco, corrido, tango, bolero, chacarera, cielito, candombe. Cuban author Alejo Carpentier, who wrote extensively about Latin American music, describes how interpretive styles change the sense and meaning of a melody: "A well-known Colombian 'romanza' passed as Cuban, for a long time, once it was re-edited in Havana, with slight rhythmic modifications in the accompaniment. [...] The 'Dies Irae' of Gregorian chant becomes a magnificent Argentinian tango when it is played, on the bandoneon, with a 'porteño' rhythm [...]."[5]

The instruments also reveal the intangible flow history of Latin America; thus the fusion of Spanish guitar, African drums, and Andean flutes testifies to the encounters of those civilizations as they were experienced on American soil. This symbiosis occurred in various ways, as we see in the Afro-Cuban rhythms contrasted with those of the Brazilian samba de enredo[6] or with the Uruguayan candombe.[7] We can also consider the indigenous influence in the carnavalitos or other Andean folklore, the predominant European music in the zamba, chacarera, or bambuco, or the absorption of the classical European waltz into valses criollos of Peru, Venezuela, Mexico, and the River Plate countries.

From the beginning there was an element of revolt in this new music. For example, in colonial Montevideo, the African rhythms in the beat of the drums were considered heretic by the colonial authorities but eventually permitted for Sunday morning parades to prevent secret meetings. It was also around walls of that besieged plaza in the 1810s that the independence movement found a native voice in Bartolomé Hidalgo. An early composition is believed to have been sung on 1 May 1813, when besiegers, gathered close to the walls of the Montevideo fort from the darkness of night, sang these verses with guitar accompaniment to tease the besieged Spaniards[8]: "Cielito de los gallegos / ¡Ay¡ cielito del Dios Baco / Que salgan al campo limpio / Y verán lo que es tabaco"[9] ('Cielito of the Galicians (Spanish) / Oh! cielito of the God Bacchus / May they jump into the clean countryside / And see what tobacco is'). Using the cielito musical form, Hidalgo commented on the political climate of his day: "Cielito, cielo que sí, / no se necesitan Reyes / para gobernar los hombres / sino benéficas leyes,"[10] stating that there is no need of kings to rule men but rather beneficent laws. According to the Uruguayan musicologist Lauro Ayestarán, the cielito, which was primarily a dance, did assume many times a lyrical form that was meant only to be sung. It is considered a musical descendant of the European Minuet, gradually taking on a criollo character, and reaching by 1830 a completely different form from its ancestor.[11]

Later examples are the corridos of the Mexican Revolution, and particularly of the incursions of Pancho Villa, or the "sons" written by the Cuban Nicolas Guillén. In general, however, the traditional music and songs of protest faded during most of the first part of the twentieth century, as regional societies became more adept at incorporating foreign music from Europe and the United States. The traditional musical forms were conceded a lesser status in academic and performance circles. This meant that usually there were parallel repertoires, where popular and elite ("culto") manifestations of art forms coexisted in different places. The bifurcation between the high/low classification of the arts, including music and songs, eventually dissolved, especially during the second half of the twentieth century, with the development of the mass media.

THE CHALLENGES OF THE LATE TWENTIETH CENTURY

The second half of the twentieth century witnessed many changes – post-World War II reconstruction and restructuring of Europe and the cold war – that affected Latin America in various ways. First, cold war politics caused the United States to look at containing or eliminating any manifestations of anti-capitalist tendencies or other perceived dangers to the balance of power. One of the first threats to U.S. policy came from Cuban revolution and the restlessness there for national independence, cultural pride, and freedom from imperialist manipulation. For fear of this action spreading to other parts of Latin America, the United States mounted a campaign to control the Latin American area. By means of military and other policing forces, its government tried to control the economic structure of the region and prevent cultural messages transmitted through the mass media. This last area, the more difficult to trace and steer, is by far the most serendipitous yet far reaching in its fundamental influence on the citizens of a nation. It was not until the 1960s, however, when the revolution of ideologies started to turn resolvedly against the U.S. power centre from within its own borders, that music started to take the reigns of its own development worldwide; it then stood as a formidable counterpoint to the dominant voice of imperialist tendencies. Throughout the second half of the century, Latin American countries suffered systematic intrusions into their political, economic, social, and cultural spheres, under the guise of policies in defence of "freedom."

The two decisive political incursions by the U.S. in Latin America have been in Cuba and Chile, but all other countries were also affected by the development of military dictatorships. The consequences of these actions were the persecution of persons supporting any intellectual activity not conforming to the orthodoxy, and quite often their death or disappearance. Let us examine the effects of this experience in some of these regions of Latin America in greater detail, so that the role of music and its eventual disappearance from the political arena can be seen more clearly as economically/politically orchestrated manipulation.

One of the strongest responses to this imperialistic challenge was the emergence of the "New Song" or "Nueva Trova" movement in various countries. Exponents of this type of early protest music include representatives from all across the region: Carlos Puebla, Silvio Rodríguez, and Pablo Milanés in Cuba; Violeta Parra, Victor Jara, and the groups Inti-Illimani, Illapu, and Quillampallí in Chile; Mercedes Sosa and Atahualpa Yupanqui in Argentina; Daniel Viglietti, Alfredo Zitarrosa and the duo Los Olimareños in Uruguay; Benjo Cruz and Nilo Soruco in Bolivia, for instance. As Murray Luft comments,

The Cuban Revolution of 1959 nourished the roots of Latin American protest music even more profoundly [than the music of Spanish Civil War (1936–39)]. The voice of revolutionary Cuban singer Carlos Puebla, one of the troubadours in the old style, was popular in South America in the 1960s. During the

1970s, Cuba's socialist musical renaissance, known as the "Nueva Trova," acquired a following among Bolivia's [and other Latin American nations'] progressive sectors increasingly opposed to de facto military regimes and 'Yankee imperialism.'[12]

The "Nueva Trova" in Cuba, as Luft aptly describes, "proved to be an exciting experiment in the construction of a Latin American musical tradition that was both politically progressive and esthetically pleasing."[13] The predominance of lyrics over solely musical preoccupations is one of the most outstanding features of this music with a social message. Examples abound, but we can illustrate this with the lyrics of the following composition in "son" form by Pablo Milanés, entitled "Son de Cuba a Puerto Rico":

Cuando se alzó mi bandera	When my flag was raised
la tuya lo haría igual	yours would do the same
y fue esa vez la primera	and that was the first time
que juntos quisimos volar.	that together we wished to fly.
Más tarde una voz amada	Later a beloved voice
gritó con mucha razón:	shouted with great reason:
Cuba y Puerto Rico son	Cuba and Puerto Rico are
de un pájaro las dos alas.	two wings of one bird.

This tends to be the type of music favoured when music is created with a marked sociopolitical theme. However, music does not necessarily need text to be subversive. As Rothstein describes in relation to classical music in various contexts of political censorship (the Ukraine, China, the Soviet Union), music's capacity to communicate on a deeper level can threaten the status quo to the extent of becoming dangerous for composers to select certain arrangements or melodic nuances. Nevertheless, during the decades of the 1960s, 1970s, and into the 1980s, the trends in the music of social change and protest tended to emphasize verbal expression, even when the message was indirect or hidden. In Latin America, the songs that were most censored were those that were verbally powerful, and censorship focused mainly on the words of the text.

Although some songs are directed to the external dominator, such as in the songs of Carlos Puebla, most of the songs cry for a liberation from the internal dominance of the upper classes and for the affirmation of values that are felt to be threatened, including the brotherhood of the region. This is elegantly shown in a well-known song entitled "Canción con Todos" (Song with Everyone) by Chilean composers A. Tejada Gómez and César Isella, first sung in the 1960s. The region is described as an organic whole in spite of its diversity:

Salgo a caminar	I set out to walk across
Por la cintura cósmica del sur	The cosmic belt of the south
Piso en la región	I step upon the most fertile region
Más vegetal del viento y de la luz	Of the wind and the light
Siento al caminar	I sense as I walk
Toda la piel de América en mi piel	All of the skin of America in my skin
Y anda en mi sangre un río	And in my blood a river flows
Que libera en mi voz, su caudal.	That sets free in my voice, its abundance.[14]

Musically, the melody initiated in this verse is composed as a milonga[15] that, together with an arpeggio-style guitar accompaniment, renders a meditative approach to the theme. The reflective form of these verses sets the stage for listeners to embrace a humanistic world vision, grounded in unity, interconnection, and freedom to roam the natural world they have inherited. The unity among peoples stems from a respect for the diversity of the region, which is itself rooted in an appreciation of the natural abundance and variations of the geography:

Sol de alto Perú,	Sun of regal Peru,
Rostro Bolivia, estaño y soledad;	The face of Bolivia, tin and solitude;
Un verde Brasil	One green Brazil
Besa a mi Chile, cobre y mineral.	Kisses my Chile, copper and mineral.
Subo desde el sur	I move up from the south
Hasta la entraña de América total,	Up to the entrails of all America,
Pura raíz de un grito	A pure root of a shout
Destinado a crecer y a estallar.	Which is destined to grow and explode.

The poetic voice presents the region through the use of certain well-recognized symbols of the various facets of the region. It is interesting to note that the movement of "high to low" is also compounded in the contrast between the heights of mountain and the depths of the mines (tin, copper). In the final verses, the release of the voice ushers the flow of energy upwards again. The musical accompaniment parallels this movement when, at this moment in the song, the minor key shifts to a major, and the chorus is released in a spirit of unity and collective power emphasized by the repetition of "all" ("todas/toda"):

Todas las voces, todas;	All the voice, all of them;
Todas las manos, todas;	All the hands, all of them;

Toda la sangre puede	All the blood can become
Ser canción en el viento.	A song in the wind.
Canta conmigo, canta,	Sing with me, sing,
Hermano americano.	(Latin) American Brother
Libera tu esperanza	Liberate your hope
Con un grito en la voz.	With a shout in your voice.

It is important to note that the musical form, which started as a song, has solidified in the chorus into the form of a zamba, which possesses a heartier rhythmic structure. This modulation lifts the song to a higher level of collective engagement that follows from a more stressed beat. The use of a folkloric rhythm recalls the popular roots of the history of ordinary people, united by a common experience. "Canción con Todos" is a collective song brought forth by the identity of Latin America, and its call for the brotherhood/sisterhood of "hermanos americanos," impresses the need to unite and to sing for liberation. This common thread in Latin American music most clearly refers to the social aspects of its experience within the world order as it has evolved until today.

Another exponent of the New Song is Violeta Parra, who was very active between 1960 and 1973 and died prior to the dictatorship of Augusto Pinochet. A singer-poet and composer, Parra's music is representative of the key role alloted to meaningful lyrics in the Latin America folk song of the era. As Gina Cánepa-Hurtado explains, the core dynamic inherent in the musical structure of the folkloric song resides in that "its schematic simplicity, and functional symmetry is superedited by the importance of the verbal text."[16] In Parra's repertoire of folkloric music, this simplicity is reflected in "an accentuated diatonic structure, intervalic leaps which are not too vast, [...]. The rhythms are mainly binary."[17] Though there are certain exceptions, these characteristics describe the majority of her musical compositions. Notably, the strength of the simple structure anchors the solid message of her lyrics, which are often of such poetic quality as to warrant universal appeal. To cite one of her pieces, "Gracias a la vida," we see that Parra's focus is to communicate certain values, which are symbolically represented in the many things she has received in life:

Gracias a la vida que me ha dado tanto	Thanks to life which has given me so much
Me ha dado el sonido y el abecedario	it has given me sound and the alphabet
con él las palabras que pienso y declaro:	and with it the words which I think and declare:

madre, amigo, hermano, y luz	mother, friend, brother, and
alumbrando	the light
la ruta del alma del que estoy	which illuminates the path to the
amando.	soul of whom I love.

The basic zamba structure of the song is maintained with no variation into a chorus, or key change, for example. As a result, the main focus is on the verbal text. The zamba rhythm sweeps the listener along the shared testimony of life's abundant gifts toward a final sense of communion created among singer, song, and community, when Parra states that the people's singing is her own, and vice versa. Evident in this final image of "Gracias a la vida" is Parra's belief that her direct contact with the people of Chile informed her work. Parra herself states that "[w]hen could I have imagined that as I set out to collect my first song [...] I would learn that Chile is the best book of folklore ever written."[18] As Cánepa-Hurtado comments, Parra "considers folklore, not as isolated arqueological survival that develops in a dominated culture standing before the dominant culture, but rather as a cultural phenomenon that corresponds with certain social forms and which is transformed or nullified in relation to that correspondence. Beyond that, it seems, that the concept of the folkloric culture transcends the areas of the plastic arts, literature, and music and refers to a global attitude towards life, a conception of the universe, a peculiar religion, which manifest itself also in colloquial language."[19] The reactivation and revaluation of popular or folkloric[20] forms that emerged as a strong current during the 1960s can now signal an alternative way to finetune the current vision of the various parts of sociopolitical and cultural dimensions of the New World Order.

What Violeta Parra achieved for social awareness through music from her Chilean perspective, Atahualpa Yupanqui did from Argentina; both were to have a major influence on a large number of Latin American musicians and folk-singers. As Rodolfo Pino-Robles states, many folk groups followed the example of Parra and Yupanqui, and

'discovered' Indigenous instruments of the Andes region. Thus, audiences learned about 'charangos, quenas, antaras (zampoñas), quenachos, pinkullos, etc.' We could remember 'Los Calchaquís' from Argentina, 'Quilapayún' from Chile, and 'Inti-Illimani' and 'Illapu' from Chile, both groups borrowing the Quechua or Aymara language and deities to name themselves. [...] Indigenous peoples of Argentina and Chile also had been [...] equated with the generic economic and political concept of campesino (peasant). In any event, a large public became familiar with the musical forms such as 'Yaravies,' 'Carnavalitos,' 'Morenadas,' 'Huayños,' 'Bailecitos,' all Indigenous Andean music hitherto virtually unknown except to the peoples of the highlands of Peru, Bolivia, Ecuador, Argentina and, to a certain extent, northern Chile.[21]

As a result, folkloric forms merged with socially aware lyrics to give voice to political views opposing the dominant shift towards totalitarian powers of the governing bodies. As Luft recounts, "[f]ollowing the Chilean military takeover [in 1973], Argentina assumed a position of prominence in the dissemination of protest music."[22] This included the rise to popularity of musicians/singers such as Mercedes Sosa, Horacio Guaraní, Piero, Eduardo Falú, and, later in the 1980s, Leon Gieco and Victor Heredia. After the military coup and "the subsequent 'dirty war' against Argentina's organized left (1976–83), [there was] [...] further constriction of the New Song in the Southern Cone. This was a period in which some 30,000 persons 'disappeared' in Argentina,' as is witnessed in a popular song performed by Mercedes Sosa, "Sólo le pido a Diós," written by Silvio Rodríguez: " I only ask God, that the war will not make me indifferent! / It's a huge monster that steps clumsily, / On a poor and innocent people."[23]

In Uruguay, political persecution and censorship after 1973 eventually meant exile for the majority of the best known artists of the time. Among those exiled were musicians associated with the "Nueva Trova" such as Daniel Viglietti, Alfredo Zitarrosa, and the duo Los Olimareños, as well as writers such as Mario Benedetti, Juan Carlos Onetti, Cristina Peri Rossi, Carlos Martínez Moreno, Saúl Ibargoyen, and Eduardo Galeano. Viglietti had composed songs like "A desalambrar," a call for liberation from the abuse of personal property, and Zitarrosa had renewed many traditional rhythms with expressive songs such as "Doña Soledad" ("Madam Solitude") and "Adagio a mi país" ("Adagio for my country"):

Dice mi pueblo que puede leer	My people say that they can read
en su mano de obrero el destino	destiny in the palm of the worker's hand
y que no hay adivino ni rey	and there is no fortune-teller or king
que le puedan marcar el camino.	that could set its path.

The duo Los Olimareños had teased the political conservative structures with songs such as "Cielito del 69."[24] With the exile of these artists, a new generation quickly gained a significant audience, but their work was suffocated by censorship of their texts and performances. In this climate, audiences became adept at "listening between the lines"[25] and musical notes for hidden messages that alluded to the current times. The "Canto Popular Uruguayo" or CPU reached new heights during this period in which it became difficult for Uruguayans to remain neutral about this tendency in the music. Indeed, it maintains a politically and ideologically charged dimension in the present, despite the fact that not all the songs were of a political nature.

Some of the best known songs of the CPU are collaborations between poets and musicians, whose solidarity grew out of the common foe of the dictatorship. In one example, a text by poet Circe Maia, "Otra voz canta" ("Another Voice Sings"), set to music and sung by Daniel Viglietti (1978), speaks indirectly about the disappearances of people that occurred during the military regime in Uruguay, which could also apply to the experiences of other countries. In a well-known performance of the piece in 1994 in Mexico, Viglietti sang with Mario Benedetti, who interwove verses from his poem "Desparecidos" ("Disappeared Ones"), thereby creating a triangular structure and making the references more explicit. The performance begins with the sung portion of Maia's text:

Por detrás de mi voz	From behind my voice
– escucha, escucha –	– listen, listen –
otra voz canta.	Another voice sings.
Viene de atrás, de lejos;	I comes from behind, from far away;
viene de sepultadas	it comes from entombed
bocas, y canta.	Mouths, and sings.
Dicen que no están muertos	They say they're not dead
– escúchalos, escucha –	– listen to them, listen –
mientras se alza la voz	while the voice is lifted
que los recuerda y canta.	Which remembers them and sings.

Benedetti's verses then amplify the sense of absence and emptiness: "cuando empezaron a desaparecer / [...] / a desaparecer como sin sangre / como sin rostro y sin motivo"[26] ("when they started to disappear / [...] / to disappear as if without blood / as if without face and without reason"). In the face of this loss and not finding a reason to justify it, the poet's verses reiterate the song's expression for the need to remember these people and to incorporate this experience in the soul of those who are listening: "están en algún sitio / nube o tumba/ están en algún sitio / estoy seguro / allá en el sur del alma"[27] ("they are in some place / cloud or tomb / they are in some place / I am sure / there in the southern portion of the soul").

Throughout the 1960s and 1970s, the community of artists in Latin America responded to the environment of dictatorship. Luft explains the scenario:

As monolithic police states became the norm in more and more South American countries, subtle expressions of freedom remained incredibly persistent. Despite systematic human rights abuses, the New Songs were still hummed and sung. Like the ubiquitous signs of graffiti painted on city walls, music gave hope to a suffering people. In Bolivia, as in Argentina, protest music was equated with 'building resistance.' It was focused on one over-riding objective – to return Latin America to democracy![28]

In general, therefore, the power of music to sustain a people through turbulent times has been recorded in the testament left by the overwhelming amount of New Songs created and shared during this period. Not to be underestimated, these songs succeeded in "harnessing the energy, purpose, and spirit of pro-democratic forces."[29]

The 1980s saw a lessening of political tensions and new directions began to emerge; this gave way to a more economic focus. As Luft suggests,

Neo-liberal economic policies inevitably accompanied the return to democracy in [... various countries in the region]. Without a viable socialist option, Latin Americans were forced to meekly accept international capitalism as 'the only game in town.' Beginning in 1985, for example, Bolivia's government passed a series of Draconian structural laws. Designed by the International Monetary Fund (IMF), and reinforced by powerful governments and corporations to the North, these new economic policies had a devastating effect on the welfare of the poor. Massive layoffs in parastatal industries and the government bureaucracy created unprecedented social dislocations throughout the country.[30]

Music's role in the search for independence – during colonial periods and afterwards as a way of liberating Latin American countries from imperialist *encrutements* – has been as an alternative perspective from which to analyze the unfolding of the community, and to give voice to the values and beliefs of a people.

THE PLAYING FIELD
OF THE NEW WORLD ORDER:
RECREATION VERSUS CONSUMPTION

Globalization, according to Keith Ellis in this collection, has become the new face of imperialism; it is the means by which markets are directed and the resources of various regions manipulated. In recent years, the term "globalization" entered our vocabulary in relation to of the New World Order. The Brazilian academic Maria de Lourdes Sekeff, in "As artes, Universidade e a globalizacïo" (1998), discusses how the economic definition of globalization has robbed the term of its all encompassing meaning:

Discussing the phenomenon of 'globalization' – that movement which some believe to be an invention of Neo-liberalism – has usually entailed circumscribing it to the area of economics. However 'globalization' is present in other dimensions, such as the ecological, the social, the artistic, the musical, with consequences which are difficult to predict in the economic field, in such a way that it has been dividing leadership.[31]

Sekeff suggests that within its broader framework there exist many possibilities for the arts, particularly in conjunction with universities, to harness the effects of globalization for their own evolution:

In relation to the arts, the university, stimulated by new directions in development and in the economy, has begun to confer to them their rightful place – well-deserved through their own merit – as the new matrices of knowledge which indeed they are. As a result, the university invests in the reengineering of arts and music education, in this way favouring sectors which were previously 'marginalized' from the academic forum, and emphasizing quality and 'flexibilization.' In the end, the achievement of qualification is not merely a question of technical ability, but also of 'flexibilization' and possessing an awareness of the new directions that transcend the walls of academia.[32]

Viewed from this perspective, with a focus on ways that foster relations between the disciplines to enrich our way of being in the world, globalization seems to offer favourable possibilities for music. Notwithstanding, when the economic aspects of globalization are set above all other considerations, these benefits fade from view.

It is perhaps this multivocal sense of leadership in the other fields that provides an outlet for alternative voices, if not to be heard equally, at least to coexist. The interdisciplinary approach favoured in the arts and the plurality of voices it promotes, therefore, can be seen as a positive side of globalization, where there is a growing sense of interdependence and connection. This became an important issue during the final decades of the twentieth century. Unfortunately, economic considerations remain, if not the only criteria, then at least the most predominant.

Marshall McLuhan predicted the emergence of the global village, envisioning the closing of distances, both geographically and perceptively, through the rapidly evolving mass communication systems that stretch across the planet. Yet his assumption in seeing the world as a village proved somewhat optimistic. In lieu of a village, or closely-knit community,[33] what we experience in the world today is more akin to a network of systems that link those in power and privilege to commercial aspects of relations between the various parts of the globe. That is to say, the structure of communications has been secularized to such an extent that what has been lost along the way is a vision that could incorporate a sense of unity at a deeper level. Music, particularly as song, is a way of creating a sense of unity, if not one of community. In this way, the songs that began to emerge as waves of new musical movements across Latin America revealed a predominant focus on collective cultural expression as a means of self-preservation in the face of a common threat.

MUSIC'S SOCIAL AND COMMUNICATIVE POWER

In times of relative political stability and less ideological polarization, there is still a role for music to play. Music should never be underestimated as a social force and a source of communicative power, even when the structure of the commercial system does not support all of its manifestations. In the 1990s, we began to witness the downsides of runaway commercialism and a focus on material growth. This in turn was coupled with a rising interest in the issues of spirituality and a search for greater health and well-being. In this way, globalization has encouraged more curiosity about other communities with greater evolved spiritual growth within their cultures. But this is still occurring mainly by means of consumption of goods and has not yet become engaged in fuller dialogue. For Latin America in the last decade, globalization has meant substituting sociopolitical ideology with economics. By submerging ideological questions in economic paradigms, the solutions spell out the advantages of globalization and increased trade, measured in terms of quantifiable profits. However, no measure is taken of the more subtle sides of the equation. Who is really profiting from all the increased trade? And where is music's stand on all of this?

Fortunately, songs of deeper resonance have not disappeared. They exist as alternative voices, even if most do not receive sufficient media support to channel them to a larger forum. Environmental issues, women's issues, and poverty issues appear in the contemporary repertoire of Latin American musicians. Although, as Luft suggests, "the stereotypical 'protest musician' is no longer easily identifiable" in Latin America, we find traces of social commitment in other ways; "[a]s in Canada, contemporary folk musicians in South America may selectively incorporate specific protest issues into their song portfolios, largely guided by personal convictions, social/political circumstances, and audience approval factors."[34] He gives as an example the Bolivian musician Luis

Rico, previously imprisoned for his music, who "is highly respected by his colleagues for being unwilling to compromise, [and ...] continues to compose on political subjects."[35] Other best-known Bolivian musicians who "have written and performed issue-based, socially committed songs [...] are Manuel Monroy, Adrien Barrenechea, Matilde Casazola, Canto Popular and Ernesto Cavour."[36] There have also been events such as the "Todas las voces todas" ("All the Voices All") concert held in 1996 in Quito, which featured performances by Mercedes Sosa, Silvio Rodríguez, Fito Páez, Inti-Illimani, César Isella, Joaquín Sabina, León Gieco, Victor Heredia, and the group Fortaleza. These musicians and newer groups continue to put their music at the service of a deeper message. Even less verbal music can be subversive; the musical forms themselves speak volumes on behalf of certain values and beliefs that they represent, such as Andean music performed by Inti-Illimani. These forms incorporate developments in the rest of the world, evident in the re-interpreting, Latin-American style, of innovations from jazz, rock, pop, folk, reggae, and rap music.

It is also promising that the voices of Latin American music are heard now more commonly in North America than before, and this is increasing with the growth of the Spanish-speaking population in the United States. What is still unclear is what issue(s) will unify the voices, and what vision is being put forward. Where are the values? How are they to be identified? Something in the music speaks to us profoundly. As Luft believes, "[t]he future of Latin American protest music [and all music with a deeper message] has as much to do with listening audiences, as with musicians. Make no mistake about it – Latin Americans love music! Indeed, in 1994, they spent $1,900 million on cassettes, CDs, and LPs. Rock music makes up a major share of this burgeoning market. Increasingly, the music consumed is in English and is imported from the United States."[37] A notable exception is Brazil, where more national music is consumed than that from other countries. For example, in a recent tour of the Portuguese-speaking country, Alanis Morissette's music had difficulty entering the market, and over $1 million had to be spent on publicity alone to facilitate sales.

It is not a question of condemning music whose purpose is purely for entertainment value. As Silvio Rodriguez points out, citing Bertolt Brecht: "art should entertain as well as educate; it fails when it doesn't entertain!"[38] Certain sections of music produced in Latin America address those issues that lie beyond mere entertainment for its own sake, and seek to consider the values and principles our lives can represent. There do exist artists who still raise questions about the directions that the New World Order is taking, particularly with regard to issues such as environmental protection, poverty, women's rights, the funding of education, among others that have become more pressing in recent years. The modern rock Mexican group Maná, for example, sings about the environment in such a song as "Dónde jugarán los niños," the title-track for an album the band released in 1992. The song, co-written by two of the band's members (Alejandro González and Fernando Olivera), deals with the destruction of the environment, told through the eyes of a grandfather in the spirit of storytelling in the oral tradition:

Cuenta el abuelo que de niño el jugó	Grandfather tells us that as a child he used to play
Entre árboles y risas y alcatraces de color	Among trees and laughter and colourful pelicans
Recuerda un río transparente sin olor,	He remembers a transparent river, without odour
Donde abundaban peces, no sufrían ni un dolor.	Where an abundance of fish lived never suffering any pain.

The second verse continues this structure, telling of "very blue" skies where this grandfather would fly kites he himself had made. As time passes, and this elder dies, and the singer poses the following question, as much to the listeners as to himself:

Y hoy me pregunté después de tanta destrucción	And today I asked myself, after so much destruction,
¿Dónde diablos jugarán los pobres niños?	Where in hell will the poor children play?
¡Ay ay ay! en dónde jugarán	Ay ay ay! Where will they play
Se está pudriendo el mundo	The world is rotting
Ya no hay lugar.	There is no more room.

The lack of space for children's playgrounds, described in the five lines of the chorus, alludes to a diminishing land allotted to non-commercial use; this image ties in with the previous allusions to the pollution of the waterways and the skies, and the general deterioration of the earth. The third verse continues to add to the list of destruction:

La tierra está a punto de	The earth is on the brink
Partirse en dos	Of breaking in two
El cielo ya se ha roto	The sky has already broken
El llanto gris	With gray tears
La mar vomita ríos de aceite	The sea vomits rivers of oil
Sin cesar	Unendingly

As the song returns to the chorus, we have a clear sense of how futile is this cycle of environmental abuse, but it is left up to us to find a way out. The song lays out for us the reality of the situation, and leaves us to ponder the question of "where the children will play"? In essence, it places the responsibility in our hands. Yet it harmonizes this social concern with an upbeat, popular musical style that has been described as "a mix of fresh eclectic pop-rock with reggae and Afro-Latin rhythms" of Cuban-Colombian roots. Certainly part of the song's appeal to a large audience is this unique style which accounts for the enormous commercial success of the album, which in turn implies that its message has reached a widespread audience. Maná's *Dónde jugarán los niños*[39] surpassed 1.5 million units in sales in their native Mexico. By 1997, it had exceeded 3.5 million units sold worldwide, as cited on their website (www.mana.com.mx). The group's latest album, *Sueños Líquidos* (1997), gained Maná increased international kudos, such as two nominations for the Grammy Award's "Best Latin Rock/Alternative" category in December 1998, and several projects with MTV, the international vehicle for music promotion. In sum, the band is referred to as the best-known pop-rock Latin group in the world. Clearly, it seems entertainment and social consciousness can share space in songs and still achieve a large audience.

In Brazil, the arts – social poetry and music, for instance – began to solidify as a voice of social change in the 1960s. In a discussion of the socially committed arts, Charles Perrone states that one of the best examples is a publication entitled *Violïo de Rua* (1962–63). This three-volume anthology brings together poets of the Generation of '45 with the new voices of the time, all under the umbrella of "ideological verse."[40] The work was produced by the "Centro Popular de Cultúra," created by the UNE (National Student Union) with the purpose of propagating "arte popular revolucionária," which included popular music as well (Perrone, 32–3). As Perrone observes, the sociopolitical objectives of this collection are evident in the subtitle of the first volume: *Poemas para a Liberdade* (*Poems for Freedom*). One of the main themes of the texts in this volume is solidarity in the effort to defend the rights of the "camponeses."[41]

Caetano Veloso is one of these artists who founded the "Tropicalismo" movement in 1968. This "musical revolution combined highly politicized lyrics, traditional Brazilian music and Western rock elements. Perceiving his music as a national threat, the military regime arrested Veloso, in 1969, and forced him to seek exile in London. His provocative and innovative music is generally described as a cross between Bob Dylan, John Lennon and Prince."[42] To illustrate, let us take his "Tropicália":

O monumento náo tem porta	The monument has no door
A entrada é uma rua antiga	The entrance is an old street,
estreita e torta	narrow and curved
e no joelho uma criança	and upon bended knee a smiling
sorridente feia e torta	child ugly and lame
Estenda a mão	Extends his hand
Viva a mata ta ta	Long live the forest [aliteration]
Viva a mulata ta ta ta ta.	Long live the mulatta ta ta ta ta.

Popular Brazilian musician and composer Gilberto Gil, also one of the founders of "Tropicalismo" was arrested in 1969 and held in the same prison as Veloso, "Vila Militar de Deodoro" in Rio de Janeiro. They composed several songs inside the prison, but perhaps the most astonishing fact was that Gil was asked to give a concert in the prison for 150 soldiers and officers of a regiment of paratroopers in February of 1969. Included among the songs he performed were his recent successes and several "tropicalista" songs such as "Geléia Geral" and "Soy Loco por ti América," the latter written in Spanish as a tribute to Che Guevara and as a reflection of the symbolism of Cuba and Latin America's struggle for sociopolitical and cultural independence. No censorship was made of the repertoire Gil played that night in prison – such was the popularity of the songs – and he played for over an hour, until a commandant in charge arrived to bring the performance to a close.

These experiences were all brought to light again in the public sphere following the great success of the documentary film *Buena Vista Social Club* (1998). Awareness of the current situation of musicians shed light on social issues of Cuban culture. Projects such as this impact the world as they raise questions and inform audiences. That success, coupled with a trip to Cuba undertaken by Caetano Veloso in 1999 – forty years after the revolution – made the connection between Cuba and music with a social voice current again in Brazil. Veloso admits that he had been reluctant to travel to Cuba, afraid he would feel frustrated with what he found there,[43] yet once there he admits things were in better condition than he expected. What drew him to the island was the musical link. Veloso explains that, since his adolescence, Cuban music has influenced his artistic development and his thinking on social values and systems. In an interview for the Brazilian newspaper *O Globo*, Veloso confirms that "[e]ven when, in 1968, Caetano and Gil were imprisoned by the military and asked to go into exile, the 'Tropicalistas' were already not subscribing to leftist orthodoxy. However as Caetano recalls now, the references to the Caribbean island on the album-manifesto "Tropicália" were obvious."[44] For example, it contained a song entitled "Três caravelas," a Cuban song that Veloso sings in Spanish while Gil sings the Portuguese version in "Joïo de Barro," an intended irony: "People saw the Cuban revolution as a mirage of hope, while Brazil was held under a right-wing dictatorship."[45] Poignantly, thus, in Veloso's experience of Brazilian music, "Cuba was a reference made through songs heard as a child. And the revolution seemed much more interesting precisely because it was in Cuba. [...] in cultural terms, Cuba is closer to us [than Chile for instance]. The force of Cuban music is only paralleled by Brazilian music and that of the United States."[46] This connection stems from an awareness of the musical structures of those countries, which reflect certain similar historical trajectories, including ethnic diversity and the religious and racial experiences of communities of African origin that contribute to the character of a people.

The core identity reflected within a shared experience of a community and its evolution toward its unique expression can be contained in music. Once its uniqueness has been determined to its finer dimensions, it then has the necessary inner power to enter into truer dialogue with other identities. Thus, music in Latin America has given the various communities a way of revaluing themselves and maintaining their spirit in the face of encroachments and influences from outside their region or within amidst their own fears. And it reaches beyond these questions of identity to include and defend those issues that are becoming significant to the survival of the world as a whole. If we are to strengthen our support for values that have fallen to the wayside as our desire for financial abundance grows, we must tune in to what these other voices are saying, or rather, singing. As Uruguayan writer Eduardo Galeano is quoted as saying in *Presencia* of 20 October 1995: "Things are unbearable as they are now – poisoned souls, poisoned air, poisoned waters! [...] We are being obliged to accept a world without soul as the only one possible. In this system, there are no *pueblos* (peoples), only markets; no citizens, only consumers; no nations, only companies; no cities, only conglomerations; no human relations, only economic competitions! [...] We will have to invent something as an alternative to the present system."[47] Argentine popular singer Fito Paez also offers a sense of hope for another alternative to the way things are in the current world climate. In his song, "Yo vengo a ofrecer mi corazón," he says that in the face of despair, he will offer his heart, citing the title of the song.

Latin American music has shown how vital a force it can be as a defender of core values that contribute to the well-being of each society and of the world order. We need to focus on abundance in a fuller sense, to channel the pursuit of wealth in ways that nurture spirit and everyone's dignity, physical well-being, and capacity to self-realize. The respect for cultural identity in all of its manifestations is achieved in a spirit of plurality and interdependence. Music allows us to rise above the mundane, pragmatic view of things and builds a connection between us as individuals and as societies, bridging inner worlds and not just fostering our outer conditions. More particularly, the emphasis of Latin American songs on the human voice expresses an alternative perspective, manifesting a sense of being through collectivity and connectivity. By fostering an integrated approach to voicing views on world issues, music in Latin America has shown how sustaining a force this can be, as a power for social change and for developing the vital expression of a people. The songs of social message in Latin America beckon us to another way of seeing the possibilities for the New World Order. Music is a sign of life and a sign that there are deeper questions to be explored. If that is silenced, there remains little reason for continuing to evolve. Many Latin Americans are familiar with the refrain from a song by the Argentinian Horacio Guaraní that says: "Si se calla el cantor, calla la vida," that is, "if the singer falls silent, so does life." To perceive music as a vital necessity is a fundamental belief in Latin America, as witnessed by the way music permeates all of life in the various countries in the region, and how its value is appreciated across the world. The weight given to music in Latin America as a means of survival and for elucidating meaning in life is a lesson from which the world could benefit, if taken to heart. Latin American music is a voice for values that stand as an alternative to those that prioritize economic viability over the quality, indeed, the sanctity of life.

NOTES

1 Key examples will be taken mainly from South America and the Caribbean, though references will also be made to Mexico and Central America.

2 This and the following quotations from Edward Rothstein are my translations of passages from his article, "La música amenaza a los dictadores," *Relaciones* 140–1 (1996), 27–8.

3 Michael Chanan, *Musica Practica: The Social Practice of Western Music from Gregorian Chant to Postmodernism*, New York: Verso, 1994, 11.

4 Adorno in Rothstein, "La música amenaza a los dictadores," 28.

5 Alejo Carpentier, "América Latina en la confluencia de coordenadas y su repercusión en la música," in Manuel R. Castro Lobo, ed., *La música latinoamericana y sus fuentes: Textos elegidos*. San José, Costa Rica: Editorial Alma Mater, 1985, 13.

6 The Brazilian samba is said to have evolved from the northeastern state of Bahia (though originally stemming from Africa) and later became

prevalent in a place known as "Cidade Nova" ["New City"], later the neighbourhood of Estácio, located on the outskirts of Rio de Janeiro. This area was a main point of convergence for migrations of population at the end of the nineteenth century in search of work in urban centres. For cultural and economic reasons, the city of Rio de Janeiro attracted many former slaves, as well as European immigrants, the majority of them Portuguese. This also meant it was a point of convergence of several cultures. People gathered around musical groups to dance, sing, and celebrate life, each group bringing its cultural element to this "festa." Those of African origin came with their rhythms, percussion, and the custom of playing music as a community; the Portuguese brought poetic songs and melodies rich in melancholic beauty.

7 A Latin American dance of African origin, marked by pronounced rhythms of the tamboril and marimba instruments. The term "candombe," though generally used in Uruguay to refer to dance of African origin, appears to have derived from two types of Afro-Uruguayan dances and ceremonies known as "La Chica" and "La Bámbula" (circa 1820–1888); the latter disappeared in the nineteenth century.

8 Lauro Ayestarán, *El folklore musical uruguayo*, Montevideo: Arca, 1971, 112.

9 Ibid., 111.

10 Cédar Viglietti, *Folklore musical del Uruguay*, Montevideo: Ediciones del Nuevo Mundo, 1968, 43.

11 Ibid., 41.

12 Murray Luft, "Latin American Protest Music – What Happened to 'The New Songs'?" *Bulletin de musique folklorique canadienne* 30, no. 3 (1996), 10.

13 Ibid., 11.

14 All translations of song lyrics are mine, unless otherwise noted.

15 The "milonga" is a musical form that appeared in folkloric repertoires of the River Plate circa 1870. In the nineteenth century it was at once a dance, a "payada de contrapunto" – a form of musical duel – as well as an indigenous song that could adapt to verses of four, six, eight, and ten syllables (see Ayestarán, 65). Carlos Vega, Argentine musicologist, defines the milonga as "the only disseminated form of colonial two-four or binary type of song in Argentina and Uruguay during the last decades of the last century. In temporal measure it is equal to the [Panamanian] 'Tamborito,' the [Cuban] 'Son,' and the [Brazilian] 'Modiña' (in certain cases), etc., and it also applies to the melody" (Carlos Vega, *Panorama de la música popular argentina, con un ensayo sobre la ciencia del folklore*, Buenos Aires: Editorial Losada, S.A., 1944, 245).

16 Gina Cánepa-Hurtado, *La canción de lucha en Violeta Parra*, Odense: Romansk Institut, 1981, 14.

17 Ibid., 14.

18 Translated from Rodolfo Pino-Robles, "Music and Social Change in Argentina and Chile: 1950–1980 and Beyond," paper presented at the Canadian Association for Latin American and Caribbean Studies (CALACS) conference in Ottawa, Canada, 2 October 1999.

19 Cánepa-Hurtado, La cancíon de lucha, 1.

20 "Folklore" and "folkloric" in the Latin American context differs from the North American usage of the term; in this study we refer to these terms as the traditions that reach back to the early incarnations of their respective cultural regions and are continually revisited, thus nourishing the identity of the community.

21 Pino-Robles, "Music and Social Change," 3.

22 Luft, "Latin American Protest Music," 11.

23 Translated in Ibid., 12.

24 "Cieilito cielo que sí / cielo del 69 / con el arriba nervioso / y el abajo que se mueve" ("Little cielo, cielo oh yes / cielo of 69 / with the above levels nervous / and those below on the move") / "Mejor se ponen el sombrero / que el aire viene de gloria / si no los despeina el viento / los va a despeinar la historia" ("Better put on your hats / for the wind is coming from glory / and if the wind doesn't ruffle your hair / it will be tousled by history"). This song is registered with AGADU (the General Association of Uruguayan Authors) as #22.660; the text is by Mario Benedetti and the music by Héctor Numa Moreas, 1970.

25 See Daniel Viglietti, "Vigencia de la nueva canción: raíz, rama, y otros vuelos," La del taller 2 (February-March 1985), 22–4.

26 Mario Benedetti y Daniel Viglietti, A dos voces, Buenos Aires: RCA Ceibo, 1992, 39.

27 Ibid.

28 Luft, "Latin American Protest Music," 12.

29 Ibid.

30 Ibid, 14.

31 This and the subsequent Sekeff quotations are my translations of passages from Maria de Lourdes Sekeff, "As Artes, a Universidade e a Globalizaçïo," Revista da Academia Nacional de Música, volume 9, Rio de Janeiro, 1998, 100.

32 Sekeff, "As Artes," 100.

33 In this context, the meaning of "community" encompasses various dimensions: a social group whose members reside in a specific locality, who share government, and have a cultural and historical heritage; and a shared identity.

34 Luft, "Latin American Protest Music," 15.

35 Ibid.

36 Ibid.

37 Ibid., 17.

38 Translated in ibid., 17.

39 Maná, *Dónde Jugarán Los Niños*, Mexico: Warner Music, 1992.

40 Charles A. Perrone, *Letras e Letras da Música Popular Brasileira*, translated by José Puiz Paulo Machado, Rio de Janeiro: Editora e Distribuidora Ltda, 1988, 32.

41 Ibid., 33.

42 "Pride of Brazil," *EnRoute Magazine*, October 1999, 184.

43 See Antonio Carlos Miguel, "Uma outra vista do trópico: De volta de sua primeira viagem a Cuba, Caetano Veloso fala da cultura e socialismo," 'Segundo Caderno,' *O Globo,* 12 December 1999, 1–2.

44 Ibid., 2.

45 Ibid.

46 Ibid. See also "A nova geraçïo cubana," *Veja Rio* 10, no. 5 (2 February 2000), Separata, 60.

47 Luft, "Latina American Protest Music," 17.

Higher Education
in the New World Order

EDWARD VARGO

At the United Nations Conference on Trade and Development (UNCTAD) meeting in Bangkok early in the new millennium, United Nations Secretary-General Kofi Annan proposed a "Global New Deal" of debt relief and better access to foreign markets for poor countries that followed certain economic policies.[1] At the same time, Thailand's Foundation for International Human Resource Development organized Leadership Forum 2000, a gathering of academics, business leaders, and government officials to consider cooperative strategies for the Greater Mekong Sub-Region. In the forum's workshop on Education/Knowledge, academics from Australia, England, India, New Zealand, and the United States presented crucial changes in management that higher education has experienced in their own countries. The unexamined assumption was that Asian countries should make the same adjustments in education structures and teaching systems as these countries have done to cope with the challenges of globalization. Such promoters of the New World Order for higher education are distant relatives to the missionaries who purveyed Western culture hand in hand with earlier subjugators and colonizers of Asian and African peoples. However, in the drive towards profit and efficiency, today's secular educators are exporting a more soulless agenda.

What alternatives are available in an age when unchallenged power-brokers take it for granted that the rest of the world must inevitably follow their lead? To what extent can universities buy into the culture of profit-making and not lose their souls? The presentations in Leadership Forum 2000 offer a microcosm of what has been happening in higher education across the world in the 1990s: what is being accepted as inevitable, what is being left unquestioned. In counterpoint, an increasing number of commentators warn against the uncritical acceptance of narrow business models into higher education. Among them, the World Bank's recently published *Higher Education in Developing Countries: Peril and Promise* includes some significant correctives to past directions.[2] Further antidotes to current trends in higher education emerge from looking at counter-movements to "business as usual" in the world of commerce and industry. As Margaret J. Wheatley has written, "The old story [of dominion and control and all-encompassing materialism] has failed abysmally even in the for-profit sectors where it still dominates. Why would we continue to let such thinking move unchallenged into other kinds of organizations?"[3]

LEADERSHIP FORUM 2000

In the opening session, Professor Donald Hellman, director of the University of Washington's APEC Center, argued that American post-cold-war triumphalism is setting the terms of globalization. Smug in its dominance, the United States behaves a bit like a bully but still expects to convert the world to its views with pious calls for "free" trade. Western macroeconomists who do not understand the social and cultural factors active in different countries control the International Monetary Fund. Unfair as this may seem, it is futile to resist globalization, Hellman bleakly concluded, because we live in an interdependent though non-convergent world.[4] Narrowing the focus, Peter Brimble, president of the Bangkok consulting firm The Brooker Group, noted several global trends in higher education. Among them, the increasing integration of higher education into national economic structures has promoted a worldwide tendency towards applied research, an orientation to technology, and vocationalism in university curricula. Governments, commerce, and industry have called for greater accountability regarding the use of funds, and taxpayers have increasingly questioned the public benefits of higher education.[5] Di Yerbury, vice-chancellor of MacQuarie University, offered a specific example of these global trends. During Australia's economic decline in the 1980s, government policymakers began demanding stronger "skills formation" from education and training. Consequently, higher education shifted to "more specifically vocational" learning to produce a more highly skilled workforce and to improve "productivity, efficiency and innovation." These priorities have continued into the 1990s.[6] Speaking from the context of developing countries, S. Neelamegham of the University of Delhi accepted globalization's demands for "change in the existing

structure, management and mode of delivery of the education system."
His belief was that program development must keep market forces and
funding needs in mind. Moreover, universities in developing countries
will have to forge new links with business and industry, focusing specifically on "consultancy, problem solving, meeting the requirements of
industry in the areas of applied science and engineering, and earning
revenue."[7]

According to Yerbury, the "knowledge- and information-based society" of the New World Order in the twenty-first century is creating a
global economy for higher education that includes "global labor markets, global student markets, global distribution by transnational
providers" (4). Accepting "the 'user-pays' principle" that has forced
Australian universities to gain income through increasing foreign student enrollment and other "entrepreneurial endeavours," she invited
forum participants to profit from the opportunities provided by
globalization, technological advances, and growing competition (5).
In a similar vein, Neelamegham argued that "market driven forces
such as managerial efficiency, cost effectiveness, executive leadership,
strategic planning and control" must become more central to the management of universities (7). For Jack Wood of Australia's Monash
University, competition in the global "knowledge marketplace" is also
the central reality.[8] Viewing knowledge as a commodity to be sold and
purchased, he concluded that we need improved measures to assess its
"production, diffusion, use and depreciation" (7). While he rejected
"traditional human capital indicators" as inadequate tools, Wood still
called upon higher education to find a "formula" that would ensure
faster, more appropriate responses to the needs of knowledge-based
economies (13).

Taking the above as *contextual imperatives*, most speakers at the
Education/Knowledge Workshop followed the mindset and rhetoric of
business models in their observations and proposals. Concepts repeatedly related to higher education reform included the buying and selling
of commodities, economies of scale, alliances, flexibility, efficiency,
accountability, quality control, and meeting market needs.[9] Here I limit
discussion to what the speakers had to say about alliances, university
leaders, and students.

The Asian Development Bank's attempts to introduce autonomy into
Thailand's state universities provide an interesting case study in how
some alliances operate in the New World Order. In 1994, the Bank
put forth a plan "to support post-graduate centers of excellence" that
would inspire further movement towards autonomy in Thailand's
universities. After several years of preparation, a local screening committee rejected the foreign borrowing project just months before the

economic crisis began in mid-1997 (Brimble 14). But when the Thai government turned to the Asian Development Bank for a Social Sector Program Loan in 1998, it had to agree to make all its universities autonomous by the year 2002 as a condition for receiving the loan (10). This agreement then made it possible to reactivate the former proposal. In fact, Peter Brimble's well-researched paper was originally written to support the ADB's reappraisal mission for that Higher Education Development Project (1). Elsewhere, Noam Chomsky has argued that the worldwide movement to privatize universities is part of an effort "to create a socio-economic order which is under the control of private concentrated power."[10] Even though the university autonomy being evolved in Thailand is procedural rather than substantive,[11] Brimble's final recommendations feed into that "private" agenda. Among them, he argues that university personnel will need extensive training in finance, developing linkages with industry, marketing, "outreach" strategies, and commercializing the results of research and development (18–20). In remarks at an after-dinner speech, Prime Minister's Office Minister Abhisit Vejjajiva was more cautionary. He foresaw problems with the process of privatizing education if the focus was confined to economic issues and did not include the education of well-rounded citizens. As he put it, the government still has to assure the training of artists and historians for the needs of the nation.

Yerbury proposed "local, national and international strategic alliances" with other educational and commercial organizations to meet the demands for change coming from the New World Order (8). Neelamegham called for "mutually satisfactory exchange agreements" between supply and demand to keep more flexible contenders from rival sectors at bay (10). In contrast, Neil Quigley of New Zealand's Victoria University stressed that universities do not forget their mission to educate individuals while establishing affiliations with other organizations. Through such alliances universities gain insight into the challenges other organizations face; in return, they offer "the benefits that flow from the focus on analytical capability and critical thinking skills." In Quigley's judgment, those companies that develop their own "in-house universities" tend to "become captive of the status quo, and become focused on information and training rather than understanding." As a result, they lose the ability to respond innovatively.[12]

Several speakers described the kind of leaders needed to fulfil the New World Order's agenda for higher education. Pennsylvania's Robert Zemsky predicted that "in the management of their own human resources, [universities] will come increasingly to resemble other enterprises in which professional managers dominate." In a market-smart world, academic managers will have to be highly skilled in what their product costs and what to charge. In a shift from the democratizing tendencies of previous decades, "the faculty [will] become the expert providers (respected and protected but not in control)."[13] Neelamegham claimed that hierarchical, rigidly centralized organizational structures will break down under a special breed of leaders "gifted with strategic vision, well versed with financial management and resource allocation, capable of leading a team" as well as directing traditional functions like curriculum planning and research development (7). Considering the resistance to institutional change found in many universities, Jack Wood argued that leaders should dis-establish entrenched thinking through fragmentation, a time-honoured if manipulative method of generals and executives. *Divide et impera.*

Neil Quigley was about the only speaker to relate leadership issues in higher education to moral development. Although he stated that "[t]he best of leaders are both transactional and transformational," he emphasized the crucial – and rare – presence of transformational leadership. Transactional leaders focus "on the implementation of incentive and monitoring systems" in which "decision-making is confined to a narrow framework designed to implement the status quo." In contrast, "transformational leaders promote change by acting as a role model and an inspiring and challenging visionary, ... encourage critical and lateral thinking, facilitate innovation and reward the pursuit of new ways of doing things" (2–3). While Quigley did not explicitly say so, transactional leadership operates on the level of pre-conventional moral development normal for a pre-adolescent child. It involves "instrumental compliance with exchange agreements" and has "enforcible contracts and job descriptions" as its moral referents. On the other hand, transformational leadership operates on the level of postconventional moral development achieved by the fully mature adult. It takes the "cost and benefits for all stakeholders" as its moral referents. It also draws on "self-chosen, universal ethical principles to seek creative solutions to ethical dilemmas that serve the common good while respecting the individual rights of all interested parties (including self)."[14] Even though the other speakers might seek the results that come from transformational leadership, they for the most part proposed business models for higher education that follow a more narrow transactional style.

When students came into the picture at all, the overriding concern was preparing them for usefulness to the marketplace. Wood's discussion of two-tier organizational design revealed exactly what that means. The first tier, "the inner core workforce," consists of "high knowledge value adding employees." The second tier, the outer ring workforce, often referred to as "the contingent workforce," consists of employees usually hired on a part time or casual basis. The attraction of the core-ring organization is its flexibility in meeting market demand. The contingent workforce can be expanded or contracted as needed. The result for Australia, encapsulated in a cold statistic, is that part-time employment has more than doubled over the past two decades, with one-fourth of the workforce now falling into this category (18). Human beings have become as disposable as nappies. Not much concern for the individual quality of life of students/workers beyond their service to market forces is evident in this spiritually bankrupt approach to education.

In the forum's Final Plenary Session, former Australian diplomat Richard Woollcott reminded the participants that the major burden of the Asian economic crisis fell on those least able to bear it, the workers who were laid off. *True* development needs to address poverty and equity. We cannot presume that technology carries human solutions within it. A human perspective needs to replace a blind belief in the marketplace. A speaker from the floor added that the American system, out of which globalization has emerged, not only pushes free enterprise, market forces, and new technologies, but also has a concern for human rights, democracy, and social justice. To trust this latter agenda to the free market or to the foreign policies of corporations driven by self-interest is a fool's errand. We can no longer allow the market economy to proceed on its own without a concern for the *public good*. A growing number of commentators in the United States itself are drawing attention to the negative consequences of uncritically accepting narrow business models into higher education.[15] Human beings come first. The World Bank's Task Force on Higher Education and Society made that very point in listing the desirable features of a higher education system: "Higher education is focused on people – regulations need to foster, not hamper, human potential" (52).

HIGHER EDUCATION IN DEVELOPING COUNTRIES AND THE WORLD BANK

Although it employs the same socioeconomic discourse favoured by the forum speakers introduced above, this task force takes a generally more holistic approach and recommends several critical shifts in the World Bank's previous policies on higher education. These correctives call for greater support from the World Bank and other international donors for higher education as a public good, a renewed emphasis upon general education in addition to specialized training, and some back-tracking on the myth of the free market. In the task force's judgment, narrow, misleading economic analysis promoted the view that public investment in higher education only "magnifies income inequality" and brings fewer returns to society than investment targeting primary and secondary schools (10). Policies based on such an analysis resulted in a substantial lack of funding and development for higher education institutions in developing nations at a time when developed countries keep raising the ante. For its own part, the task force believes that "the social returns to investment are substantial and exceed private returns by a wider margin than was previously believed" (20). Because the demands of globalization make higher education a crucial factor in the advancement of any given country, it cannot simply be dismissed as "a small cultural enterprise for the elite" (27). As for the claim that "public investment in higher education is socially inequitable" because university graduates tend to come from the upper classes, the task force argues that higher education has helped many "disadvantaged groups" come into their own (40).

In the past decade or so, the World Bank based "its lending strategy" on rate-of-return studies of labour economists. It chose to place primary education high and higher education low on its development agenda. Many other donors followed its influential lead. The task force rejects the reasoning behind this strategy because "standard rate-of-return analyses" failed to consider other benefits of higher education than "incremental earnings." Educated people are also valuable for their input into building up the institutions and structures needed for business to thrive. Moreover, the research undertaken by universities has "far-reaching social benefit" for a nation's economy, another factor missed by rate-of-return analysis (39–40).

In their new, more balanced vision, the task force proposes two major directions for higher education in developing countries: training in "specialized skills" for a greater number of students *and* a new kind of "general education" (10). They came to these conclusions from the belief that "in the knowledge economy, highly trained specialists and broadly educated generalists will be at a premium, and both will need to be educated more flexibly so that they continue to learn as their environment develops" (14).

With regard to specialized skills, the task force notes that developing countries increasingly lag behind industrial countries in terms of science and technology. Because "many areas of scientific inquiry that hold great promise for the development of international public goods are receiving inadequate attention," the gap will widen between the standards of living for rich and poor nations (81). As an example, they cite the disparities between funding for AIDS and malaria research. Even though the two diseases have approximately the same annual mortality rate, AIDS research gets much more funding because the disease is more common than malaria in richer countries. The task force believes that national governments and international organizations must counter such market failures as well as adequately recognize "the global public benefits of scientific inquiry and education" (71). It also supports the alliances for the development of new technologies that are emerging between governments seeking economic benefit for the nation, academic researchers, and businesses on the lookout for quick commercial development of that research (73).

In making the case for liberal or general education, the task force is sensitive to the controversy they might arouse because of its Western origins and its associations with colonial rule in some countries. What they hope for is an educational approach tailored to the culture of each country yet providing "a broad, flexible, interactive education that addresses the whole human being" beyond mere job orientation. Nonetheless, much of the argument still remains within the framework of socioeconomic development to which the World Bank is committed. The task force argues that general education is an excellent preparation for the "flexible, knowledge-based careers" ever more available on the top tiers of today's workforce (83–4, 89). They offer the example of a liberal arts university being planned by the Bangladesh Rural Advancement Committee to fit local needs. The curriculum design fuses two years of liberal arts schooling centred on development studies with another two years of specialized technical training. Thus, the Bangladesh Committee hopes to provide not only a better general education but also a readiness to take up jobs requiring specific skills (85–6).

Among the significant benefits to be gained from a general education, the task force draws attention to the aptitude for "lifelong learning" and the promotion of "social equity and mobility" (87). In addition to providing a basis for further specialization, it constitutes the common ground for interaction between all kinds of specialists. It can "promote responsible citizenship, ethical behavior, educational ambition, professional development in a broad range of fields, and even global integration." In this way, it facilitates the consideration of moral issues posed by new development endeavours, thus safeguarding a country's long-term interests (89).

As much as the task force employs the discourse of business and links higher education to economic development, its members do not count among "true believers" in market forces. Rather, they consistently point out the market's limitations. For instance, they state that government policymakers need to lend support to areas neglected by private funding, such as basic scientific research, the humanities, and scholarships for the inclusion of "underrepresented groups" (17). Noting the difficulties of private, for-profit higher education institutions to maintain first-rate programs, the task force dispels the myth that market forces automatically ensure quality: "To the extent that competition is driven by cost alone, it is likely to abet the provision of low-quality education" (32).

In arguing for greater public interest in higher education, the task force also undercuts the currently popular *user-pays* principle. It stresses the benefits that flow to society at large from the benefits gained by better educated individuals, for they can contribute to improvements in such areas as health care and institutional capital, to mention only a few. They also point out the consequences of the increasing reliance on fee-based education in developing countries. As market forces predominate, the focus falls upon short-term gains, and people lose sight of public responsibilities for higher education. The task force remains convinced that the public sector retains an indispensable role in higher education because the myth of the free market does not translate easily from developed to developing countries. In poorly functioning markets, a host of problems follow: misused resources, the exclusion of talented students with limited resources, the continued survival of "weak, exploitative institutions," and the profit-driven tendency to "underinvest in certain subjects and types of higher education, even if these are important to the well-being of society as a whole."[16]

As throughout, the task force tries to be fair to both sides. In this case, they conclude that the higher education system needs the active involvement of both commerce and government, with neither dominating: "Too close a reliance on market forces reduces public benefits," but "the compelling logic of private investment for private benefit" also has its advantages (45). Among its responsibilities to higher education, the government needs to ensure the preservation of the public interest, especially equity for all, provide those elements of higher education ignored by the market, and support those areas of basic research crucial for society. Private financing does ease the government's financial burden, and it can guarantee that those who gain the benefits of higher education pay the costs. However, private philanthropy toward higher education is not in the traditions of most developing countries, and some students will fall between the cracks. In the end, government "[p]olicymakers must decide on the extent to which they will guide the development of their country's higher education sector, and the extent to which they think market forces will lead to the establishment and operation of a viable system" (58).

Good governance is a major issue for the task force. Many current commentators, like some of the forum speakers, expect higher education institutions to ape the management practices of the world's best business and government organizations. In contrast, the task force recognizes that there cannot be a one-to-one correspondence: "Higher education institutions rely on individual initiative and creativity, and these need time and space to develop. The institutional time horizon is usually much longer than in industry, with the bottom line blurred. Collegiality is a value to be cultivated, alongside considerable academic autonomy" (59).

The task force's comprehensive approach to higher education in developing countries corrects and broadens the narrow vision of earlier World Bank policies that many foreign experts are still foisting upon these countries. Even so, the report is imbedded in the limiting context of development economics. Thus, the greatest peril for higher education in developing countries is the increasing disparity between the richest and the poorest peoples in the world. The greatest hope is that strengthening higher education systems can halt further deterioration in relative incomes while positioning developing countries "on a higher and more sharply rising development trajectory" (97).

Can one dismantle the master's house with the master's tools? As much as the task force challenges the premises of certain business models, it is still reporting to the World Bank and willy-nilly may be serving the interests of "private concentrated power," as Chomsky has claimed. Saying so is not meant to belittle the healthy correctives offered in *Higher Education in Developing Countries: Peril and Promise*. Rather, it is meant to highlight "the current hegemony of managerial discourse" in many circles of higher education.[17] Business and economics have their own valid forms of discourse, but they cover only one small corner of the total picture. As some of the presentations at Leadership Forum 2000 suggest, a certain brand of business rhetoric is in danger of stifling all other forms of discourse in the field of higher education. Hand in hand with the rhetoric goes a problematic "growth of a managerial mentality" in university administration. Collegial and bureaucratic "decision-making styles" are being demonized in favour of a sometimes self-serving managerial style. Moreover, as the task force itself has argued, too exclusive a concentration upon the instrumental goals of higher education ignores its other critical goals, such as the promotion of culture, values, religion, nation, and citizenship. Significant losses are occurring for questionable gains.

ALTERNATIVES TO THE NEW WORLD ORDER'S AGENDA FOR HIGHER EDUCATION

What alternatives are available in an age when the drive of the profit motive seems unstoppable? Some answers emerge from looking at counter-movements to "business as usual" in the world of commerce and industry itself. Even as higher education was embracing narrow business models in the past ten years, there have been growing movements to re-humanize or reinstate the place of spirituality in business cultures. These humanistic alternatives to currently prevalent business models regard "organizations as a culture, a matrix of personal relations, a way of life" and "trace productivity to relationships, collaboration, and creativity rather than to sheer efficiency and economy."[18]

Millions are familiar with the work of M. Scott Peck, Stephen Covey, and Deepak Chopra, popularizers of spiritual values in business. Other authors influential among business organizations like Peter Block, Ken Blanchard, Max DePree, and Peter Senge have proposed management paradigms like "total quality management," "learning organizations," and "community-building." W. Edwards Deming, the famous proponent of quality in manufacturing, ultimately believed that "quality was about the human spirit."[19] Bill Bottum, an executive in the construction industry, has been drawing practical business strategies out of the Sermon on the Mount for over forty years. He relates the impulse to "team building, partnering, strategic alliances, and total quality management" in the 1990s to values found in the Eight Beatitudes.[20] In the last five years before his death in 1970, psychologist Abraham Maslow studied "people who had made the greatest contributions to the world" and concluded that they were "self-transcenders ... inspired by spiritual 'Being Values.'"[21] Robert Greenleaf, whose Servant-Leadership movement still thrives today, argued in "The Servant as Leader" (1970) that "the most effective leaders are those motivated not by power and greed, but by a desire to serve. This desire to serve almost always comes from deep transcendent spiritual impulses." The litmus test for such leadership "is the effect it has on its followers."[22] In this final section, I will highlight proposals from Servant-Leadership that are relevant to unbalancing trends in higher education today. Such solutions offer hope for a healthier, *new* New World Order. The starting point lies in shifting our premises and widening our vision. Here I take my lead from the editor of this volume: "If the technologically oriented culture of today were to work together with the wisdom of traditional, religious and intuitive cultures, the two could wonderfully complement each other and create a holistic society where neither body nor soul

... would suffer in isolation" (Yovanovich). Secularized consumer society – which is obsessed with life-destroying technology, seeks profit above all, and depends too exclusively upon the power of reason – needs a new flowering of "spiritual awareness" that goes beyond the old sectarian oppression and deformation of individuals.

Even as higher education prepares students to live in the age of globalization, it must address every aspect of their development "so that they can lead a desirable way of life and live in harmony with other people."[23] Students can hardly prepare for a better quality of life when they are narrowly conceptualized as cogs in a socioeconomic machine forever out of their control. Only teaching that has its foundation in caring can enable them to take on new dynamic roles boldly and responsibly. If universities want to survive and grow within a highly competitive global marketplace, they are well advised to align their structures, systems, and management style so as to activate the creative talents and loyalties of their people. As Stephen Covey has written, "Synergy comes from the balance and integration of the four basic needs of life – physical, social, mental, and spiritual."[24] In any organization, making money is only one of these needs and usually serves "only one need of one stakeholder" (xiii). There are many other needs and stakeholders in any enterprise. Higher education institutions need to develop "high-trust cultures" in which everyone is motivated more "by coaching, empowerment, persuasion, example, modeling" than by fragmentation, performance measures, and similar controls (xi–xii). The basic business model developed in Greenleaf's Servant-Leadership movement fits these criteria. It is an institutional model "based on teamwork and community, one that seeks to involve others in decision making, one strongly based in ethical and caring behavior, and one that is attempting to enhance the personal growth of workers while improving the caring and quality of our many institutions."[25] Above all, Servant-Leadership "holds that the primary purpose of a business should be to create a positive impact on its employees and community, rather than using profit as the sole motive" (7). Management models currently gaining the upper hand in higher education tend to skew those priorities.

Because it is easier to manage *things*, administrators speak of faculty as "tools" and students as a "workforce." However, one cannot really *manage* people; beyond measurements and controls, it takes a special kind of *leadership* to inspire the most effective performances in people. Instead of a one-way look backwards, such leadership encourages people to "fail forward." It operates from a two-way, open-ended, ongoing paradigm; its driving forces are interdependency, connection, and power sharing. It builds on mutual respect and promotes multi-directional accountability.[26] In a system that leaves no room for self-creation, self-organization, or self-correction, however, leadership has to exhaust itself providing everything: organizational mission and values, structure, plans, and supervision. Because human beings conceived as machines are expected to conform to these plans and comply with this supervision, key human traits pose special problems. The only option in these "machine-organizations" is to stamp out individuality in order to meet goals set from the top, squelch uniqueness for control, and sell creativity short for petty performance measures. In Margaret Wheatley's words, only a full appreciation of our expansive human capacities can save us from our constraining organizations.[27]

Easier said than done. As Wheatley has described it, the *old story* of mechanistic mastery continues to hold us in its hypnotic power. We still trust in technical solutions to bail us out from "the earthly mess we've created." We now expect genetic engineering "to yield unsurpassed benefits in health and longevity, and all because we are such smart engineers of the human body." In higher education, too, the managerial mentality encourages us to focus "on creating better functioning machines. We replace the faulty part, reengineer the organization, install a new behavior or attitude." Most perniciously, we have come to "believe we can ignore the deep realities of human existence" in our organizational lives together. By reducing the complexity of human life into a story of simple dimensions, we can control others to perform with the efficiency and predictability of machines. The only thing is: "[P]eople *never* behave like machines" (341–2).

In counterpoint, Wheatley proclaims a *new story* emerging from the work of modern science. Interestingly, it reinscribes an *ancient* story found in early primal wisdom traditions, among modern indigenous tribes, as well as in most spiritual and poetic thought of all ages. Life scientists today observe "a world where creative self-expression and embracing systems of relationships are the organizing energies, where there is no such thing as a separate individual, and no need for a leader to do it all" (344). They observe life "processes that inflame, breed more life and wildness, create more deepness and mystery" – quite the opposite of sterile, constraining organizational charts (345). Applying this story to our organizational lives suggests an alternative scenario in which diversity and uniqueness are seen positively.

Primary forces in this story of life are constant creativity and space to evolve: "Many designs, many adaptations are possible, and organisms enjoy far more freedom to experiment than we humans, with our insane demand to 'Get it right the first time.'" Other great forces are connectedness and self-organization: "Everywhere we look, we see complex, tangled, messy webs of relationships .... Organisms shape themselves in response to their neighbors and their environments. All respond to one another, coevolving and cocreating the complex systems of organization that we see in nature" (346). Organization is not an imposition but a natural outgrowth from the interactions and needs of those that have come together. In suggesting new models to replace well-planned, well-orchestrated, well-supervised but ultimately deadening strategies, Wheatley presents the following summary:

Life seeks organization, but it uses messes to get there. Organization is a process, not a structure. Simultaneously, and in ways difficult to chart, the process of organizing involves creating relationships around a shared sense of purpose, exchanging and creating information, learning constantly, paying attention to the results of our efforts, coadapting, coevolving, developing wisdom as we learn, staying clear about our purpose, being alert to changes from all directions. Living systems give form to their organization, and evolve those forms into new ones, because of exquisite capacities to create meaning together, to communicate, and to notice what's going on in the moment. These are the capacities that give any organization its true liveliness, that support self-organization. (347–8)

Traditionally, higher education institutions were founded to achieve some special purpose or call. Most people who chose professions in higher education saw the fit with their own aspirations and believed in the greater effectiveness of collaboration. The new story takes their hopes and desires into account. But when higher education institutions revert to rigid "machine ideas about structures, roles, designs, [and] leaders," they become a major obstacle to the flowering of creativity and fulfillment of purposeful dreams (347). Their detailed plans and controls damage the organization's need for individuals to go beyond the rules in unpredictable crisis situations. Higher education institutions also deny the system-seeking forces of creativity and connectedness when they exploit a dog-eat-dog mentality to raise performance. The black hole that will ultimately consume such organizations, as it has other experiments in narrow social engineering, is its denial of human spirit. Life-giving servant-leaders allow for the human ability to surprise, to "create wisely and well," to cooperate in seeking the best interests of the organization (350).

Generally speaking, universities have tended to follow a *traditional not-for-profit enterprise strategy*, which aims at maximizing social benefits for the community at the lowest possible cost, or a *profligate not-for-profit enterprise strategy*, which aims to do the same *"without* regard to economic cost." Today, when many reformers of higher education look primarily to the interests of private investment, a more preferable strategy is the *balanced stakeholder service enterprise strategy*, which aims at "positive net value for all stakeholders ... so that no stakeholder group is used purely instrumentally to serve others."[28] This is a most challenging strategy because it encourages all stakeholder groups to have long-term expectations but is likely to experience short-term conflicts over priorities between various interest groups. Such an organization "must have distinctive abilities both at managing conflict and at adapting successfully to change over time so that it prospers indefinitely in its environment" (154). Bill Bottum looks to the governance structure prevailing in European companies like Unilever, Royal Dutch Shell, and Phillips as examples of servant-leadership. These companies have inside boards that choose their managing directors, who thus become directly responsible to their peers. In such councils of equals, consensual decisions will likely be based on intuition and empathy as well as rational, linear thinking. A very different style emerges when power is concentrated in the hands of professional managers alone. Bottum concludes that organizations will activate more creativity in all their members when they discover "the productive power of self-directed work teams, councils of equals, and alliances in which everyone is serving and accountable to the others" (169). Although several forum speakers stressed alliances as the wave of the future, they did not go far enough in examining which of a university's many stakeholders these alliances will serve.

What may frighten many away from such a model "is the need for each member of their council to have an inner journey and quest, perhaps even a contemplative practice, leading toward authenticity and mutual understanding" (167). As Parker J. Palmer writes, "[i]t is easier to spend your life manipulating an institution than dealing with your own soul." It is more comfortable to believe that the only changes that really matter are those that fit into measurements and statistics. In the Western managerial models now being propagated to universities throughout the world, leaders gain "power by operating very competently and effectively in the external world, sometimes at the cost of internal awareness." Those considering the adoption of these managerial models should remember that they grow out of "an American culture that wants to externalize everything, that wants (just as much as Marx ever did) to see the good life more as a matter of outer arrangements than of inner well-being."[29] Too many leaders who follow this line trust in the external world so much that they dismiss any talk of the inner life as illusion. Yet the bottom line is that neither individuals nor organizations can ultimately escape their inner lives.[30]

In the virtual organization, which Thomas A. Bausch claims to be the pace-setting model for the future, authority comes not from structures but from developing open relationships with others. Consequently, Bausch maintains, servant-leadership "must begin with a deep understanding of the human person as the basis, and the only source of sustainable competitive advantage as we enter the new millennium."[31] With the primacy of the person as the foundation-stone for building up organizations, he raises several key issues. Organizations need to face the corrupting nature of purposeless, money-driven work and "the unethical nature of financial marketplaces that reward executives for firing people rather than making them productive and the companies profitable." Higher education must search for "entirely new models of education that focus on the needs of persons rather than the vested rights of the providers" (236). The real genius of the capitalist system is not the efficiency that so obsesses current managerial discourse, but its remarkable ability to release the greatest of all assets – unpredictable human creativity. If one considers the *function* of work as well as its remuneration, process, and product, then the only way to release full potential in an organization is to "form community" (242).

Creativity and community. As both Wheatley and Palmer have pointed out, the *new story* embraces the insight "that creation comes out of chaos, and that even what has been created needs to be turned to chaos every now and then so that it can be re-created in a more vital form." A higher education that encourages such thinking involves not only skills with which to manipulate the external world but also "the personal and corporate disciplines of the inner world."[32] Moreover, higher education that cultivates self-esteem, integrity, initiative, and mutual trust can infuse in all its members the vitality, enthusiasm, and spirit needed to acquire true excellence.[33] With such values and processes, higher education will not become a slave to dehumanizing forces but will serve to renew the life of the world.

NOTES

1 "Annan Proposes New Deal for Poor Nations," *Bangkok Post*, 13 February 2000, 1.
2 Task Force on Higher Education and Society, *Higher Education in Developing Countries: Peril and Promise*, Washington: World Bank, 2000.
3 Margaret J. Wheatley, "What Is Our Work?" in Larry C. Spears, ed., *Insights on Leadership: Service, Stewardship, Spirit, and Servant–Leadership*, New York: John Wiley & Sons, 1998, 350.

4 Donald Hellman, "New Realities of the Global Economy in the 21st Century: Implications for Human Resource Strategies," Panel Discussion, Leadership Forum 2000, Imperial Queen's Park Hotel, Bangkok, 16 February 2000.

5 Peter Brimble, "University Autonomy in Thailand: An Issues Paper," Education/Knowledge Workshop, Leadership Forum 2000, Imperial Queen's Park Hotel, Bangkok, 17 February 2000, 4.

6 Di Yerbury, "Changing Global Characteristics and Societal Priorities, and the Implications for Education and Knowledge," Education/Knowledge Workshop, Leadership Forum 2000, Imperial Queen's Park Hotel, Bangkok, 16 February 2000, 2.

7 S. Neelamegham, "Education and Management in Higher Education for the Globalised World," Education/Knowledge Workshop, Leadership Forum 2000, Imperial Queen's Park Hotel, Bangkok, 17 February 2000, 2.

8 Jack Wood, "Research and Development Issues for Knowledge Based Economies," Education/Knowledge Workshop, Leadership Forum 2000, Imperial Queen's Park Hotel, Bangkok, 16 February 2000, 16.

9 See Brimble, 8, Neelamegham, 7, Yerbury, 8–9.

10 Noam Chomsky, "Assaulting Solidarity – Privatizing Education," *Znet Updates*, 22 May 2000, http://znetupdates@tao.ca.

11 See Brimble 6, 9.

12 Neil Quigley, "The Role of Universities in the Development of Leadership and Management Skills in Business and Government," Education/Knowledge Workshop, Leadership Forum 2000, Imperial Queen's Park Hotel, Bangkok, 16 February 2000, 5.

13 Robert Zemsky, "Higher Education and Human Resource Management," abstract, Education/Knowledge Workshop, Leadership Forum 2000, Imperial Queen's Park Hotel, Bangkok, 16 February 2000.

14 Jill W. Graham, "Servant-Leadership and Enterprise Strategy," in Spears, *Insights*, 152–3.

15 See Phyllis R. Brown's excellent review-essay, "The Business of Higher Education in America: Some Hopeful Prospects," review of *Literature: An Embattled Profession* by Carl Woodring, *Cultivating Humanity: A Classical Defense of Reform in Liberal Education* by Martha C. Nussbaum, *The Pleasures of Academe: A Celebration and Defense of Higher Education* by James Axtell, *Chalk Lines: The Politics of Work in the Managed University*, ed. Randy Martin, in *College English 62*, no. 4 (March 2000), 511–23.

16 Task Force, 38. See page 43 for comments on the occasionally negative impact of Western franchise universities in developing countries.

17 Jan Currie and Lesley Vidovich, "The Ascent toward Corporate Managerialism in American and Australian Universities," in Randy Martin,

ed., *Chalk Lines: The Politics of Work in the Managed University,* Durham: Duke University Press, 1998, 139, Brown qtd. 520.

18 Christopher Newfield, "Recapturing Academic Business," in Martin, *Chalk Lines,* 82, Brown qtd. 519.

19 Wheatley, 349.

20 Bill Bottum with Dorothy Lenz, "Within Our Reach: Servant-Leadership for the Twenty-First Century," in Spears, *Insights,* 158. Among key influences upon the evolution of his own thinking, Bottum has cited *The Functions of the Executive* (1938), in which AT&T's Chester Barnard opposed then dominant "theories of scientific management and mechanistic behavioral ideas," and *The Human Side of Enterprises* (1960), in which Douglas McGregor argued that managers' beliefs about people determine the manner in which they supervise workers (160).

21 Bottum, 160.

22 Bottum, 161. Other bestselling books that have proposed "'a management model filled with heart – and soul'" are *Spirit at Work: Discovering the Spirituality in Leadership* by Jay Conger, *Leadership Jazz* by Max DePree, *The Soul of a Business* by Tom Chappell, *Stewardship: Choosing Service Over Self–Interest* by Peter Block, and *Making the Grass Greener on Your Side: A CEOs Journey to Leading by Serving* by Kendrick Melrose (see James Conley and Fraya Wagner-Marsh, "The Integration of Business Ethics and Spirituality in the Workplace," in Spears, *Insights,* 251–7). Also see Caryle Murphy, "Workers Taking Religion to the Office," *Washington Post,* 12 September 1998, B1 and Michelle Conlin, "Religion in the Workplace," *Business Week,* 8 November 1999, 81–6.

23 Nuchanart Vanichbutr, "Education with a Heart," *Bangkok Post,* 7 May 2000, Perspective, 6.

24 Stephen R. Covey, foreword, "Servant-Leadership from the Inside Out," in Spears, *Insights,* xv.

25 Larry C. Spears, introduction, "Tracing the Growing Impact of Servant-Leadership," Spears, *Insights,* 1.

26 See Ann McGee-Cooper, "Accountability as Covenant: The Taproot of Servant-Leadership," in Spears, *Insights,* 77–84.

27 See Wheatley, 343–4.

28 Jill W. Graham, "Servant-Leadership and Enterprise Strategy," Spears, *Insights,* 148. For some writings that have focused on "the ethical underpinnings of strategy" in the last two decades, see Spears, *Insights,* 367n1.

29 Parker J. Palmer, "Leading from Within," Spears, *Insights,* 200–2.

30 In "Leading from Within," Parker J. Palmer argues that the most effective leaders are willing to do the "inner work" necessary to confront

the *shadows* in their lives: insecurity, competition, workaholism, "fear of the natural chaos of life," fear of failure, and the denial of death (see 204–6). In "Healing Leadership," Judith A. Sturnick discusses the kind of renewal leaders themselves need to go through in order to facilitate transformation of the quality of life and work within dysfunctional organizations. In particular, she identifies six "components of healing wisdom": respecting boundaries, releasing destructive perfectionism, seeking creative responses to ambiguity, acknowledging some spiritual reality within the organization, fostering experimentation, and maximizing elements of discovery and surprise (Spears, *Insights*, 192).

31 Thomas A. Bausch, "Servant-Leaders Making Human New Models of Work and Organization," Spears, *Insights*, 231.

32 Palmer, 206–7.

33 See Conley and Wagner-Marsh, 254–5.

About the Contributors

JOHN MCMURTRY, professor of philosophy at the University of Guelph, most recently published *Unequal Freedoms: The Global Market as an Ethical System*, (1998) *The Cancer Stage of Capitalism*, (1999) and *Value Wars: The Global Market Versus the Life Economy*, (2002). He is a Fellow of the Royal Society of Canada.

JAMES BISSET spent thirty-seven years as a public servant in the Government of Canada's Department of Citizenship and Immigration and Foreign Affairs. He was appointed head of the Immigration Foreign Service in 1974 and became assistant under-secretary of state for Social Affairs in 1980. In the early 1970s he served at the Canadian High Commission in London, England. He was appointed Canadian high commissioner to Trinidad and Tobago in 1982 and served there until 1985, when he was seconded to the Department of Employment and Immigration as executive director to help steer new immigration and refugee legislation through Parliament. In 1990 he was appointed Canadian ambassador to Yugoslavia, Bulgaria, and Albania.

MICHAEL MANDEL, professor of law at Osgoode Hall Law School of York University in Toronto, has taught and lectured at many universities abroad, especially in Italy, (Bologna, Torino, Bolzano, Trento, Padova) and also in Israel, at the Hebrew University in Jerusalem. His book *The Charter of Rights and the Legalization of Politics in Canada* is now in its second edition and has been translated into French. He is a frequent contributor to the op-ed pages of Canada's newspapers and

if often heard on radio and television. In May 1999, he led an international team of lawyers who brought formal complaints of war crimes
against sixty-eight NATO leaders before the International Criminal Tribunal for the former Yugoslavia.

JORGE NEF, professor of politics, international development, and rural
extension studies at the University of Guelph, has been a visiting professor in numerous Canadian and foreign universities and institutes. In
1999–2000 he was the director of the School of Government, Public
Administration, and Political Science at the University of Chile and
taught at the Institute of International Studies of the same university.
Professor Nef has edited and written over a dozen books and mono-
graphs and published over eighty articles in refereed journals in the fields
of Latin American politics and development. His most recent book,
Human Security and Mutual Vulnerability, was published in 1999.

JENNIFER SUMNER is a postdoctoral fellow and teaches at the University of Guelph. Her work on education has been published in *Open
Leaning, The Canadian Journal for the Study of Adult Education*, and
the *Australian Journal of Adult Learning*, as well as in edited volumes
dealing with environmental adult education and alternative educational
policy.

MEENAKSHI BHARAT, professor of English literature at the University
of New Delhi, India, has contributed to the Routledge *Who's Who on
Postcolonial Women Writers* (in press), written extensively (almost the
entire section on India) for the *Cambridge Guide to Children's Literature*, reported and written for *Bookbird* (Baltimore, U.S.) in the Special
issue on Postcolonial Children's Literature, and published "Dual Read-
ership: Continuing Concerns in Swami and Friends and A Strange and
Sublime Address" in the Swedish journal *Halva Varldens Litteratur*
(April 1997) and "Gender and Beyond: The Girl Child in the English
Novel from the Indian Subcontinent in the Past Decade" in a special
issue of the *World Literature Written in English*. Bharat has also presented conference papers all over the world.

TERISA E. TURNER, associate professor of sociology and international
development at the University of Guelph, is the author of *Counterplan-
ning from the Commons: Gendered Class Analysis and Globalization
from Below, Arise ye Mighty People! Gender, Class and Race in Popular Struggles*, and *Oil and Class Struggle*. Professor Turner has published widely in scholarly journals and authored many United Nations
and other governmental reports, as well as many consultancy reports.
Leigh S. Brownhill is a Ph.D. candidate at the Ontario Institute for

Studies in Education at the University of Toronto. She has written a number of scholarly articles and conference papers on social movements and feminist politics in Kenya and Canada.

KEITH ELLIS, professor of Spanish at the University of Toronto, is the author of *Critical Approaches to Rubén Darío*, *El arte narrativo de Francisco Ayala*, *Cuba's Nicolás Guillén*, and *Nicolás Guillén: New Love Poetry*. Ellis is internationally recongnized for his numerous articles and public conferences. He is a Fellow of the Royal Society of Canada.

MARÍA FIGUEREDO, obtained her Ph.D. from the University of Toronto. Her thesis topic was *Poesia y Musicalización Popular: Selección y Recepción del Texto Poético en Forma Musicalizada*. Dr Figueredo's book and articles on the topic of Latin American music are forthcoming.

EDWARD VARGO, professor of English and a former dean of Arts at the Assumption University in Bangkok, Thailand, is the author of *Rainstorms and fire: Ritual in the Novels of John Updike*, and numerous articles published in international journals.

GORDANA YOVANOVICH, associate professor of Latin American literature at the University of Guelph, has published *Julio Cortázar's Character Mosaic, Play and the Picaresque*, and a number of articles on various topics in Latin American literature.